STUDY GUI

Lynn Mazzola
Nassau Community College

Introduction to
FINANCIAL ACCOUNTING

SEVENTH EDITION

HORNGREN   SUNDEM   ELLIOTT

Prentice Hall, Upper Saddle River, NJ 07458

Acquisitions editor: Deborah Emry
Associate editor: Natacha St. Hill Moore
Senior editorial assistant: Jane Avery
Project editor: Richard Bretan
Manufacturer: Quebecor Printing Group

Printed in the United States of America

10 9 8 7 6 5 4 3

ISBN 0-13-974296-4

Prentice-Hall International (UK) Limited, *London*
Prentice-Hall of Australia Pty. Limited, *Sydney*
Prentice-Hall Canada Inc., *Toronto*
Prentice-Hall Hispanoamericana, S.A., *Mexico*
Prentice-Hall of India Private Limited, *New Delhi*
Prentice-Hall of Japan, Inc., *Tokyo*
Simon & Schuster Asia Pte. Ltd., *Singapore*
Editora Prentice-Hall do Brasil, Ltda., *Rio de Janeiro*

CONTENTS

Preface

This Study Guide will assist you in mastering *Introduction to Financial Accounting, Seventh Edition*, by Charles T. Horngren, Gary L. Sundem, and John A. Elliott. The fourteen chapters of this Study Guide correspond to the fourteen chapters in the textbook. THIS STUDY GUIDE IS A SUPPLEMENT TO AND NOT A SUBSTITUTE FOR YOUR TEXTBOOK. It has been designed as an aid to understanding the concepts and practices presented by the text authors. Using this Study Guide should reinforce what you have read in the textbook and help you prepare for examinations. Each chapter of this Study Guide contains the following sections:

Learning Objectives

This section identifies the important areas of study that your instructor will expect you to understand by the end of the chapter.

Pretest and Answers to Pretest

This section consists of two multiple-choice questions for each learning objective in a chapter. The Pretest is designed to help you in identifying those learning objectives for which you need additional review and study. Answers with explanations are provided, and are referenced to the appropriate learning objective.

Key Concept Review by Learning Objectives

This section is organized by learning objective and provides a concise outline of the major points of each learning objective. References to examples, illustrations, or exhibits in the textbook are highlighted in the shaded boxes.

Test Yourself

This section consists of a variety of questions, exercises and problems, and a matching section and ten multiple-choice questions. The questions, exercises and problems, and the multiple-choice questions are designed to improve your comprehension of key concepts presented in the textbook. The matching part is designed to test your comprehension of the new terminology introduced in the chapter. Answers are provided at the end of the chapter after Test Yourself with reference to the appropriate learning objective.

Accounting is important to understanding the world of business. If you read and study the textbook and Study Guide, and answer the questions, exercises and problems in the textbook and Study Guide on a regular basis, you should be able to understand the concepts and practices in accounting that are basic to business.

I would like to thank everyone at Prentice Hall for their support and guidance in preparing this Study Guide. A special thanks to my children, Justin and Lindsey, and my parents for their encouragement and cooperation.

Lynn Mazzola
Nassau Community College

Chapter 1

ACCOUNTING: THE LANGUAGE OF BUSINESS

I. Learning Objectives

The purpose of accounting is to provide useful information in an effective, relevant, and reliable way for a wide variety of decisions.   Anyone involved in making financial decisions of any kind — business or personal — should have a clear understanding of accounting theories and practices. Use the following learning objectives as an aid for your study of Chapter 1, which is designed to introduce you to accounting — the language of business.

1. Explain how accounting information assists in making decisions.

2. Describe the components of the balance sheet.

3. Analyze business transactions and relate them to changes in the balance sheet.

4. Compare the features of proprietorships, partnerships, and corporations.

5. Describe auditing and how it enhances the value of financial information.

6. Distinguish between public and private accounting.

7. Evaluate the role of ethics in the accounting process.

II. Pretest

SELECT THE BEST ANSWER AND ENTER THE IDENTIFYING LETTER IN THE SPACE PROVIDED.

_____ 1. Which of the following is *not* true of accounting?

    a.   It is an aid to decision making.
    b.   It is a measure of financial success.
    c.   It is useful *only* to managers of the organization.
    d.   It is the major means of organizing information about economic activities.

_____ 2. Analysis of financial statements:

    a.   Helps managers to manage the business.
    b.   Allows investors to select among investments.
    c.   Provides elected officials critical information to use in directing government.
    d.   All of the above are true of analysis of financial statements.

_____ 3. A balance sheet *does not:*

    a.   Show the financial status of a business entity.
    b.   Present revenues and expenses of a business entity.
    c.   Have two counterbalancing sections.
    d.   Represent a particular instant in time.

_____ 4. The balance sheet equation may *not* be expressed as:

    a.   Owners' Equity = Liabilities - Assets
    b.   Assets = Liabilities + Owners' Equity
    c.   Liabilities = Assets - Owners' Equity
    d.   All of the above are expressions of the balance sheet equation.

_____ 5. A transaction must:

    a.   Affect the financial position of an entity.
    b.   Be reliably recorded in terms of money.
    c.   Maintain the equality of the balance sheet equation.
    d.   All of the above are true of a transaction.

_____ 6. A summary record of the changes in a particular asset, liability, or owners' equity is known as:

    a.   An entity.
    b.   A transaction.
    c.   An account.
    d.   None of the above.

_____ 7. A proprietorship is an organization:

    a.   With a single owner.
    b.   That joins two or more individuals together as co-owners.
    c.   That is an "artificial being" created by individual state laws.
    d.   Owned by a family.

_____ 8. The form of organization that has limited liability of owners is a:

    a.   Proprietorship.
    b.   Partnership.
    c.   Corporation.
    d.   All of the above forms of organization have limited liability.

_____ 9. A Certified Public Accountant (CPA) in the United States must have:

    a.   Met educational requirements.
    b.   Qualifying experience.
    c.   Passed a national examination.
    d.   All of the above are requirements for a CPA.

_____ 10. An audit _does not:_

    a.   Assess management's financial disclosure.
    b.   Examine every transaction included in the financial statements.
    c.   Become the basis of the CPA's independent opinion.
    d.   All of the above meet the definition of an audit.

_____ 11. Private accountants:

    a.   Work for businesses, government, or other organizations.
    b.   Offer services on a fee basis.
    c.   Cannot be Certified Public Accountants.
    d.   All of the above are true of private accountants.

_____ 12. Public accountants:

    a.   Work for businesses, government, or other organizations.
    b.   Offer services on a fee basis.
    c.   Cannot be Certified Public Accountants.
    d.   All of the above are true of public accountants.

_____ 13. Professional ethics are:

    a.   The result of public attitude surveys.
    b.   A code of professional conduct.
    c.   Limited only to public accountants.
    d.   Mandated by the United States government.

_____ 14.   Professional ethics:

    a.   Guarantee that financial statements are accurate.
    b.   Have no relationship to accounting.
    c.   Promote confidence in the credibility of accounting information.
    d.   None of the above statements are correct.

III. Answers to Pretest

1. c   Accounting provides information useful to a variety of decision makers, not only managers. (L. O. 1)

2. d   The study of accounting is important to everyone even if they do not plan to become accountants or enter the field of business. (L. O. 1)

3. b   Revenues and expenses are presented on the income statement. (L. O. 2)

4. a   b and c are correct expressions of the balance sheet equation. (L. O. 2)

5. d   a, b, and c must be present in a transaction. (L. O. 3)

6. c   (L. O. 3)

7. a   (L. O. 4)

8. c   Only the corporate form of organization has limited liability. Proprietorships and partnerships typically have *unlimited* liability of owners. (L. O. 4)

9. d   (L. O. 5)

10. b   Audits are an examination of transactions and financial statements in accordance with generally accepted auditing standards, which do not require every transaction to be reviewed. (L. O. 5)

11. a   Any type of accounting other than public accounting is considered private accounting. (L. O. 6)

12. b   Public accountants offer their services on a fee basis and *may* be CPAs but do not have to be. (L. O. 6)

13. b   (L. O. 7)

14. c   (L. O. 7)

EVALUATION

The pretest contained two questions for each learning objective. If you did not answer both questions correctly for each learning objective, you should review the appropriate section of the textbook and study guide before you attempt the material after Part IV.

IV. Key Concept Review by Learning Objectives

L. O. 1: Explain How Accounting Information Assists in Making Decisions

A. The Nature of Accounting

   1. **Accounting** is a process of identifying, recording, summarizing and reporting economic information to decision makers.

   2. **Financial accounting** focuses on the specific needs of external (outside) decision makers, such as shareholders, suppliers, banks, and government agencies.

   3. Financial statements, the output of the accounting process, are the result of the accountant's ability to analyze, record, quantify, accumulate, summarize, classify, report, and interpret economic events and their financial effect on an organization.

B. Accounting as an Aid to Decision Making

   1. Accounting information is useful to anyone who must make decisions that have economic consequences. Managers, owners, investors, and politicians all use accounting information to make decisions.

   2. Accounting information may be used to help predict future effects of decisions, confirm or reject past predictions, and show where and when money has been spent and commitments have been made, by evaluating performances, and by indicating the financial implications of choosing one plan over another.

C. Financial and Management Accounting

   1. Both financial accounting and managerial accounting use financial data related to a particular entity, and share many of the same accounting procedures. The difference between the two is their use by different types of decision makers.

   2. **Management accounting** serves internal (inside) decision makers, such as top executives, department heads, and people at other management levels within an organization.

   3. Accounting, through financial statements, performs a scorekeeping function. It answers the questions of: What is the financial picture of the organization on any given day?   How well did it do during a given period?

   4. There are three major financial statements:

      a. The *balance sheet* focuses on the financial picture as of a given day.

      b. The *income statement* and the *statement of cash flows* focus on performance over time.

   5. The **annual report** is a document prepared by management and distributed to current and potential investors to inform them about the company's past performance and future prospects.

L. O. 2: Describe the Components of the Balance Sheet

A. The Balance Sheet

    1. The **balance sheet** is the financial statement that shows the financial position of a business at a *particular point in time.* It is also known as the **statement of financial position** or **statement of financial condition.**

    2. The balance sheet has two counterbalancing sections, which form the **balance sheet equation:**

$$\text{Assets} = \text{Liabilities} + \text{Owners' Equity}$$

    3. The right side of the balance sheet equation represents outsider and owner "claims against" the total assets shown on the left side of the equation.

    4. **Assets** are economic resources that are expected to increase or cause future cash inflows or reduce or prevent future cash outflows.

    5. **Liabilities** are economic obligations of the organization to outsiders, or claims against its assets by outsiders. **Notes payable** are promissory notes that are evidence of a debt and state the terms of payment.

    6. **Owners' equity** is the *residual interest* in, or remaining claims against, the organization's assets after deducting all liabilities. This may be expressed as:
$$\text{Owners' Equity} = \text{Assets} - \text{Liabilities.}$$

STOP & REVIEW:

Before continuing, review the accounting equation and its major components.

> **STUDY TIP:**
> Quiz yourself on all the new terms introduced to this point.

L. O. 3: Analyze Business Transactions and Relate Them to Changes on the Balance Sheet

A. Balance Sheet Transactions

    1. An **entity** is an organization or a section of an organization that stands apart from other organizations and individuals as a separate economic unit.

    2. A **transaction** is any event that both affects the financial position of an entity and can be reliably recorded in terms of money.

    3. Each transaction requires two counterbalancing entries so that the equality of the balance sheet equation is maintained. That is, total assets must always equal the total of liabilities and owners' equity.

B.   Transaction Analysis

     1.   An **account** is a summary record of the changes in a particular asset, liability, or owners' equity. An *account balance* is the total of all entries to the account to date.

     2.   The analysis of transactions is the heart of accounting. For each transaction you must determine:

          a.   Which specific accounts are affected.

          b.   Whether the account balances are increased or decreased.

          c.   The amount of the change in each account balance.

     3.   Additional new terms introduced in this section.

          a.   **Inventory** is goods held by the company for the purpose of sale to the customers.

          b.   An **open account** means buying or selling on credit, usually by just an "authorized signature" of the buyer.

          c.   An **account payable** is a liability that results from a purchase of goods or services on open account.

          d.   A **compound entry** is a transaction that affects more than two accounts.

          e.   A **creditor** is one to whom money is owed.

          f.   A **debtor** is one who owes money.

STOP & REVIEW:

Before continuing, carefully review each of the individual transactions in **Exhibit 1-2 in the text.**

STUDY TIP:
Quiz yourself on the additional new terms introduced.
Remember, *each* transaction must *balance*.

C.   Preparing the Balance Sheet

     1.   Remember that the balance sheet represents the financial impact of the accumulation of transactions at a specific point in time. Therefore, the totals of each account (account balances) are used to prepare the balance sheet.

     2.   A balance sheet could be prepared after each transaction, but this is unnecessary. Balance sheets are usually produced once a month.

STOP & REVIEW:

Review "Preparation of the Balance Sheet" in the text.

L. O. 4: Compare the Features of Proprietorships, Partnerships, and Corporations

A.   Types of Ownership

    1.   A **sole proprietorship** is a separate organization with a single owner.

    2.   A **partnership** is a special form of organization that joins two or more individuals who act as co-owners.

    3.   A **corporation** is an organization that is an "artificial being" created by individual state laws that is a separate *legal* entity from its owners. Corporations may be:

        a.   **Publicly owned** in that shares in the ownership are sold to the public who are known as *shareholders* or *stockholders*.

        b.   **Privately owned** by a family, a small group of shareholders, or a single individual, where shares of ownership are not publicly sold.

B.   A Note on Nonprofit Organizations

    1.   Fundamental accounting principles also apply to nonprofit (or not-for-profit) organizations.

    2.   Managers and accountants in hospitals, universities, government agencies, and other nonprofit organizations also use financial statements in decision making.

C.   Advantages and Disadvantages

    1.   Corporations have **limited liability** (corporate creditors ordinarily have claims against the corporate assets only), while the owners of proprietorships and partnerships typically have *unlimited liability*.

    2.   It is also easier for corporations to transfer ownership and raise ownership capital than for proprietorships and partnerships. **Capital stock certificates** (or simply **stock certificates**) are issued as formal evidence of ownership.

    3.   The corporation continues to exist even if its ownership changes, while proprietorships and partnerships officially terminate upon the death or complete withdrawal of an owner.

    4.   A corporation is taxed as a separate entity, but the income earned by a proprietorship or partnership is distributed to the owners, where it is taxed on their personal tax returns.

D.   Accounting for Owners' Equity

    1.   The basic accounting concepts that underlie owners' equity are the same whether the organization is a proprietorship, a partnership, or a corporation.

    2.   Owners' equities for proprietorships and partnerships are often identified by the word **capital,** while owners' equity for a corporation is usually called **stockholders' equity or shareholders' equity.**

    3.   The total capital investment in a corporation by its owners is called **paid-in capital,** which is recorded in two parts:

a. Capital stock at par value. (The term **common stock** is sometimes used instead of capital stock.)

b. Paid-in capital in excess of par value.

E. The Meaning of Par Value

1. **Par value** or **stated value** is the nominal dollar amount printed on stock certificates that is established by the board of directors of the corporation.

2. Stock is usually sold at a price higher than its par value. The difference between the total amount received for the stock and the par value is called **paid-in capital in excess of par value.**

STUDY TIP:
Quiz yourself on all the new terms introduced in this section.

L. O. 5: Describe Auditing and How It Enhances the Value of Financial Information

A. Credibility and the Role of Auditing

1. The credibility of financial statements is the ultimate responsibility of the managers who are entrusted with the resources of the organization.

a. In proprietorships and partnerships, the top managers are usually the owners.

b. In corporations, the stockholders elect and delegate to the board of directors the responsibility for management. The board of directors then appoints the managers.

2. Boards of directors and external users of financial statements need third party assurance about the credibility of the financial statements. The **auditor** examines the information used by managers to prepare the financial statements and attests to the credibility of those statements.

B. The Certified Public Accountant

1. To assure expertise and integrity, public accountants are certified. This adds credibility to the public accountants' opinions on financial statements.

2. A **certified public accountant (CPA)** in the United States earns this designation by a combination of education, qualifying experience, and the passing of a national written examination.

C. The Auditor's Opinion

1. To assess management's financial disclosure, public accountants conduct an **audit,** which is an examination of transactions and financial statements made in accordance with generally accepted auditing standards.

2. The examination, or audit, is described in the **auditor's opinion** (also called an **independent opinion**) that is included with the financial statements in an annual report issued by the corporation.

L. O. 6: Distinguish Between Public and Private Accounting

A. The Accounting Profession

1. **Public accountants** are accountants whose services are offered to the general public on a fee basis. Such services include auditing, income taxes, and management consulting.

2. **Private accountants** work in all the other areas of employment such as businesses, government agencies, and other nonprofit organizations.

B. Public Accounting Firms

C. Other Opportunities for Accountants

L. O. 7: Evaluate the Role of Ethics in the Accounting Process

Professional Ethics

1. Members of the American Institute of Certified Public Accountants must abide by a code of professional conduct to help assure public confidence in the integrity and independence of the CPA.

2. The emphasis on ethics extends beyond public accounting. Auditors and management accountants, as well as all other accountants, have professional responsibilities regarding competence, confidentiality, integrity, and objectivity.

3. Professional accounting organizations and state regulatory bodies have procedures for reviewing behavior alleged to violate codes of professional conduct.

STOP & REVIEW:

Before continuing, review the objectives for this chapter and make sure you have a good understanding of each one.

V. Test Yourself

Questions

1. Briefly explain how accounting information assists in making decisions.

2. Identify and explain the major components of the balance sheet.

3. Identify and discuss at least three advantages of the corporate form of organization.

4. Explain how auditing enhances the value of financial information.

5. Discuss the role of professional ethics in accounting.

Exercises and Problems

1. For each of the following prepare the appropriate owners' equity section of the balance sheet.

   a. Richard Randall decided to open his own management consulting practice as a sole proprietorship. Richard contributed $85,000 from his personal savings to start the business.

   b. Janet Cassagio, Howard Director, and Fannie Davis formed a partnership to open an accounting practice. Total contributed capital was $540,000, with Cassagio contributing $255,000; Director, $135,000; and Davis, $150,000.

   c. On January 1, 19X9 Susan Newman incorporated her new business. The board of directors issued 15,000 shares of $5 par common stock for $125,000.

2. Artisan Corporation's balance sheet for December 31, 19X9 is presented below in random order:

Accounts receivable	$ 25,000	Stockholders' equity	$ 363,000
Notes payable	70,000	Accounts payable	87,000
Merch. inventory	175,000	Equipment	350,000
Long-term debt payable	290,000	Land	200,000
		Cash	60,000

Prepare in good form the balance sheet for December 31, 19X9.

3. Certain amounts are omitted in the following balance sheets. Determine the missing amounts.

	Mets Company	Braves Company	Dodgers Company
Total Assets	$ (A)	$75,000	$ 89,000
Total Liabilities	24,000	23,000	(C)
Total Owners' Equity	73,000	(B)	45,000

4. Analyze the following transactions using the accounting equation format for March for Corel Company. Then prepare a balance sheet as of March 31, 19X8. Corel was founded on March 1.

March 1   Issued 2,500 shares of $3 par common stock for cash, $37,500.

2   Purchased equipment for $18,000, paying $7,000 now and agreeing to pay $11,000 on account later.

3   Paid $4,000 on open account.

4   Borrowed cash from a bank, signing a note for $15,000.

5   Sold equipment on account at cost, $5,000.

6   Collected cash on account, $2,000.

5. The balances of each item in Ridgewood Company's accounting equation are given below for May 31 and for each of the next nine business days. State briefly what you think took place on each of these nine days, assuming that only one transaction occurred each day.

Date	Cash	Accounts Receivable	Inventory	Equipment	Accounts Payable	Owners' Equity
May 31	$ 3,000	$ 7,000	$11,000	$ 9,000	$14,000	$16,000
June 1	13,000	7,000	11,000	9,000	14,000	26,000
2	13,000	7,000	10,000	9,000	13,000	26,000
3	3,000	7,000	14,000	15,000	13,000	26,000
4	9,000	1,000	14,000	15,000	13,000	26,000
5	6,000	1,000	14,000	15,000	10,000	26,000
6	8,500	2,500	14,000	11,000	10,000	26,000
7	8,500	2,500	16,000	11,000	12,000	26,000
8	7,500	2,500	16,000	11,000	12,000	25,000
9	7,500	2,500	16,000	13,000	14,000	25,000

Matching

MATCH EACH TERM WITH ITS DEFINITION BY WRITING THE APPROPRIATE LETTER IN THE SPACE PROVIDED.

Terms

_____ 1. Account

_____ 2. Accounting

_____ 3. Account payable

_____ 4. Assets

_____ 5. Annual report

_____ 6. Audit

_____ 7. Balance sheet

_____ 8. Capital

_____ 9. Common stock

_____ 10. Compound entry

_____ 11. Corporation

_____ 12. Entity

_____ 13. Financial accounting

_____ 14. Inventory

_____ 15. Liabilities

_____ 16. Limited liability

_____ 17. Management accounting

_____ 18. Notes Payable

_____ 19. Owners' equity

_____ 20. Paid-in capital

_____ 21. Paid-in capital in excess of par value

_____ 22. Partnership

_____ 23. Par value

_____ 24. Sole proprietorship

_____ 25. Stockholders' equity

_____ 26. Transaction

Definitions

A. The field of accounting that serves internal decision makers.

B. A liability that results from a purchase of goods or services on open account.

C. An organization that is an "artificial being" created by individual state laws.

D. The nominal dollar amount printed on stock certificates.

E. Any event that affects both the financial position of an entity and can be reliably recorded in money terms.

F. An examination of transactions and financial statements made in accordance with generally accepted auditing principles.

G. Claims against an organization's assets by outsiders.

H. The excess of assets over liabilities of a corporation.

I.   A separate organization with a single owner.

J.   The residual interest in the organization's assets after deducting liabilities.

K.   A term used to identify owners' equities for proprietorships and partnerships.

L.   A summary record of the changes in a particular asset, liability, or owners' equity.

M.   Stock representing the class of owners having a "residual" ownership of a corporation.

N.   A financial statement that shows the financial position of a business at a particular instant in time.

O.   When issuing stock, the difference between the total amount received and the par value.

P.   An organization that is a separate economic unit.

Q.   An organization that is co-owned by two or more individuals.

R.   The field of accounting that serves external decision makers.

S.   A feature where the owners' personal assets are not subject to creditors' claims.

T.   The total capital investment in a corporation by its owners.

U.   Economic resources that are expected to provide future benefits.

V.   Goods held by a company for the purpose of sale to customers.

W.   Written promises that are evidence of a debt and state the terms of payment.

X.   A combination of financial statements and management discussion and analysis that is provided annually to investors.

Y.   A transaction that affects more than two accounts.

Z.   A process of identifying, recording, summarizing and reporting economic information to decision makers.

Multiple Choice

_____ 1.   The financial statement that shows the financial position of a business at a particular point in time is the:

        a.   Income statement.
        b.   Statement of cash flows.
        c.   Balance sheet.
        d.   None of the above are correct.

_____ 2.   The balance sheet equation is best expressed as:

        a.   Owners' equity = assets - liabilities
        b.   Assets + liabilities = owners' equity
        c.   Assets = liabilities - owners' equity
        d.   Owners' equity + assets = liabilities

_____ 3.   Which of the following statements is true?

        a.   If there is an increase in an asset account, there could be an increase in a liability account.
        b.   If there is an increase in an asset account, there could be a decrease in another asset account.
        c.   If there is an decrease in a liability account, there could be a decrease in an asset account.
        d.   All of the above statements are correct.

_____ 4.   Which of the following statements is false?

        a.   A transaction can increase the balance in one account and decrease the balance in another account.
        b.   A transaction can increase the balance in two accounts.
        c.   A transaction can increase the balance in two accounts and decrease the balance in one account.
        d.   A transaction must increase and decrease the same number of accounts.

_____ 5.   Which of the following transactions would increase the cash account and increase notes payable?

        a.   Purchasing inventory on account.
        b.   A bank loan.
        c.   Payment on account.
        d.   Collection on account.

_____ 6.   Paula is trying to decide which form of organization she should adopt for her new business. She is worried about the effect on her personal assets if a customer should be injured in her store and sued her company. Which form of organization should she adopt?

        a.   Partnership.
        b.   Corporation.
        c.   Sole proprietorship.
        d.   Limited partnership.

_____ 7.   The published financial statements are the responsibility of the :

a.   Corporate managers.
b.   Auditors.
c.   Securities and Exchange Commission.
d.   Certified public accountant.

_____ 8.   The major difference between financial and managerial accounting is the:

a.   Use of financial data of the business.
b.   Absence of similar procedures for analyzing and recording transactions.
c.   Ultimate user of the information.
d.   None of the above is correct.

_____ 9.   Which of the following is _not_ an advantage of the corporate form of organization?

a.   Limited liability.
b.   Easy transfer of ownership.
c.   Continuous existence.
d.   All of the above are advantages of the corporate form of organization.

_____ 10.   If a certified public accountant owned shares of stock in a client's business it might be a violation of:

a.   The entity concept.
b.   Professional ethics.
c.   The reliability principle.
d.   None of the above are correct.

VI. Solutions to Test Yourself

Questions

1. Accounting is the major means of organizing and summarizing information about the economic activities of a business. Accounting systems are designed after considering the types of information desired by managers and all other decision makers. Accountants then analyze, record, quantify, accumulate, summarize, classify, report, and interpret the information that is provided to decision makers in the form of financial statements. (L. O. 1)

2. The major components of the balance sheet are assets, liabilities, and owners' equity. Assets are the economic resources that are expected to provide future benefits to the organization. Liabilities and owners' equity represent claims against these resources (assets). Liabilities are claims by outsiders and owners' equity is the owners' claim or residual interest in the organization. (L. O. 2)

3. Advantages of the corporate form of organization are:

   1. *Limited liability.* The owners' personal assets are not subject to the claims of creditors.
   2. *Easy transfer of ownership.* Ownership is represented by shares of stock that may be sold and resold.
   3. *Ease in raising ownership capital.* Hundreds to thousands of potential stockholders may buy stock in a corporation.
   4. *Continuity of existence.* The life of the corporation continues even if ownership changes. (L. O. 4)

4. Auditing enhances the value of financial information by providing interested parties with information about the credibility of financial statements. Certified public accountants issue an auditor's opinion on financial statements. (L. O. 5)

5. The users of financial information need assurance that accountants have high ethical standards. All accountants have professional responsibilities regarding competence, confidentiality, integrity, and objectivity. Professional accounting organizations and state regulatory bodies have procedures for reviewing behavior alleged to violate codes of professional conduct. (L. O. 7)

Exercises and Problems

1. a. <u>Owner's Equity</u>   (sole proprietorship)

        Richard Randall, capital   <u>$85,000</u>

    b. <u>Owners' Equity</u>   (partnership)

        Janet Cassagio, capital $255,000
        Howard Director, capital   135,000
        Fannie Davis, capital   <u>150,000</u>
            Total partners' capital   <u>$540,000</u>

    c. <u>Stockholders' Equity</u>   (corporation)

        Paid-in capital:
          Common stock, 15,000 shares issued
            at par value of $5 per share $ 75,000
          Paid-in capital in excess of par value   <u>50,000</u>
          Total paid-in capital $125,000

2.

Artisan Corporation
Balance Sheet
December 31, 19X9

<u>Assets</u>		<u>Liabilities &</u> <u>Stockholders' Equity</u>	
		Liabilities:	
Cash	$ 60,000	Accounts payable	$ 87,000
Accounts receivable	25,000	Notes payable	70,000
Merchandise inventory	175,000	Long-term debt payable	<u>290,000</u>
Equipment	350,000	Total liabilities	$447,000
Land	<u>200,000</u>	Stockholders' equity	<u>363,000</u>
		Total liabilities &	
Total assets	<u>$810,000</u>	stockholders' equity	<u>$810,000</u>

3. A $97,000 (liabilities $24,000 + owners' equity $73,000)
    B $52,000 (assets $75,000 - liabilities $23,000)
    C $44,000 (assets $89,000 - owners' equity $45,000)

4.

	Cash	Accounts Receivable	Equipment	Accounts Payable	Notes Payable	Stock-holders' Equity
1	+37,500					+37,500
2	-7,000		+18,000	+11,000		
3	-4,000			-4,000		
4	+15,000				+15,000	
5		+5,000	-5,000			
6	+2,000	-2,000				
	43,500	3,000	13,000	7,000	15,000	37,500
		59,500			59,500	

Corel Corporation
Balance Sheet
March 31, 19X8

Assets		Liabilities & Stockholders' Equity	
		Liabilities:	
Cash	$43,500	Accounts payable	$ 7,000
Accounts receivable	3,000	Notes payable	15,000
Equipment	13,000	Total liabilities	$22,000
		Stockholders' Equity:	
		Paid-in capital	37,500
		Total liabilities &	
Total assets	$59,500	stockholders' equity	$59,500

5.   June 1   Owners invested $10,000 additional cash in Ridgewood Company.

June 2   Ridgewood returned $1,000 in inventory to a supplier for credit against accounts payable.

June 3   Ridgewood paid $10,000 in cash to purchase additional inventory of $4,000 and equipment worth $6,000.

June 4   Ridgewood collected $6,000 cash on accounts receivable.

June 5   Ridgewood paid $3,000 on accounts payable.

June 6   Ridgewood sold $4,000 of equipment for $2,500 cash and $1,500 accounts receivable.

June 7   Ridgewood purchased inventory on account for $2,000.

June 8   Owners withdrew $1,000 cash from Ridgewood Company.

June 9   Ridgewood purchased $2,000 of equipment on account.

Matching

1.	L	L .O. 3		10.	Y	L .O. 3		19.	J	L. O. 2
2.	Z	L .O. 1		11.	C	L. O. 4		20.	T	L. O. 4
3.	B	L .O. 3		12.	P	L. O. 3		21.	O	L. O. 4
4.	U	L. O. 2		13.	R	L. O. 1		22.	Q	L. O. 4
5.	X	L .O. 1		14.	V	L. O. 3		23.	D	L. O. 4
6.	F	L. O. 5		15.	G	L. O. 2		24.	I	L. O. 4
7.	N	L. O. 2		16.	S	L. O. 4		25.	H	L. O. 4
8.	K	L. O. 4		17.	A	L. O. 1		26.	E	L. O. 3
9.	M	L. O. 4		18.	W	L .O. 2				

Multiple Choice

1.   c   The income statement and statement of cash flows focus on *performance over time*, not at a particular point in time.   (L. O. 1)

2.   a   Assets = liabilities + owners' equity can be stated as assets - liabilities = owners' equity. (L. O.2)

3.   d   All the answers are correct. (L. O.3)

4.   d   a, b, and c are true. (L. O. 3)

5.   b   a, c, and d are incorrect. (L. O. 3)

6.   b   A corporation would probably be the best choice because of the limited liability feature of the corporate form of organization. (L. O. 4)

7.   a   The financial statements are the responsibility of the management of the organization. (L. O. 5)

8.   c   Both financial and managerial accounting use financial data for an organization and share many of the same procedures for analyzing and recording transactions. (L. O. 1)

9.   d   (L. O. 5)

10.   b   Certified public accountants have a professional code of ethics or conduct to maintain competence, confidentiality, integrity, and independence. If a CPA owned stock in a client's business there could be a question of a violation of ethics. (L. O. 7)

Chapter 2

MEASURING INCOME TO ASSESS PERFORMANCE

I. Learning Objectives

The measurement of income is one of the major ways of evaluating the performance of a business. This chapter addresses the basics of measuring income, with a special focus on revenues and expenses. It also defines three additional financial statements — the income statement, the statement of cash flows, and the statement of retained income. Financial ratios used by decision makers are also introduced in this chapter. Use the following learning objectives as stepping stones in completing your study of this chapter.

1. Explain how income is measured using both the accrual basis and cash basis accounting methods.

2. Use the concepts of recognition, matching, and cost recovery to record revenue and expenses.

3. Prepare an income statement and show how it is related to a balance sheet.

4. Prepare a statement of cash flows and show how it differs from an income statement.

5. Account for cash dividends and prepare a statement of retained income.

6. Compute and explain earnings per share, price-earnings ratio, dividend-yield ratio, and dividend-payout ratio.

II. Pretest

_____ 1. Which of the following is *not* a part of the definition of revenues?

    a.   Gross decreases in owners' equity.
    b.   Increases assets.
    c.   For the delivery of goods or services to customers.
    d.   All of the above are a part of the definition of revenues.

_____ 2. Income is:

    a.   Additional owners' equity generated by revenues.
    b.   The excess of expenses over revenues.
    c.   The excess of revenues over expenses.
    d.   None of the above are correct.

_____ 3. The recording of expenses in the same time period as related revenues is known as:

    a.   Operating cycle.
    b.   Matching.
    c.   Cost recovery.
    d.   Cash basis.

_____ 4. The concept of recognizing expense in the accounts is called:

    a.   Product costs.
    b.   Period costs.
    c.   Recognition.
    d.   Cost recovery.

_____ 5. A report of all revenues and expenses pertaining to a specific time period is the:

    a.   Balance sheet.
    b.   Income statement.
    c.   Statement of retained income.
    d.   Statement of cash flows.

_____ 6. The excess of expenses *over* revenues is:

    a.   Retained income.
    b.   Net income.
    c.   Net loss.
    d.   Not possible.

_____ 7. Which of the following is *not* true of the statement of cash flows?

    a.   It is for a specific point in time.
    b.   It reports cash receipts and payments.
    c.   It is separated into three categories.
    d.   It details the changes in the cash account.

_____ 8.   The sale and the purchase or production of goods and services, including collections from customers, and payments to suppliers or employees, are:

   a.   Financing activities.
   b.   Investing activities.
   c.   Operating activities.
   d.   Not reported on the statement of cash flows.

_____ 9.   Distributions to stockholders that reduce retained income are known as:

   a.   Withdrawals.
   b.   Expenses.
   c.   Payments.
   d.   Dividends.

_____ 10.   Which of the following is *not* true of the statement of retained income?

   a.   It is dated for a specific point in time.
   b.   It lists the beginning balance of retained income.
   c.   It includes all changes in retained income.
   d.   It states the ending balance of retained income.

_____ 11.   The only financial ratio that is required as a part of the body of a financial statement is:

   a.   Price-earnings ratio (P-E).
   b.   Dividend-yield ratio.
   c.   Earnings per share (EPS).
   d.   Dividend-payout ratio.

_____ 12.   The ratio that measures how much the investing public is willing to pay for the company's prospects for earnings is the:

   a.   Price-earnings ratio (P-E).
   b.   Dividend-yield ratio.
   c.   Earnings per share (EPS).
   d.   Dividend-payout ratio.

III. Answers to Pretest

1.   a   Revenues are gross *increases* in owners' equity, not decreases. (L. O. 1)

2.   c   Income results when revenues are more than expenses. (L. O. 1)

3.   b   The matching of revenue and related expenses in the same time period is the basis of accrual accounting. (L. O. 2)

4.   d   Under the cost recovery concept, some costs are recorded as assets until their benefit is realized in future periods. At that time, transactions to decrease the assets and increase expense accounts are recorded. (L. O. 2)

5.   b   Only the income statement reports all revenues and expenses. (L. O. 3)

6.   c   Net loss occurs when expenses for an entity exceed its revenues for the same period. This is the exact opposite of net income. (L. O. 3)

7.   a   The statement of cash flows summarizes cash activities over a *span of time*, not at a specific point in time. (L. O. 4)

8.   c   All transactions that relate to the operation of the business are operating activities. (L. O. 4)

9.   d   Distributions to stockholders of a corporation are called dividends. (L. O. 5)

10. a   The statement of retained income is also for a *span of time*, not at a specific point in time. (L. O. 5)

11. c   Because of the importance of the income statement and earnings, accounting regulators have required earnings per share (EPS) to be shown on the face of the income statement of publicly held corporations. (L. O. 6)

12. a   (L. O. 6)

EVALUATION

The pretest contained two questions for each learning objective. If you did not answer both questions correctly for each learning objective, you should review the appropriate section of the textbook and study guide before you attempt the material after Part IV.

IV. Key Concept Review by Learning Objectives

L. O. 1: Explain How Income Is Measured Using Both the Accrual and Cash Basis Accounting Methods

A.   Introduction to Income Measurement

    1.   *Income* is generally regarded as a measure of the increase in the "wealth" of an entity over a period of time.

    2.   Accountants have agreed on a common set of rules for measuring income so that all decision makers can more easily compare the performance of one company with that of another.

B.   Operating Cycle

    1.   An **operating cycle** is the time span during which cash is used to acquire goods and services, which are sold to customers, who then pay for their purchases with cash.

    2.   An operating cycle is also called a *cash cycle* or *earnings cycle*.

C.   The Accounting Time Period

    1.   Most companies use a calendar year, but many companies use a **fiscal year** (the year established for accounting purposes that ends on some date other than December 31) for measuring income or profit.

    2.   Companies may also prepare financial statements for **interim periods**, which are the time spans established for accounting purposes that are less than one year.

D.   Revenues and Expenses

    1.   Revenues and expenses are the key components in measuring income.

        a.   **Revenues** (inflows) increase the owners' interest (equity) in the business.

        b.   **Expenses** (outflows) decrease the owners' interest (equity) in the business.

        c.   Together, these items define the fundamental meaning of **income** (or **profit** or **earnings**), which is simply the excess of revenue over expenses.

    2.   The additional owners' equity generated by income or profits is called **retained income** (or **retained earnings** or **reinvested earnings**).

STOP & REVIEW:

Before continuing, carefully review each of the individual transactions in **Exhibits 2-1 and 2-2 in the text**.

L. O. 2: Use the Concepts of Recognition, Matching, and Cost Recovery to Record Revenues and Expenses

A. Accrual Basis and Cash Basis

1. There are two basic methods of measuring income: the accrual basis and the cash basis. The basic difference between the two methods is the timing associated with a transaction's effect on financial statements.

2. The **accrual basis** recognizes the impact of transactions on the financial statements in the time periods when *revenues are earned* and *expenses are incurred* — not necessarily when cash changes hands.

3. The **cash basis** recognizes the impact of transactions on the financial statements only when *cash is received or disbursed*.

B. Recognition of Revenues

1. A major convention used to measure income on an accrual basis is recognition of revenues.

2. **Recognition** of revenues is a test for determining whether revenues should be recorded in the financial statements of a given period. To be recognized, revenues must meet *both* of the following criteria:

   a. Be *earned*. Revenues are considered earned when a company delivers goods or services to a customer.

   b. Be *realized*. Revenues are realized when cash or claims to cash are received in exchange for goods or services. The usual evidence is a market transaction where the buyer pays or promises to pay cash and the seller delivers merchandise or services.

C. Matching and Cost Recovery

1. There are two types of expenses in every accounting period:

   a. **Product costs** are costs linked with revenues and charged as expenses when the related revenue is recognized. **Cost of goods sold** (or **cost of sales**), which is the original acquisition cost of the inventory that was sold to customers during the reporting period, and sales commissions are good examples.

   b. **Period costs** are items identified directly as expenses of the time period in which they are incurred.

2. **Matching** is the recording of expenses in the same time period as the related revenues are recognized.

3. **Cost recovery** is the concept by which some purchases of goods or services are recorded as assets because their costs are expected to be recovered in the form of cash inflows or reduced cash outflows in future periods. An example would be *prepaid rent*.

D. Applying Matching and Cost Recovery

1. As an asset is being used, more and more of its original cost is transferred from an asset account to an expense account.

2. The purchases and uses of goods and services usually consist of two basic steps:

    a. The *acquisition* of the assets.

    b. The *expiration* of the assets as *expenses*.

3. **Depreciation** is the systematic allocation of the cost of long-lived or fixed assets to the expense accounts of the particular periods that benefit from the use of the asset.

E. Recognition of Expired Assets

1. Assets such as inventory, prepaid rent, and equipment may be thought of as stored costs that are carried forward to future periods and recorded as expenses in the future. Assets have future potential to produce revenues.

2. Some of the most difficult issues in accounting center on *when* an unexpired cost expires and becomes an expense.

3. The balance sheet equation shows revenue and expense items as subparts of owners' equity. The income statement just collects all of these changes in owners' equity for the accounting period and combines them in one place.

    a. Revenue and expense accounts are nothing more than subdivisions of stockholders' equity — temporary stockholders' equity accounts.

    b. Their purpose is to summarize the volume of sales and the various expenses so that income can be measured.

4. The striking feature of the balance sheet equation is its universal applicability. No transaction has ever been conceived, no matter how simple or complex, that cannot be analyzed via the equation.

STUDY TIP:
Quiz yourself on all the new terms introduced to this point.

L. O. 3: Prepare an Income Statement and Show How it Is Related to a Balance Sheet

A. The Income Statement

1. An **income statement** is a report of all revenues and expenses pertaining to a specific time period. Income statements measure performance for a *span of time*, whether it be a month, a quarter, or longer.

2. **Net income** is the famous "bottom line" on an income statement — the remainder after all expenses have been deducted from revenue.

3. By tracking net income from period to period, comparing changes in net income to economy wide and industry averages, and examining changes in the revenue and expense components of net income, investors and other decision makers can evaluate the success of the period's operations.

B.   Relationship Between Income Statement and Balance Sheet

    1.   The income statement is the major link between two balance sheets.

    2.   Remember that the balance sheet provides a snapshot of an entity's financial position at an *instant* of time. In contrast, the income statement provides a moving picture of events over a *span* of time.

    3.   The balance sheets show the financial position of the company at discreet points in time, and the income statement explains the changes that have taken place between those points.

L. O. 4: Prepare a Statement of Cash Flows and Show How it Differs from an Income Statement

Income Versus Cash Flows

    1.   Income is a measure of the entity's performance in generating net assets. Increases in assets or decreases in liabilities accompany increases in retained income. However, income does not measure the entity's performance in generating cash.

    2.   The **statement of cash flows** (or **cash flow statement**) is a required statement that reports the cash receipts and cash payments of an entity during a particular period (over a span of time).

    3.   The statement of cash flows gives a direct picture of where cash came from and where it went. The fundamental approach to the statement of cash flows is simple:

        a.   List the activities that increased cash (cash inflows) or decreased cash (cash outflows).

        b.   Place each cash inflow and outflow into one of three categories according to the type of activity that caused it: operating activities, investing activities, and financing activities.

    4.   *Operating activities* include the sale and the purchase or production of goods and services, including collections from customers, payments to suppliers or employees, and payments for items such as rent, taxes, and interest.

    5.   *Investing activities* include acquiring and selling long-term assets and securities held for long-term investment purposes.

    6.   *Financing activities* include obtaining resources from owners and creditors and repaying amounts borrowed.

STOP & REVIEW:

Review **Exhibit 2-4** in the text.

STUDY TIP:
Study the "Summary Problem for Your Review" and its solution including Exhibits 2-5 and 2-6 in the text before going on.
Quiz yourself on all the new terms introduced to this point.

L. O. 5: Account for Cash Dividends and Prepare a Statement of Retained Income

A. Accounting for Dividends and Retained Income

1. A corporation's revenues and expenses for a particular time period are recorded in the stockholders' equity account, Retained Income.

2. Retained Income is increased by the net income for the period or decreased by the period's net loss.

B. Cash Dividends

1. **Cash dividends** reduce Retained Income and are paid out to stockholders to provide a return on the stockholders' investment in the corporation.

2. Cash dividends are not expenses and should not be deducted from revenues because dividends are not directly linked to the generation of revenues or the costs of operating activities.

3. Cash dividends are not "paid out of retained income"; they are distributions of assets that reduce a portion of the ownership claim. This distribution is made possible by both profitable operations *and* the existence of cash.

C. Dividend Transactions

1. There are three important steps or dates related to dividends:

    a. The board of directors declares (announces its intention to pay) a dividend on the *date of declaration*

    b. Payable to those stockholders on record as owning the stock on the *record date*

    c. And actually pays the dividend on the *payment date*.

2. Accounting transactions are required:

    a. On the date of declaration as the declaration affects the corporation's financial position because the shareholders also become creditors for the amount of the legally declared dividends.

    b. On the payment date as the resulting liability is reduced only when the cash is disbursed.

D. Retained Income and Cash

1. The existence of retained income enables the board of directors to *declare* a dividend. The existence of cash enables the corporation to *pay* the dividend.

2. Cash and Retained Income are two entirely separate accounts sharing no necessary relationship.

E. Statement of Retained Income

1. The **statement of retained income** lists the beginning balance in Retained Income, followed by a description of any changes that occurred during the period and the ending balance.

2. When the statement of retained income is added to the bottom of the income statement, the combined statement is called a **statement of income and retained income**.

🛑 **& REVIEW:**

Review **Exhibits 2-7** and **2-8** in the text.

F. Customs of Presentation

> **STUDY TIP:**
> Study the "Summary Problem for Your Review" and its solution
> in the text before going on.
> Quiz yourself on all the new terms introduced to this point.

L. O. 6: Compute and Explain Earnings Per Share, Price-Earnings Ratio, Dividend-Yield Ratio, and Dividend-Payout Ratio

A. Because stock market prices are quoted on a per-share basis, many ratios are expressed per share (and after taxes). A financial ratio is computed by dividing one number by another.

B. Earnings Per Share (EPS)

1. Earnings per share data is required to be presented on the face of the income statement of publicly held corporations. This is the only instance where a financial ratio is required as a part of the body of financial statements.

2. The earnings per share computation:

$$EPS = \frac{Net\ Income}{Average\ Number\ of\ Shares\ Outstanding}$$

C. Price-Earnings Ratio (P-E)

1. Price-earnings ratio measures how much the investing public is willing to pay for a chance to share the company's potential earnings.

2. The P-E calculation:

$$P\text{-}E = \frac{Market\ Price\ Per\ Share\ of\ Common\ Stock}{Earnings\ Per\ Share\ of\ Common\ Stock}$$

D. Dividend-Yield Ratio

1. Dividend-yield ratio gives an indication of the return or profitability, in the form of dividends, of a stock relative to the current market price of the stock.

2. The dividend-yield ratio is computed as follows:

$$Dividend\ Yield = \frac{Common\ Dividends\ Per\ Share}{Market\ Price\ Per\ Share}$$

E.   Dividend-Payout Ratio

    1.   The dividend-payout ratio gives an indication of the percentage of earnings that will be distributed to the shareholders in the form of dividends.

    2.   Dividend-payout ratio is computed as follows:

$$Dividend\text{-}Payout\ Ratio = \frac{Common\ Dividends\ Per\ Share}{Earnings\ Per\ Share}$$

F.   The Language of Accounting in the Real World

    1.   Organizations use different terms to describe the same concept or account.

    2.   Exhibit 2-9 in the text presents synonyms for various accounting terms.

G.   Accounting for Nonprofit Organizations

STUDY TIP:
Study the "Summary Problem for Your Review" and its solution in the text before going on.

STOP & REVIEW:

Before continuing, review the objectives for this chapter and make sure you have a good understanding of each one.

V. Test Yourself

Questions

1. Explain how income is measured.

2. Distinguish *accrual* basis accounting from *cash* basis accounting.

3. Discuss the convention of revenue recognition.

4. Briefly explain the concept of cost recovery.

5. Identify the three categories of cash flows found on the statement of cash flows, and list two activities that might appear in each of the categories.

Exercises and Problems

1. Certain amounts are omitted for each of the following companies. Determine the missing amounts.

	Lakers Inc.	Kings Inc.	Sonics Inc.	Suns Inc.	Nets Inc.
	125			-	
Total Assets	**(A)**	**(C)**	775	680	**(H)**
Total Liabilities	30	40	250	384	119
Paid-in Capital	-0-	50	**(E)**	77	44
Beg. Retained Income	100	30	**(F)**	185	156
Revenue	85	**(D)**	675	983	323
Expenses	-0-	70	600	935	**(I)**
Dividends	**(B)**	10	25	**(G)**	34
End. Retained Income		60	425	210	174

Data for use with #2 - #4

The following information is available for Midnight Express for 19X9:

    a.   The business generated revenues of $558,000. All but $175,000 were for cash or were collected by December 31, 19X9.

    b.   Rent expense of $210,000 was paid.

    c.   Depreciation expense was $90,000.

    d.   Other operating expenses of $96,000 were incurred and paid during 19X9 except for $35,000 still owed to suppliers on December 31, 19X9.

    e.   An additional $100,000 in common stock was issued to help finance equipment purchases of $225,000. The difference needed to purchase the equipment was funded with a loan from the bank.

    f.   The Cash balance on January 1, 19X9 was $23,000, and the Cash balance at December 31, 19X9 was $95,000.

    g.   The beginning balance in Retained Income was $420,000 and dividends of $40,000 were declared and paid during the period.

2.   Using the above information, prepare, in good form, an income statement for Midnight Express for 19X9.

3.   Prepare, in good form, a statement of retained income for Midnight Express for 19X9 using the given data.

4.   From the given information, prepare, in good form, a statement of cash flows for Midnight Express for 19X9.

5.   Sunset Software Company's annual report showed earnings of $1,580 million. Cash dividends per share were $1.85. Sunset had 436,100 average number of common shares outstanding. No other type of stock was outstanding. The market price of the stock at the end of the year was $68 per share.

    Compute (1) earnings per share, (2) price-earnings ratio, (3) dividend-yield ratio, and (4) dividend-payout ratio.

Matching

MATCH EACH TERM WITH ITS DEFINITION BY WRITING THE APPROPRIATE LETTER IN THE SPACE PROVIDED.

Terms

_____ 1. Accrual basis

_____ 2. Cash basis

_____ 3. Cash dividends

_____ 4. Cost of goods sold

_____ 5. Cost recovery

_____ 6. Depreciation

_____ 7. Expenses

_____ 8. Fiscal year

_____ 9. Income

_____ 10. Income statement

_____ 11. Interim periods

_____ 12. Matching

_____ 13. Net income

_____ 14. Operating cycle

_____ 15. Period costs

_____ 16. Product costs

_____ 17. Recognition

_____ 18. Retained income

_____ 19. Revenues

_____ 20. Sales

_____ 21. Statement of cash flows

_____ 22. Statement of retained income

Definitions

A.   A test for determining whether revenues should be recorded in the financial statements of a given period. To be this, revenues must be earned and realized.

B.   The time span during which cash is used to acquire goods and services, which in turn are sold to customers, who in turn pay for their purchases.

C.   The systematic allocation of the acquisition cost of long-lived or fixed assets to the expense accounts of particular periods that benefit from the use of the assets.

D.   Recognizes the impact of transactions on the financial statements only when cash is received or disbursed.

E.   A statement that lists the beginning balance in retained income, followed by a description of any changes that occurred during the period, and the ending balance.

F.   Gross increases in owners' equity arising from increases in assets received in exchange for the delivery of goods or services to customers.

G.   Costs that are linked with revenues and are charged as expenses when the related revenue is recognized.

H.   A required statement that reports the cash receipts and cash payments of an entity during a particular period.

I.   Additional owners' equity generated by income or profits.

36

J.   The original acquisition cost of the inventory that was sold to customers during the reporting period.

K.   The recording of expenses in the same time period as the related revenues are recognized.

L.   Recognizes the impact of transactions on the financial statements in the time periods when revenues and expenses occur.

M.   Distributions of cash to stockholders that reduce retained income.

N.   The concept by which some purchases of goods or services are recorded as assets because their costs are expected to be recovered in the form of cash inflows or reduced cash outflows in future periods.

O.   Decreases in owners' equity that arise because goods or services are delivered to customers.

P.   A report of all revenues and expenses pertaining to a specific time period.

Q.   Items identified directly as expenses of the time period in which they are incurred.

R.   A synonym for revenues.

S.   The excess of revenues over expenses.

T.   The time spans established for accounting purposes that are less than one year.

U.   Is the remainder after all expenses have been deducted from revenue.

V.   The year established for accounting purposes that ends on some date other than December 31.

Multiple Choice

_____ 1.   The accounting system that recognizes revenue and expenses when they occur is:

      a.   Cash basis.
      b.   Accrual basis.
      c.   Cost recovery.
      d.   Recognition.

_____ 2.   The systematic allocation of the cost of long-lived or fixed assets to expense accounts over the assets' useful lives is known as:

      a.   Matching.
      b.   Recognition.
      c.   Depreciation.
      d.   Accrual accounting.

_____ 3.   In order to be recognized on an accrual basis, revenues must ordinarily be:

      a.   Earned.
      b.   Realized.
      c.   Both a. and b.
      d.   None of the above are correct.

_____ 4.   Which of the following is _not_ part of the income statement?

      a.   Date at a point in time.
      b.   Revenues.
      c.   Expenses.
      d.   Net income.

_____ 5.   The income statement is:

      a.   The only financial statement decision makers use.
      b.   Not related to the statement of retained income.
      c.   Useful only when prepared annually.
      d.   The major link between two balance sheets.

_____ 6.   Which of the following is _not_ part of the statement of cash flows?

      a.   Operating activities.
      b.   Cash flow activities.
      c.   Investing activities.
      d.   Financing activities.

_____ 7.   The statement of cash flows would include:

      a.   The purchase of equipment for cash.
      b.   The declaration of dividends.
      c.   Sales on account.
      d.   Depreciation.

_____ 8. Which of the following is *not* related to dividends?

    a. Declaration date.
    b. Liability date.
    c. Record date.
    d. Payment date.

_____ 9. The statement of retained income includes:

    a. Net income or net loss.
    b. Dividends.
    c. Ending balance of retained income.
    d. All of the above are included on the statement of retained income.

_____ 10. Financial ratios are:

    a. Computed by dividing one number by another.
    b. Used by decision makers.
    c. Often quoted on a per share basis.
    d. All of the above are true of financial ratios.

VI. Solutions to Test Yourself

Questions

1. Revenues are the gross increases in owners' equity arising from increases in assets received in exchange for the delivery of goods or services to customers. Expenses are decreases in owners' equity that arise because goods or services are delivered to customers. Together these items define the meaning of income, which is simply the excess of revenues over expenses. (L. O.1)

2. The accrual basis recognizes the impact of transactions on the financial statement in the time periods when revenues and expenses occur. That is, revenue is recorded as it is earned, and expenses are recorded as they are incurred — not necessarily when cash changes hands.

   In contrast, the cash basis recognizes the impact of transactions on the financial statements only when cash is received or disbursed. (L. O. 1)

3. Revenue recognition is a convention used to measure income on the accrual basis. It is a test for determining whether revenues should be recorded in the financial statements of a given period. To be recognized, revenues must ordinarily be earned and realized. (L. O. 2)

4. Cost recovery is the concept by which some purchases of goods or services are recorded as assets because their costs are expected to be recovered in the form of cash inflows or reduced cash outflows in future periods. When the good or service is used, the asset account is reduced and an expense is recorded. (L. O. 2)

5. The categories on the statement of cash flows and activities that might appear in each category are:

   1. *Operating activities*: Collections from customers and payments to suppliers.
   2. *Investing activities*: Acquiring and selling long-term assets, and acquiring and selling securities held for long-term investment purposes.
   3. *Financial activities*: Selling and repurchasing stock, and borrowing from and repaying creditors. (L. O. 4)

Exercises and Problems

1.	Lakers Inc.	Kings Inc.	Sonics Inc.	Suns Inc.	Nets Inc.
Total Assets	125	**150**	775	680	**337**
Total Liabilities	**80**	40	250	384	119
Paid-in Capital	30	50	**100**	77	44
Beg. Retained Income	-0-	30	**375**	185	156
Revenue	100	**110**	675	983	323
Expenses	85	70	600	935	**271**
Dividends	-0-	10	25	**23**	34
End. Retained Income	**15**	60	425	210	174

(A) = 125 - (30 + [100 - 85]) = **80**

(B) = 0 + (100 - 85) - 0 = **15**

(C) = 40 + (50 + 60) = **150**

(D) = (60 - 30) + 70 + 10 = **110**

(E) = 775 - (250 + 425) = **100**

(F) = 425 + 25 - (675 - 600) = **375**

(G) = 185 + (983 - 935) - 210 = **23**

(H) = 119 + 44 + 174 = **337**

(I) = 156 + 323 - 34 - 174 = **271**

2.

Midnight Express
Income Statement
For the period ended December 31, 19X9

Service revenue		$588,000
Expenses:		
Rent expense	$210,000	
Depreciation expense	90,000	
Other operating expenses	96,000	
Total expenses		396,000
Net income		$ 162,000

3.

Midnight Express
Statement of Retained Income
For the period ended December 31, 19X9

Retained income, January 1, 19X9	$420,000
Net income	162,000
Total	$582,000
Dividends declared	40,000
Retained income, December 31, 19X9	$542,000

4.

Midnight Express
Statement of Cash Flows
For the period ended December 31, 19X9

CASH FLOWS FROM OPERATING ACTIVITIES	
Cash collections for revenues	$ 383,000
Cash payment for rent	(210,000)
Cash payment for other operating expenses	(61,000)
Net cash provided by operating activities	$ 112,000
CASH FLOWS FROM INVESTING ACTIVITIES	
Cash payments for purchases of equipment	$(225,000)
CASH FLOWS FROM FINANCING ACTIVITIES	
Proceeds from sale of stock	$ 100,000
Proceeds from bank loan	125,000
Cash payment for dividends	(40,000)
Net cash provided by financing activities	$ 185,000
Net increase in cash	$ 72,000
Cash balance, January 1, 19X9	23,000
Cash balance, December 31, 19X9	$ 95,000

5. Answers are rounded.

1.
$$EPS = \frac{\$1,580,000}{436,000} = \$3.62$$

2.
$$P\text{-}E = \frac{\$68}{\$3.62} = 18.8$$

3.
$$Dividend\ yield = \frac{\$1.85}{\$68} = 2.7\%$$

4.
$$Dividend\ payout = \frac{\$1.85}{\$3.62} = 51.1\%$$

Matching

1.	L	L .O. 2	8.	V	L. O. 1	15.	Q	L. O. 2
2.	D	L. O. 2	9.	S	L. O. 1	16.	G	L. O. 2
3.	M	L. O. 5	10.	P	L. O. 3	17.	A	L. O. 2
4.	J	L. O. 2	11.	T	L. O. 1	18.	I	L. O. 1
5.	N	L. O. 2	12.	K	L. O. 2	19.	F	L. O. 1
6.	C	L. O. 2	13.	U	L. O. 3	20.	R	L. O. 6
7.	O	L. O. 1	14.	B	L. O. 1	21.	H	L. O. 4
						22.	E	L. O. 5

Multiple Choice

1. b   The accrual basis of accounting recognizes the impact on financial statements of revenues and expenses in the time period in which they occur but not necessarily when cash changes hands. (L. O. 2)

2. c   (L. O. 2)

3. c   To be recognized in an accrual system, revenues ordinarily must be *earned* and also must be *realized*. (L. O. 2)

4. a   An income statement measures performance for a *span or period of time*; not at a specific point in time. (L. O. 3)

5. d   The income statement is the major link between two balance sheets. It is only one of several financial statements decision makers use; it is related to the other financial statements; and it is useful for interim or annual time periods. (L. O. 3)

6. b   Cash flow activities is not a defined category of the statement of cash flows. (L. O. 4)

7. a   The purchase of equipment for cash is the only item listed that impacts directly on cash. (L. O. 4)

8. b   At the declaration date, the entity records a liability to stockholders. Therefore, there is *no* liability date. (L. O. 5)

9. d   (L. O. 5)

10. d   (L. O. 6)

Chapter 3

RECORDING TRANSACTIONS

I. Learning Objectives

Many financial statement readers focus entirely on the output of an accounting system, the financial statements. While this is natural, a good understanding of the supporting theories and procedures is needed to be an effective user of the information presented on the face of those statements. This chapter focuses on the methods used to record and analyze the data in the financial statements — in particular, the double-entry accounting system. Use the following learning objectives to help coordinate your study of the material presented and aid your progress toward a better understanding of the accounting function.

1.   Use double-entry accounting.

2.   Analyze and journalize transactions.

3.   Post journal entries to the ledger.

4.   Prepare and use a trial balance.

5.   Correct erroneous journal entries and describe how errors affect accounts.

6.   Use T-accounts to analyze accounting relationships.

7.   Explain how computers have transformed processing of accounting data.

II. Pretest

_____ 1.   Which of the following is *not* true of the double-entry accounting system?

         a.   It affects at least two accounts for each transaction.
         b.   It is a systematic method of recording transactions.
         c.   It is useful only in manual accounting systems and not in computerized systems.
         d.   All of the above are true of the double-entry accounting system.

_____ 2.   The collection of accounts that accumulates the amounts reported in the financial statements is the:

         a.   T-accounts.
         b.   General ledger.
         c.   General journal.
         d.   Source documents.

_____ 3.   An analysis of the effects of a transaction on the accounts, usually accompanied by an explanation, is:

         a.   A journal entry.
         b.   A ledger entry.
         c.   Journalizing.
         d.   Posting.

_____ 4.   The "book of original entry" is commonly known as the:

         a.   General ledger.
         b.   General journal.
         c.   Chart of accounts.
         d.   None of the above are correct.

_____ 5.   The process of transferring amounts from the journal to the appropriate accounts in the ledger is:

         a.   A journal entry.
         b.   A ledger entry.
         c.   Journalizing.
         d.   Posting.

_____ 6.   Which of the following is *not* true of revenues and expenses?

         a.   They are changes in retained income resulting from operations.
         b.   They are fundamentally a part of stockholders' equity.
         c.   They can never be recorded directly in the retained income account.
         d.   All of the above are true of revenue and expenses.

_____ 7. A trial balance:

    a.   Is a financial statement similar to the balance sheet.
    b.   Helps check the accuracy of posting.
    c.   Is the only place an account balance can be found.
    d.   All of the above statements are true of a trial balance.

_____ 8. The income statement and balance sheet:

    a.   Will be correct if the trial balance columns are equal.
    b.   And the trial balance are given to stockholders.
    c.   Can easily be prepared from the trial balance.
    d.   All of the above statements are correct.

_____ 9. When errors in one accounting period have offsetting errors in the normal bookkeeping process in the next period:

    a.   The error is counterbalanced.
    b.   It results in misstated net income for both periods.
    c.   The balance sheet for the second period is not affected.
    d.   All of the above statements are correct.

_____ 10. A correcting error:

    a.   Is made if an error is detected after posting to the ledger accounts.
    b.   Is not required; an entry can be erased or crossed out no matter when it is detected.
    c.   Is required only of counterbalancing errors.
    d.   None of the above statements are correct.

_____ 11. Sometimes financial statements need to be constructed from incomplete data because documents were:

    a.   Lost.
    b.   Destroyed.
    c.   Stolen.
    d.   All of the above.

_____ 12. Which of the following is *not* true of T-accounts and incomplete data?

    a.   T-accounts help organize an accountant's thinking.
    b.   T-accounts are the only way to reconstruct incomplete data.
    c.   T-accounts aid in the discovery of unknown amounts.
    d.   All of the above statements are true.

_____ 13. Data processing:

    a.   Refers to the computerization of an accounting system.
    b.   Systems cannot be used in all businesses.
    c.   Is all the procedures used to record, analyze, store, and report on chosen activities.
    d.   All of the above are correct.

_____ 14. Microcomputers can be used in an accounting system to:

    a. Process data more efficiently.
    b. Track inventory.
    c. Prepare monthly statements to customers.
    d. All of the above are true of microcomputers.

III. Answers to Pretest

1.   c   The double-entry accounting system is the basis of all accounting systems — manual and computerized. (L. O. 1)

2.   b   T-accounts are the simplified version of ledger accounts, but the general ledger is the *collection* of accounts. (L. O. 1)

3.   a   A journal entry is the analysis of the effects of a transaction, while *journalizing* is the process of entering the transactions into the journal. (L. O. 2)

4.   b   The general journal is the book of original entry — the place the transactions are first posted in chronological order. (L. O. 2)

5.   d   Posting is the process of transferring amounts from the journal to the appropriate accounts in the ledger. Journalizing is the process of entering the transactions into the journal. (L. O. 3)

6.   c   Revenues and expenses, as other changes are, *could* be recorded directly in retained income. However, it is *easier* to prepare an income statement if the revenues and expenses are kept in separate accounts. (L. O. 3)

7.   b   A trial balance is a list, *not* a financial statement, of account balances that proves whether total debits equal total credits. Individual account balances are also in the individual ledger accounts. (L. O. 4)

8.   c   The trial balance helps in the preparation of financial statements and is not given to stockholders. The equality of the trial balance columns *does not* assure accuracy of the recorded information or of the financial statements, just that the debits and credits equal. (L. O. 4)

9.   d   (L. O. 5)

10.   a   An entry can be erased or crossed out only if the error is detected immediately. If detected after posting to the ledger accounts, a correcting entry is made. (L. O. 5)

11.   d   (L. O. 6)

12.   b   There are many methods of reconstructing incomplete data. The use of T-accounts is an organized, convenient way to reconstruct data. (L. O. 6)

13.   c   A manual or computerized accounting system is a data processing system.(L. O. 7)

14.   d   (L. O. 7)

EVALUATION

The pretest contained two questions for each learning objective. If you did not answer both questions correctly for each learning objective, you should review the appropriate section of the textbook and study guide before you attempt the material after Part IV.

IV. Key Concept Review by Learning Objectives

L. O. 1:   Use Double-Entry Accounting

A.   The Double-Entry Accounting System

1.   The **double-entry system** is the method usually followed for recording all of a business entity's transactions. At least two accounts are always affected by each transaction.

2.   Each transaction must be analyzed to determine which accounts are involved, whether the accounts are increased or decreased, and the amount of the change in each account balance.

B.   Ledger Accounts

1.   A **ledger** contains the records for a group of related accounts kept current in a systematic manner. The ledger may be in the form of a bound record book, a loose-leaf set of pages, or some kind of electronic storage element such as magnetic tape or disk. There is one page for each account.

2.   A firm's **general ledger** is the collection of records for accounts that accumulate the amounts reported in the firm's financial statements.

3.   **T-accounts** are simplified versions of ledger accounts. A **balance** is the difference between the total left-side and right-side amounts in an account at any particular time.

4.   Asset accounts have *left-sided balances*. They are increased by entries on the left side and decreased by entries on the right side.

5.   Liabilities and owners' equity accounts have *right-sided balances*. They are increased by entries on the right side and decreased by entries on the left side.

STOP & REVIEW:

Before continuing, carefully review the textbook examples for **use of T-accounts.**

> **STUDY TIP:**
> When analyzing a transaction, ask yourself: Did cash increase or decrease?
> Then think of the effects on other accounts.

C.   DEBITS and CREDITS

1.   The term **debit**, abbreviated dr., is used to denote an entry on the left side of any account, and the term **credit**, abbreviated cr., is used to denote an entry on the right side of any account. The word **charge** is often used instead of debit.

2.   These terms by themselves have no other meaning than left (debit) or right (credit).

L. O. 2: Analyze and Journalize Transactions

A. The Recording Process

1. The sequence of steps in recording transactions is:

Transactions → Documentation → Journal → Ledger→ Trial Balance → Financial Statements
---

2. Explanations of the above steps are as follows:

a. Recording begins when the transaction is substantiated by **source documents**. Source documents are the original records of any transaction.

b. An analysis of the transaction is placed in a **general journal**, the **book of original entry**, which is a formal chronological record (somewhat like a diary) of all the transactions in an entity.

c. Transactions are then entered (posted) in the ledger.

d. A trial balance is then prepared.

e. Financial statements are prepared.

B. Journalizing Transactions

1. The process of entering transactions into the journal is called **journalizing**.

2. A **journal entry** is an analysis of the effects of a single transaction on the accounts, usually accompanied by an explanation. For each transaction, this analysis identifies the accounts to be debited and credited.

C. Chart of Accounts

1. Organizations have a **chart of accounts**, which is normally a numbered or coded list of all account titles.

2. These numbers are used as references in the Post Ref. column of the journal.

> **STUDY TIP:**
> Quiz yourself on all the new terms introduced to this point.
> Study all the transactions listed in the textbook in both T-accounts and in the general journal.

L. O. 3: Post Journal Entries to the Ledger

A. Posting Transactions to the Ledger

1. **Posting** is the transferring of amounts from the journal to the appropriate accounts in the ledger.

2. The process of numbering, dating, and/or some other form of identification to relate each posting to the appropriate journal entry is known as the **keying of entries** or **cross-referencing**. This allows users to find other parts of the transactions in the ledger no matter where they are start.

STOP **& REVIEW:**

Before continuing, carefully review **Exhibit 3-1 in the text**.

B. Running Balance Column

1. A popular ledger form adds a column to provide a *running balance*.

2. The same postings are made regardless of the account format used: T-account or running balance.

Analyzing, Journalizing, and Posting the Biwheels Transactions

A. Accountants mentally analyze transactions

1. A **simple entry** for a transaction affects only two accounts while a **compound entry** affects more than two accounts.

2. When analyzing a transaction, initially pinpoint the effects (if any) on cash. Then think of the effects on other accounts. Usually, it is much easier to identify the effects of a transaction on cash than to identify the effects on other accounts.

STOP **& REVIEW:**

Review the transactions and related analyses for Biwheels in the text as you continue your study of this section.

B. Revenue and Expense Transactions

1. Revenue and Expense accounts are part of Retained Income.

a. Any credit to Revenue is essentially a credit to Retained Income: both accounts are increased by such a credit entry.

b. A debit entry *increases* expenses although it results in a *decrease* in Retained Income.

2. The revenue and expense accounts are periodically summarized into one number, *net income* or *net loss*, which increases or decreases retained income respectively.

3. Keeping revenues and expenses in separate accounts makes it easier to prepare an income statement.

STOP & REVIEW:

Before continuing, carefully review **Exhibit 3-3 Rules of Debit and Credit and Normal Balances of Accounts in the text**.

C. Prepaid Expenses and Depreciation Transactions

1. The expiration of an asset is recorded as an increase to an expense, which is a decrease in stockholders' equity.

2. A **contra account** is a separate but related account that offsets or is a deduction from a companion account. A contra account always has a companion account and has the opposite balance of the companion account.

3. A **contra asset** account is an account offsetting an asset.

4. The **book value** (or **net book value** or **carrying amount** or **carrying value**) is defined as the balance of an account shown on the books, net of any contra accounts.

D. A Note on Accumulated Depreciation

1. An **accumulated depreciation** (sometimes called **allowance for depreciation**) account is used to record the cumulative sum of all depreciation recognized since the date of acquisition of the particular assets described.

2. This preserves the original cost in the original asset account throughout the asset's useful life. In contrast, the accumulated depreciation is an estimate, the result of a calculation whose accuracy depends heavily on the accountant's less reliable prediction of an asset's useful life.

3. Investors and others can estimate the average age of the assets by computing the percentage of the original cost that has been depreciated.

Biwheels' Transactions in the Journal and Ledger

A. Recording Transactions in the Journal

STOP & REVIEW:

Review **Exhibit 3-4 in the text**.

B.   Posting Transactions in the Ledger

 **& REVIEW:**

Review **Exhibit 3-5 in the text**.

> **STUDY TIPS:**
> It is customary *not* to use dollar signs in either the journal or the ledger.
> Negative numbers are *never* used in the journal or the ledger — debits and
> credits convey if there is an increase or decrease to the account.

L. O. 4:   Prepare and Use a Trial Balance

A.   Preparing the Trial Balance

   1.   A **trial balance** is a list of all of the accounts with their balances. The purpose of the
         trial balance is:

         a.   To help check on accuracy of posting by proving whether the total debits
               equal the total credits.
         b.   To establish a convenient summary of balances in all accounts for the
               preparation of formal financial statements.

   2.   The trial balance is normally prepared with the accounts in the following order:

         Assets → Liabilities → Stockholders' Equity → Revenues → Expenses

> **STUDY TIP:**
> The trial balance can be thought of as a kind of worksheet for checking the
> figures when preparing financial statements.

B.   Deriving Financial Statements from the Trial Balance

   1.   When a formal balance sheet is prepared, the income statement accounts (revenue
         and expense accounts) will be summarized as a single number, net income or loss,
         which then becomes part of the Retained Income account.

   2.   The financial statements are usually prepared in the following order:

                     Income statement   →   Balance Sheet

 **& REVIEW:**

Before continuing, carefully review **Exhibit 3-7 in the text**.

L. O. 5:   Correct Erroneous Journal Entries and Describe How Errors Affect Accounts

A.   Effects of Errors

    1.   When an error is detected immediately, the entry can be erased or crossed out and corrected.

    2.   If the error is detected after posting to the ledger accounts, a *correcting entry* must be made. The result of a correcting entry is that the balances in the accounts are corrected to what they should have been originally.

B.   Some Errors Are Counterbalanced

    1.   Some errors are *counterbalanced* by offsetting errors in the ordinary bookkeeping process in the next period.

    2.   Such errors misstate income in both periods, but by the end of the second period the errors counterbalance or cancel each other out, and they affect the balance sheet of only the first period, not the second.

        a.   The *total* of the incorrect pretax incomes for the two years would be identical with the *total* of the correct pretax incomes for the two years.

        b.   The retained income balance at the end of the second year would be correct on a pretax basis.

C.   Some Errors Are Not Counterbalanced

    1.   Some errors may not be counterbalanced in the ordinary bookkeeping process. Until specific correcting entries are made, all subsequent balance sheets will be in error.

    2.   For example, an error in the computation of depreciation expense in one year only would misstate pretax income, assets, and retained income in that year, and would continue to overstate assets and retained income on successive balance sheets for the life of the asset. Unless this same error was committed again, the pretax income for each subsequent year would not be affected.

L. O. 6:   Use T-Accounts to Analyze Accounting Relationships

A.   Incomplete Records

Financial statements must sometimes be constructed from incomplete data because documents may have been stolen, destroyed, or lost.

B.   T-Accounts

    1.   T-accounts help organize an accountant's thinking and aid the discovery of unknown amounts.

    2.   Enter all known items into the key T-account and find the unknown amount.

L. O. 7: Explain How Computers Have Transformed Processing of Accounting Data

A. Data Processing

1. **Data processing** is a general term referring to the procedures used to record, analyze, store, and report on chosen activities.

2. An accounting system is a data-processing system.

B. Computers

1. Computers have been refining data-processing systems including accounting systems for the last decade.

2. Today journals and ledgers are more likely to be computerized than they are to be in the traditional paper book format. Regardless of their *format*, journals and ledgers still maintain the same *form* and still require the same inputs.

STOP & REVIEW:

Before continuing, review the objectives for this chapter and make sure you have a good understanding of each one.

V. Test Yourself

Questions

1. Explain the meaning of debits and credits.

2. Discuss the sequence of steps in recording transactions.

3. Explain the relationship of revenue and expenses to stockholders' equity.

4. Explain the need for an accumulated depreciation account.

5. Discuss the relationship of the trial balance to the income statement and the balance sheet.

Exercises and Problems

Information for use with #1 - #3

O'Donnell Enterprises
Balance Sheet
July 31, 2001

Assets:			Liabilities & Stockholders' Equity:		
			Liabilities:		
Cash		$ 40,000	Accounts payable		$ 75,000
Accounts receivable		86,000	Notes Payable		65,000
Inventory		154,000	Long-term debt		360,000
Equipment	$480,000		Total liabilities		$500,000
Less: Accumulated			Stockholders'Equity:		
depreciation	(20,000)	460,000	Paid-in capital	$158,000	
			Retained income	82,000	
			Total Stockholders' Equity		240,000
			Total Liabilities and		
Total Assets		$740,000	Stockholders' Equity		$740,000

During August 2001 the following transactions occurred:

Aug. 1   Sold additional shares of stock for $60,000.

Aug. 1   Inventory of $75,000 was purchased; $35,000 was paid in cash and the balance was due in 30 days.

Aug. 1   Prepaid rent of $24,000 was paid for a 36-month period.

Aug. 3   Made sales of $40,000 to a customer on account. The original cost of the merchandise was $20,000.

Aug. 10   Received customer payments totaling $55,000.

Aug. 15   Paid wages of $2,500 to employees.

Aug. 20   Paid the outstanding balance on the note payable.

Aug. 31   Recognized depreciation expense of $2,000.

Aug. 31   Recognized this month's portion of rent expense, $1,000.

1.   Journalize the transactions for August 2001 for O'Donnell Enterprises.

2.   Enter the beginning balances and post the entries from #1 in appropriate T-accounts for
       O'Donnell Enterprises.

3.   Prepare a trial balance for August 2001 for O'Donnell Enterprises from the given information
       and from the data in #1 and #2.

4.   For each of the following, fill in the type of account (asset, liability, stockholders' equity,
       revenue, or expense), if the item has a debit or credit impact on the account, and if the normal
       balance of the account is a debit or credit.

5.   The clerk of Micro Company included the cost of a new machine, purchased on December 30
       for $35,000 to be paid in January, as an operating expense instead of as an addition to the
       proper asset account. What was the effect of this error (no effect, overstated, or understated -
       use symbols *n, o,* or *u,* respectively) on:

       A.   Operating expenses for the year ended December 31   _____

       B.   Profit from operation for the year   _____

       C.   Retained income as of December 31 after the books
              are closed   _____

       D.   Total assets as of December 31   _____

       E.   Total liabilities as of December 31   _____

Matching

Terms

_____ 1. Accumulated depreciation

_____ 2. Balance

_____ 3. Book value

_____ 4. Chart of accounts

_____ 5. Compound entry

_____ 6. Contra account

_____ 7. Contra asset

_____ 8. Credit

_____ 9. Data processing

_____ 10. Debit

_____ 11. Double-entry system

_____ 12. General journal

_____ 13. General ledger

_____ 14. Journalizing

_____ 15. Posting

_____ 16. Simple entry

_____ 17. Source document

_____ 18. Trial balance

Definitions

A. The process of entering transactions into the book of original entry.

B. The collection of accounts that accumulates the amounts shown in the firm's major financial statements.

C. A contra account that offsets an asset.

D. A list of all accounts with their balances.

E. The totality of the procedures used to record, analyze, store, and report on chosen activities.

F. The supporting original records of any transaction.

G. An entry for a transaction that affects only two accounts.

H. The difference between the total left-side and right-side amounts in an account at any particular time.

I. An entry for a transaction that affects more than two accounts.

J. The transferring of amounts from the journal to the appropriate accounts in the ledger.

K. An entry or balance on the right side of an account.

L. The most common example of a book of original entry: a complete chronological record of transactions.

M.   The balance of an account shown on the books, net of any contra accounts.

N.   The method usually followed for recording transactions, whereby at least two accounts are always affected by each transaction.

O.   The cumulative sum of all depreciation recognized since the date of acquisition of the particular assets described.

P.   A numbered or coded list of all account titles.

Q.   A separate but related account that offsets a companion account.

R.   An entry or balance on the left side of an account.

Multiple Choice

_____ 1.   Which of the following sequence of events is correct relative to the accounting cycle?

   a.   Post, journalize, trial balance, statements.
   b.   Post, trial balance, journalize.
   c.   Journalize, post, trial balance, statements.
   d.   Journalize, post, trial balance.

_____ 2.   A numbered or coded summary of all account titles is a:

   a.   Compound entry.
   b.   Chart of accounts.
   c.   Trial balance.
   d.   None of the above are correct.

_____ 3.   In a journal entry, debit and credit refer to respectively:

   a.   Right, left.
   b.   Increase, decrease.
   c.   Decrease, increase.
   d.   Left, right.

_____ 4.   Which of the following is _not_ true of accumulated depreciation?

   a.   It usually has a credit balance.
   b.   It is a contra asset.
   c.   It contains the acquisition cost of the asset.
   d.   All of the above are true of accumulated depreciation.

_____ 5.   Which of the following statements is correct?

   a.   A debit entry increases expenses, which results in a decrease in retained income.
   b.   A debit entry increases expenses, which results in an increase in retained income.
   c.   A credit entry increases expenses, which results in a decrease in retained income.
   d.   A credit entry decreases expenses, which results in an increase in retained income.

_____ 6.   When recording the sale of merchandise to a customer on credit, which of the following would be correct?

   a.   Debit Accounts Receivable and Cost of Goods Sold; Credit Sales and Merchandise Inventory.
   b.   Debit Accounts Receivable and Inventory;
          Credit Sales and Cost of Goods Sold.
   c.   Debit Accounts Receivable; Credit Sales and Merchandise Inventory
   d.   None of the above are correct.

_____ 7.   Posting reference columns are *not* used for:

    a.   Recording journal page numbers in the general ledger.
    b.   Recording general ledger account numbers in the journal.
    c.   Cross-referencing the journal and the general ledger.
    d.   All of the above are true of posting reference columns.

_____ 8.   A running balance:

    a.   Is the total of the debit or credit columns in the journal.
    b.   May be kept for ledger accounts.
    c.   Is part of the chart of accounts.
    d.   None of the above statements are correct.

_____ 9.   The balance of an account shown on the books, net of any contra accounts is the:

    a.   Normal balance.
    b.   Gross value.
    c.   Book value.
    d.   None of the above are correct.

_____ 10. Which of the following is true of counterbalancing errors?

    a.   The errors are offset by errors in the next accounting period.
    b.   Net income is misstated in both accounting periods.
    c.   Only the balance sheet of the first period is affected.
    d.   All of the above statements are true of counterbalancing errors.

VI. Solutions to Test Yourself

Questions

1. The term debit means an entry or balance on the left side of an account, while the term credit represents an entry or balance on the right side of an account. These terms by themselves have no other meaning than left (debit) or right (credit). (L. O. 1)

2. Transactions → Documentation → Journal → Ledger → Trial Balance → Financial Statements

   The recording steps begin when the transaction is substantiated by source documents. In the second step, an analysis of the transaction is placed in a book of original entry, the general journal. The third step in the recording process is entering the transactions in the ledger. The fourth step is preparing a trial balance. The final step, the culmination of the recording process, is the preparation of the financial statements, which include the balance sheet, the income statement, the statement of cash flows, and the statement of retained income. (L. O. 2)

3. The revenue account collects items that increase retained income. Any credit to revenue is essentially a credit to retained income; both revenue and retained income are increased by such a credit entry.

   The expense account collects items that decrease retained income. A debit to expense is essentially a debit to retained income. While a debit entry *increases* expenses, it results in a *decrease* in retained income. (L. O. 3)

4. Accumulated depreciation is the cumulative sum of all depreciation recognized since the date of acquisition of the particular assets described. Published balance sheets routinely report both the original cost and accumulated depreciation. Such information may be sought for reports to management, government regulators, and tax authorities.

   Moreover, the original cost is the height of accuracy; it is a reliable, objective number. In contrast, accumulated depreciation is an estimate, the result of a calculation whose accuracy depends heavily on the accountant's less reliable prediction of an asset's useful life. (L. O. 3)

5. The purpose of the trial balance is twofold: to help check on accuracy of posting by proving whether the total debits equal the total credits, and to establish a convenient summary of balances in all accounts for the preparation of formal financial statements. The trial balance is an internal report that helps accountants to prepare financial statements. The public sees only the published financial statements, not the trial balance. (L. O. 4)

Exercises and Problems

1.

Date		Debit	Credit
Aug. 1	Cash	60,000	
	Paid-in capital		60,000
Aug. 1	Inventory	75,000	
	Cash		35,000
	Accounts payable		40,000
Aug. 1	Prepaid rent	24,000	
	Cash		24,000
Aug. 3	Accounts receivable	40,000	
	Sales		40,000
3	Cost of goods sold	20,000	
	Inventory		20,000
Aug.10	Cash	55,000	
	Accounts receivable		55,000
Aug.15	Wage expense	2,500	
	Cash		2,500
Aug.20	Notes payable	65,000	
	Cash		65,000
Aug.31	Depreciation expense	2,000	
	Accumulated depreciation		2,000
Aug.31	Rent expense	1,000	
	Prepaid rent		1,000

2.   O'Donnell Enterprises general ledger:

Cash			
7/31 bal 40,000		8/1	35,000
8/1	60,000	8/1	24,000
8/10	55,000	8/15	2,500
		8/20	65,000
end bal	28,500		

Accounts Receivable			
7/31 bal 86,000		8/10	55,000
8/3	40,000		
end bal	71,000		

Inventory			
7/31 bal			
	154,000	8/3	20,000
8/1	75,000		
end bal	209,000		

Prepaid Rent			
8/1	24,000	8/31	1,000
end bal	23,000		

63

Equipment

7/31 bal 480,000	
end bal 480,000	

Accumulated Depreciation

	7/31 bal 20,000
	8/31 2,000
	end bal 22,000

Accounts Payable

	7/31 bal 75,000
	8/1 40,000
	end bal 115,000

Notes Payable

8/20 65,000	7/31 bal 65,000
	end bal -0-

Long-Term Debt

	7/31 bal 360,000
	end bal 360,000

Paid-in Capital

	7/31 bal 158,000
	8/1 60,000
	end bal 218,000

Retained Income

	7/31 bal 82,000
	end bal 82,000

Sales

	8/3 40,000
	end bal 40,000

Cost of Goods Sold

8/3 20,000	
end bal 20,000	

Wages Expense

8/15 2,500	
end bal 2,500	

Depreciation Expense

8/31 2,000	
end bal 2,000	

Rent Expense

8/31 1,000	
end bal 1,000	

3.

O'Donnell Enterprises
Trial Balance
August 31, 2001

	Debits	Credits
Cash	$ 28,500	
Accounts Receivable	71,000	
Inventory	209,000	
Prepaid rent	23,000	
Equipment	480,000	
Accumulated Depreciation		$ 22,000
Accounts payable		115,000
Notes payable		-0-
Long-term debt		360,000
Paid-in capital		218,000
Retained income		82,000
Sales		40,000
Cost of goods sold	20,000	
Wages expense	2,500	
Depreciation expense	2,000	
Rent expense	1,000	
Totals	$837,000	$837,000

4.

		Type of Account	Debit/Credit Impact	Normal Balance
a.	Decrease to **cash**	Asset	Credit	Debit
b.	Increase to **prepaid rent**	Asset	Debit	Debit
c.	Increase to **paid-in capital**	Stockholders' Equity	Credit	Credit
d.	Decrease to **accounts payable**	Liability	Debit	Credit
e.	Increase to **rent expense**	Expense	Debit	Debit
f.	Decrease to **accounts receivable**	Asset	Credit	Debit
g.	Increase to **depreciation expense**	Expense	Debit	Debit
h.	Increase to **equipment**	Asset	Debit	Debit
i.	Increase to **accumulated depreciation**	Contra Asset	Credit	Credit
j.	Decrease to **retained income**	Stockholders' Equity	Debit	Credit
k.	Increase to **sales**	Revenue	Credit	Credit

5.   A.   O   C.   U   E.   N
     B.   U   D.   U

Matching

1.	O	L .O. 3	7.	C	L. O. 3	13.	B	L. O. 1
2.	H	L. O. 1	8.	K	L. O. 1	14.	A	L. O. 2
3.	M	L. O. 3	9.	E	L. O. 7	15.	J	L. O. 3
4.	P	L. O. 2	10.	R	L. O. 1	16.	G	L. O. 3
5.	I	L. O. 3	11.	N	L. O. 1	17.	F	L. O. 2
6.	Q	L. O. 3	12.	L	L. O. 2	18.	D	L. O. 4

Multiple Choice

1.   c   The correct sequence is journalize, post, trial balance, *and* financial statements. (L. O. 2)

2.   b   A chart of accounts is a numbered or coded list or summary of all account titles. (L. O. 2)

3.   d   (L. O. 3)

4.   c   Accumulated depreciation is the cumulative sum of all depreciation recognized since the date of acquisition of the particular assets described.   The acquisition cost of the asset is in the asset account itself. (L. O. 3)

5.   a   An increase to an expense is a decrease to retained income. (L. O. 3)

6.   a   Both the sale of merchandise on credit and the recognition of cost of goods sold, with a corresponding reduction in inventory, must be recorded.   (L. O. 3)

7.   d   Posting reference columns appear in the journal and ledger accounts, and are tools for cross-referencing the two.   Therefore, statements a, b, and c are correct. (L. O. 3)

8.   b   A running balance is an account balance in the ledger. (L. O. 3)

9.   c   The book value, also known as the net book value, or carrying amount, or carrying value, is the balance of an account shown on the books, net of any contra accounts. The normal balance of an account is the increase side of an account. (L. O. 3)

10.   d   (L. O. 5)

Chapter 4

USING FINANCIAL STATEMENTS

I. Learning Objectives

The foundation of accrual accounting rests on the concepts of recognizing revenue when it is earned and recording expenses in the period that the product, service, or work is done to support contribution to revenue. This approach requires understanding the process of adjusting account balances to reflect the recognition of revenue and expense in the proper period. This chapter focuses on the concepts and practices relating to adjusting entries, the different methods of presenting balance sheet and income statement information, as well as related generally accepted accounting principles (GAAP). Utilize the following learning objectives as an outline for your study of this material.

1. Make adjustments for the expiration of unexpired costs.

2. Make adjustments for the earning of unearned revenues.

3. Make adjustments for the accrual of unrecorded expenses.

4. Make adjustments for the accrual of unrecorded revenues.

5. Describe the sequence of the final steps in the recording process and relate cash flows to adjusting entries.

6. Prepare a classified balance sheet and use it to assess solvency.

7. Prepare single- and multiple-step income statements and use ratios to assess profitability.

8. Relate Generally Accepted Accounting Principles (GAAP) to the accounting practices we have learned.

II. Pretest

SELECT THE BEST ANSWER AND ENTER THE IDENTIFYING LETTER IN THE SPACE PROVIDED.

_____ 1.   Which of the following is *not* true of adjustments? Adjustments:

    a.   Are made periodically, usually when the financial statements are about to be prepared.
    b.   Involve at least one income statement account and one balance sheet account.
    c.   Improve the matching of revenues and expenses to a particular period.
    d.   All of the above are true of adjustments.

_____ 2.   Which of the following would *never* result in an adjustment to an asset:

    a.   Passage of time.
    b.   Consumption of the asset.
    c.   Useful life.
    d.   All of the above could result in an adjustment to an asset.

_____ 3.   Revenue that is received and recorded before it is earned is:

    a.   Revenue.
    b.   Unearned revenue.
    c.   Not allowed under GAAP (generally accepted accounting principles).
    d.   None of the above are correct.

_____ 4.   Advance payments *from* customers are:

    a.   An asset.
    b.   A liability.
    c.   Stockholders' equity.
    d.   Revenue.

_____ 5.   An adjustment for accrued expenses includes a:

    a.   Debit to an expense account and a credit to a liability account.
    b.   Debit to an expense account and a credit to a stockholders' equity account.
    c.   Debit to a liability account and a credit to an expense account.
    d.   Debit to a stockholders' equity account and a credit to an expense account.

_____ 6.   Which of the following is *not* usually an example of an accrued expense?

    a.   Wages.
    b.   Income taxes.
    c.   Rent.
    d.   All of the above are examples of accrued expenses.

_____ 7.   Revenue sometimes has to be accrued to:

    a.   Show recognition of revenues that have been earned, but not yet recorded.
    b.   Match revenues to the period in which they are earned.
    c.   Bring the related asset and revenue accounts up to date.
    d.   All of the above are true for accrued revenue.

_____ 8.   Which of the following is *not* an example of an accrued revenue?

    a.   Magazine subscription.
    b.   Professional fees.
    c.   Interest.
    d.   All of the above are examples of accrued revenue.

_____ 9.   After posting transactions to the ledger, the final steps in the recording process are:

    a.   Adjusted trial balance, journalize and post adjustments, unadjusted trial balance, financial statements.
    b.   Unadjusted trial balance, financial statements, journalize and post adjustments, adjusted trial balance.
    c.   Unadjusted trial balance, journalize and post adjustments, adjusted trial balance, financial statements.
    d.   Adjusted trial balance, financial statements, journalize and post adjustments, unadjusted trial balance.

_____ 10.   Cash receipts and disbursements:

    a.   Have no relationship to adjustments.
    b.   May precede or follow the adjusting entry that recognizes the related revenue or expense.
    c.   May only precede the adjusting entry that recognizes the related revenue or expense.
    d.   May only follow the adjusting entry that recognizes the related revenue or expense.

_____ 11.   Which is *not* true of a classified balance sheet? A classified balance sheet:

    a.   Groups the accounts into subcategories to help readers quickly gain a perspective on the company's financial position.
    b.   Helps to draw attention to certain amounts or groups of accounts.
    c.   Lists assets, liabilities, stockholders' equity, revenue, and expenses to help readers of the financial statements understand the relationship of all accounts.
    d.   All of the above are true of a classified balance sheet.

_____ 12.   The current ratio is:

    a.   Used to evaluate a company's solvency.
    b.   Also known as the working capital ratio.
    c.   Is found by dividing current assets by current liabilities.
    d.   All of the above are true of the current ratio.

_____ 13.   A multiple-step income statement *does not*:

    a.   Group all revenues together.
    b.   Contain one or more subtotals that highlight significant relationships.
    c.   Show the excess of sales revenue over the cost of inventory that was sold.
    d.   All of the above are true of a multiple-step income statement.

_____ 14.   The ratio that is most useful to a retailer in choosing a pricing strategy and in judging its results is the:

      a.   Return on sales ratio.
      b.   Gross profit percentage.
      c.   Return on stockholders' equity ratio.
      d.   Current ratio.

_____ 15.   The stable monetary unit concept:

      a.   Adjusts the value of assets each year for inflation.
      b.   Is the same in all countries.
      c.   Assumes the value of the dollar does not change.
      d.   None of the above are correct.

_____ 16.   The concept that states that a financial statement item would make a difference if its omission or misstatement would tend to mislead the reader of the financial statements under consideration is the:

      a.   Going concern convention.
      b.   Materiality convention.
      c.   Cost-benefit criterion.
      d.   Entity concept.

III. Answers to Pretest

1. d   (L. O. 1)

2. d   (L. O. 1)

3. b   (L. O. 2)

4. b   Advance payments from customers is another term for unearned revenue, which is a liability. (L. O. 2)

5. a   Accrued expense adjustments include a debit or increase to an expense account, and a credit or increase to a liability account. This brings the expense and corresponding liability accounts up to date. (L. O.3)

6. c   Rent is usually prepaid, and *not* an accrued expense. (L. O. 3)

7. d   (L. O. 4)

8. a   A magazine subscription is an example of unearned revenue, *not* accrued revenue. (L. O. 4)

9. c   (L. O. 5)

10. b   Cash flows may either *precede* or *follow* the adjusting entry that recognizes the related revenue or expense. (L. O. 5)

11. c   Revenues and expenses are *never* listed on any balance sheet. (L. O. 6)

12. d   (L. O. 6)

13. a   A multiple-step income statement *has separate* sections or groupings for sales and other revenues; b and c are true of multiple-step income statements. (L. O. 7)

14. b   (L. O. 7)

15. c   The stable monetary unit in the United States is the dollar and this concept assumes the value of the dollar remains unchanged over a period of time. (L. O. 8)

16. b   (L. O. 8)

EVALUATION

The pretest contained two questions for each learning objective. If you did not answer both questions correctly for each learning objective, you should review the appropriate section of the textbook and study guide before you attempt the material after Part IV.

IV. Key Concept Review by Learning Objectives

L. O. 1: Make Adjustments for the Expiration of Unexpired Costs

A. The need for **adjusting entries** stems from the fact that some transactions are implicit rather than explicit.

    1. **Explicit transactions** are obvious events that trigger nearly all day-to-day routine entries.

    2. **Implicit transactions** are events that:

        a. Do not generate source documents or any visible evidence that the event actually happened.

        b. Are temporarily ignored in day-to-day recording procedures and are recognized only at the end of an accounting period.

B. **Adjustments** (also called **adjusting entries**) help assign the financial effects of implicit transactions to the appropriate time periods. Adjustments improve the matching of revenues and expenses to a particular period.

C. Adjustments are made at periodic intervals, when the financial statements are about to be prepared. The adjustments are made in the form of journal entries that are recorded in the general journal and then posted to the general ledger.

D. Adjusting entries are at the heart of accrual accounting. **Accrue** means the accumulation of a receivable (asset) or payable (liability) during a given period even though no explicit transaction occurs. The receivables and payables grow as the clock ticks; as some services are continuously acquired and used, so they are said to accrue (accumulate).

E. Expiration of Unexpired Costs

    1. Some costs expire because of the passage of time.

    2. Examples of expiration of unexpired costs include recognition of monthly depreciation expense and rent expense, and write-offs to expense of such assets as office supplies inventory and prepaid insurance.

F. The key characteristic of unexpired items is that an explicit transaction in the past has created an asset, and a subsequent implicit transaction serves to adjust the value of this asset.

L. O. 2: Make Adjustments for the Earning of Unearned Revenues

Earning of Unearned Revenues

    1. **Unearned revenue** (also called **revenue received in advance, deferred revenue** or **deferred credit**) is revenue that is received and recorded before it is earned. Payment is received in exchange for a commitment to provide service (or goods) at a later date.

    2. Unearned revenue is a liability because the company receiving the advance payment is obligated to deliver the service or goods, or to refund the money if the services or goods are not delivered.

3.   Stockholders' equity is not affected until the unearned revenue is earned. At that time an adjusting entry will be made to record the revenue.

 **& REVIEW:**

Review the **examples** and **journal entries** for this section in the text.

> **STUDY TIP:**
> If a contract causes one party to have a prepaid expense, it must cause the other party to have unearned revenue — as prepaid expense and unearned revenue are mirror images of each other.

L. O. 3:   Make Adjustments for the Accrual of Unrecorded Expenses

A.   Accrual of Unrecorded Expenses

Adjustments are made to bring each accrued expense (and corresponding liability) account up to date at the end of the period, just before the formal financial statements are prepared in order to match the expense to the period.

B.   Accounting for Payment of Wages

Most companies pay their employees at predetermined times, making routine entries for wage payments.

C.   Accounting for Accrual of Wages

To ensure accurate financial statements for the period, adjustments must be made to account for the accrual of any unrecorded wages which are owed, but not paid in that period.

D.   Accrual of Interest

1.   Interest on borrowed money accumulates (accrues) as time unfolds, regardless of when the actual cash for interest is paid.

2.   If an adjusting entry is omitted, both expenses and liabilities will be understated.

E.   Accrual of Income Taxes

Income tax expenses are accrued each month (not just once a year) as pretax **income** (income before taxes) is generated.

 **& REVIEW:**

Review the **examples** and **journal entries** for this section in the text.

L. O. 4:   Make Adjustments for the Accrual of Unrecorded Revenues

A.   Accrual of Unrecorded Revenues

1.   The adjusting entries show the recognition of revenues that have been earned, but not yet shown in the accounts.

2. Revenues affect stockholders' equity in the period they are earned, not the period in which they are received.

⬡ STOP **& REVIEW:**

Review the **examples** and **journal entries** for this section in the text.

STUDY TIP:
The accrual of unrecorded revenues is the mirror image of the accrual of unrecorded expenses.

L. O. 5: Describe the Sequence of the Final Steps in the Recording Process and Relate Cash Flows to Adjusting Entries

A. The Adjusting Process in Perspective

    1. In Chapter 3 the following steps in recording transactions were discussed:

Transactions → Documentation → Journal → Ledger→ Trial Balance → Financial Statements

    2. This process has a final aim: the preparation of accurate financial statements prepared on the accrual basis. To accomplish this goal, the process must include adjusting entries to record implicit transactions.

    3. The final steps in the recording process are:

	Unadjusted		Journalize		Adjusted		Financial
Ledger →	Trial	→	and Post	→	Trial	→	Statements
	Balance		Adjustments		Balance		

STUDY TIP:
An adjusting entry always affects *both* a balance sheet account — an asset or a liability — and at least one income statement account — a revenue or an expense.

⬡ STOP **& REVIEW:**

Review **Exhibit 4-1** in the text.

B. Cash Flows and Adjusting Entries

    1. Cash receipts and disbursements may precede or follow the adjusting entry that recognizes the related revenue or expense.

    2. Adjusting entries for expiration of unexpired costs and realization (earning) of unearned revenues are usually made *subsequent* to the cash flows.

    3. Adjusting entries for accrual of unrecorded expenses and revenues are made *before* the cash receipts and cash disbursements occur.

L. O. 6: Prepare a Classified Balance Sheet and Use It to Assess Solvency

A.   Classified Balance Sheet

    1.   A **classified balance sheet**, which groups the accounts into subcategories, helps readers quickly gain a perspective on the company's financial position.

    2.   Assets are frequently classified into two groupings: current assets and long-term assets.

    3.   Liabilities are similarly classified: current liabilities and long-term liabilities. This distinction is useful in assessing the company's ability to meet obligations as they fall due.

    4.   For the most part current assets will give rise to the cash needed to pay current liabilities so the relationship between these categories is important.

B.   Current Assets and Current Liabilities

    1.   **Current assets** are cash and those other assets that are expected to be converted to cash, or sold, or consumed during the next twelve months (or within the normal operating cycle if longer than a year).

    2.   **Current liabilities** are those liabilities that fall due within the coming year (or within the normal operating cycle if longer than a year).

    3.   The excess of current assets over current liabilities is known as **working capital**.

STOP & REVIEW:

    Before continuing, review **Exhibit 4-5** in the text.

C.   Current Ratio

    1.   The current ratio is widely used to evaluate a business entity's **solvency**, which is its ability to meet its immediate financial obligations with cash and near-cash assets as those obligations become due.

2.   The **current ratio** (also called the **working capital ratio**) computation is:

$$\text{Current ratio} = \frac{\text{Current Assets}}{\text{Current Liabilities}}$$

STUDY TIPS:

Other things being equal, the higher the current ratio, the more assurance creditors have about being paid in full and on time.

Conversely, a current ratio that is too high may indicate excessive holdings of cash, accounts receivable, or inventories.

D.   Formats of Balance Sheets

    1.   The **report format** is a classified balance sheet with the assets at the top.

    2.   The **account format** is a classified balance sheet with the assets at the left.

L. O. 7:   Prepare Single- and Multiple-Step Income Statements and Use Ratios to Assess Profitability

A.   Income Statement

Income statements are often considered more important than balance sheets because investors are concerned about a company's ability to produce long-run earnings, and, therefore, dividends.

B.   Single- and Multiple-Step Income Statements

    1.   A **single-step income statement** groups all revenue together and then lists and deducts all expenses together without drawing any intermediate subtotals.

    2.   A **multiple-step income statement** contains one or more subtotals that highlight significant relationships, such as gross profit and operating income.

        a.   **Gross profit** (or **gross margin**) is the excess of sales revenue over the cost of the inventory that was sold. Most multiple-step income statements start with this section.

        b.   **Operating income** (or **operating profit**) is obtained by deduction operating expenses from the gross profit.

STOP & REVIEW:

Before continuing, review **Exhibit 4-8** in the text.

C.   Examples of Actual Income Statements

D.   Profitability Evaluation Ratios

    1.   **Profitability** is the ability of a company to provide its investors with a particular rate of return on their investment.

2. Gross Profit Percentage

    a. The **gross profit percentage** is particularly useful to a retailer in choosing a pricing strategy and in judging its results.

    b. The gross profit percentage computation is:

$$Gross\ Profit\ Percentage = \frac{Gross\ Profit}{Sales}$$

3. Return on Sales Ratio

    a. Managers carefully follow the return on sales ratio from month to month.

    b. The computation for return on sales ratio is:

$$Return\ on\ Sales\ Ratio = \frac{Net\ Income}{Sales}$$

4. Return on Stockholders' Equity Ratio

    a. The **return on stockholders' equity ratio** is widely regarded as the ultimate measure of overall accomplishment.

    b. The computation for the return on stockholders' equity ratio is:

$$Return\ on\ Stockholders'\ Equity = \frac{Net\ Income}{Average\ Stockholders'\ Equity}$$

L. O. 8: Relate Generally Accepted Accounting Principles (GAAP) to the Accounting Practices We Have Learned

A. General Accepted Accounting Principles and Basic Concepts

    1. Decision makers would have difficulty using and comparing financial statements if every accountant used a different set of measurement rules. Accountants have, therefore, agreed to apply a common set of measurement principles (a common language) to record information on the financial statements.

    2. **Generally accepted accounting principles (GAAP)** is the term that applies to the broad concepts, guidelines, and practices that together make up accepted accounting practice in the United States at any given time.

B. Standard Setting Bodies

    1. GAAP in the United States have been determined primarily by two private-sector bodies:

        a. The **Financial Accounting Standards Board (FASB)** has been in existence since 1973 and its rulings on GAAP are called **FASB Statements**. **The American Institute of Certified Public Accountants (AICPA)** and other various professional accounting associations support this board.

        b. Prior to 1973, the **Accounting Principles Board (APB)** issued thirty-one rulings on GAAP called **APB Opinions**.

2. Congress has designated the **Securities and Exchange Commission (SEC)** as the agency with the ultimate responsibility for authorizing the generally accepted accounting principles for companies whose stock is held by the general investing public. The SEC works closely with the FASB and has informally delegated much power to the FASB.

3. The setting of the accounting principles is a complex process involving heavy interactions among the affected parties: public regulators (Congress and the SEC), private regulators (FASB), companies, the public accounting profession, representatives of investors, and other interested groups.

4. The **International Accounting Standards Committee (IASC)** leads the movement seeking to eliminate differences in accounting principles that are not caused by cultural or environmental differences between countries.

C. Concepts and Conventions of GAAP

   1. The Entity Concept

      a. The **entity concept** is based on the idea that an entity is an organization or part of an organization that is a separate economic unit from other organizations, or individuals such as the organization's owners.

      b. The separation of events or activities for accountability purposes is crucial if accounting is to measure the economic activity of a particular unit or business.

   2. The Reliability Concept

      a. **Reliability,** as it relates to accounting, is a quality of information that assures decision makers that the information represented in the financial records and financial statements truly represents the actual conditions and events of the reported entity.

      b. Without the reliability concept, accounting records might be based on whims and opinions open to dispute.

   3. Going Concern Convention

      a. The **going concern convention (continuity convention)** is the assumption that in all ordinary situations an entity persists indefinitely.

      b. This notion implies that existing *resources will be used* to fulfill the general purposes of a continuing entity *rather than be sold* in tomorrow's real estate or equipment markets. It also implies that existing liabilities will be paid at maturity in an orderly manner.

   4. Materiality Convention

      a. The **materiality convention** asserts that an item should be included in a financial statement, or is material (essential), if its omission or misstatement would tend to mislead the reader of the financial statements under consideration.

      b. Many acquisitions that should theoretically be recorded as assets are immediately written off as expenses because of their insignificance or immateriality. Their impact is too trivial to worry about.

   5. Cost-Benefit Criterion

      a. The **cost-benefit criterion** states that a system should be changed when the expected additional benefits of the change exceed its expected additional costs.

b. Reluctance to adopt suggestions for new ways of measuring financial position and performance is often due to the fact that the apparent benefits do not exceed the obvious costs of gathering and interpreting the information.

6. Stable Monetary Unit

a. The monetary unit (the dollar in the United States) is the principal means for measuring assets and equities. Accountants record, classify, summarize, and report in terms of the monetary unit (the dollar).

b. Accounting statements that include assets acquired in different years must be interpreted and compared with full knowledge of the limitations of the basic measurement unit.

STUDY TIP:
Study the "Summary Problem for Your Review" and solution in the text.

STOP & REVIEW:

Before continuing, review the objectives for this chapter and make sure you have a good understanding of each one.

V. Test Yourself

Questions

1. Discuss why adjustments to the accounts are important.

2. Explain the sequence of final steps in the recording process.

3. Discuss the need for a classified balance sheet.

4. Briefly explain the differences between a single-step and multiple-step income statement.

5. Discuss profitability.

Exercises and Problems

1. Analyze the effects that each independent situation given below would have on the accounting records during the adjusting process. Using I for increase, D for decrease, and NE for no effect, complete the table that follows.

    A. In August, $250,000 in advance tickets were sold to the Billy Joel concert. The concert was held on December 20.

    B. On January 5, a company purchased a new piece of equipment for $60,000. It has a useful life of ten years. Depreciation expense of $6,000 was calculated for this piece of equipment for this year.

    C. A company has not billed their clients for services totaling $82,000. These services were provided in the last quarter of this year.

    D. The total owed to employees at December 31 for unpaid wages was $23,000.

	Total Assets	Total Liabilities	Revenue	Expense	Net Income
A.	____	____	____	____	____
B.	____	____	____	____	____
C.	____	____	____	____	____
D.	____	____	____	____	____

2. Prepare the appropriate adjusting journal entry for each of the four situations in #1.

3. The adjusted trial balance for MIT Computers, Inc. is presented below. Prepare, in good form, a multiple-step income statement.

MIT Computers, Inc.
Adjusted Trial Balance
December 31, 19X9

	Debits	Credits
Cash	$65,000	
Accounts receivable	115,000	
Inventory	320,000	
Prepaid rent	40,000	
Prepaid insurance	20,000	
Land	410,000	
Equipment	350,000	
Accumulated depreciation-equipment		$125,000
Building	1,435,000	
Accumulated depreciation-building		370,000
Accounts payable		90,000
Notes payable		45,000
Accrued income taxes payable		85,000
Long-term mortgage payable		655,000
Paid-in capital		510,000
Retained income		365,000
Sales		4,350,000
Cost of goods sold	1,838,000	
Payroll expense	1,000,000	
Rent expense	400,000	
Interest expense	75,000	
Depreciation expense	100,000	
Income tax expense	334,000	
Other miscellaneous expenses	98,000	
Total	$6,595,000	$6,595,000

4. Based on the adjusted trial balance for MIT Computers, Inc. presented in #3, prepare, in good form, a classified balance sheet.

5. Use the following information for Carnegie Company to compute the current ratio, gross profit percentage, return on sales ratio, and return on stockholders' equity ratio. All the information is for year end, except as noted.

Current assets	$550,000
Total assets	$950,000
Current liabilities	$220,000
Total liabilities	$380,000
Stockholders' equity (Jan. 1)	$450,000
Stockholders' equity (Dec. 31)	$570,000
Sales	$600,000
Cost of goods sold	$350,000
Net income	$120,000

Matching

MATCH EACH TERM WITH ITS DEFINITION BY WRITING THE APPROPRIATE LETTER IN THE SPACE PROVIDED.

Terms

_____ 1. Accrue

_____ 2. Adjustments

_____ 3. Classified balance sheet

_____ 4. Cost-benefit criterion

_____ 5. Current assets

_____ 6. Current liabilities

_____ 7. Entity concept

_____ 8. GAAP

_____ 9. Going Concern convention

_____ 10. Gross profit

_____ 11. Materiality convention

_____ 12. Multiple-step income statement

_____ 13. Operating income

_____ 14. Profitability

_____ 15. Reliability

_____ 16. Single-step income statement

_____ 17. Solvency

_____ 18. Unearned revenue

Definitions

A. An income statement that groups all revenue together and then lists and deducts all expenses together without drawing any intermediate subtotals.

B. Revenue received and recorded before it is earned.

C. The assumption that in all ordinary situations an entity persists indefinitely.

D. Liabilities that fall due within the coming year or within the normal operating cycle if longer than a year.

E. The key final process of assigning the financial effects of transactions to the appropriate time periods.

F. Gross profit less all operating expenses.

G. The organization or a section of an organization that stands apart from other organizations and individuals as a separate economic unit.

H. The quality of information that assures decision makers that the information captures the conditions or events it purports to represent.

I. A term that applies to the broad concepts or guidelines and detailed practices in accounting, including all the conventions, rules, and procedures that make up accepted accounting practice at a given time.

J. Accumulation of a receivable or payable during a given period, even though no explicit transaction occurs.

K. As a system is changed, its expected additional benefits should exceed its expected additional costs.

L. An entity's ability to meet its financial obligations as they become due.

M. The concept that states that a financial statement item is important if its omission or misstatement would tend to mislead the reader of the financial statements under consideration.

N. A balance sheet that groups the accounts into subcategories.

O. Cash plus assets that are expected to be converted to cash or sold or consumed during the next twelve months or within the normal operating cycle if longer than a year.

P. The excess of sales revenue over the cost of the inventory that was sold.

Q. The assessment of the likelihood that a company will provide investors with a particular rate of return on their investment.

R. An income statement that contains one or more subtotals that often highlight significant relationships.

Multiple Choice

_____ 1.   Which of the following is *not* a principal classification for adjustments:

      a.   Expiration of unexpired costs.
      b.   Realization of unearned revenues.
      c.   Accrual of recorded expenses.
      d.   Accrual of unrecorded revenues.

_____ 2.   Adjustments:

      a.   Affect at least one income statement account and a balance sheet account.
      b.   Are for the convenience of the accountant.
      c.   May be recorded at any time during the accounting period.
      d.   All of the above are true of adjustments.

_____ 3.   The next step in the recording process after journalizing and posting adjustments is:

      a.   Unadjusted trial balance.
      b.   Ledger.
      c.   Financial statements.
      d.   Adjusted trial balance.

_____ 4.   Which is *not* a format for the classified balance sheet?

      a.   Report format.
      b.   Multiple-step format.
      c.   Account format.
      d.   All of the above are correct formats for the classified balance sheet.

_____ 5.   On a classified balance sheet, an asset that is expected to be converted to cash or sold or consumed during the next period would be classified as a:

      a.   Current asset.
      b.   Fixed asset.
      c.   Noncurrent asset.
      d.   Intangible asset.

_____ 6.   When constructing a single-step income statement, cost of goods sold is listed:

      a.   Directly below sales to determine gross profit.
      b.   In other revenues and expenses.
      c.   In a group with all the expenses listed.
      d.   None of the above are true of a single-step income statement.

_____ 7. Accountants usually show interest revenue and interest expense on a multiple-step income statement:

a. Above operating income.
b. Below operating income.
c. Below pretax income.
d. Above gross profit.

_____ 8. The ratio that is widely regarded as the ultimate measure of overall accomplishment is:

a. Return on sales ratio.
b. Gross profit percentage.
c. Return on stockholders' equity ratio.
d. Current ratio.

_____ 9. The ratio that is widely used to evaluate a business entity's solvency is the:

a. Return on sales ratio.
b. Gross profit percentage.
c. Return on stockholders' equity ratio.
d. Current ratio.

_____ 10. Which of the following is *not* true of generally accepted accounting principles? GAAP:

a. Eliminates differences in accounting principles between countries.
b. Applies to the concepts and guidelines that make up accepted accounting practices in the United States.
c. Has been determined primarily by private sector bodies — FASB and APB.
d. All of the above are true of GAAP.

VI. Solutions to Test Yourself

Questions

1. Adjustments are important because they assign the financial effects of the implicit transactions to the appropriate time periods. This helps provide a complete and accurate measure of efforts, accomplishments, and financial position. (L. O. 1)

2.

	Unadjusted		Journalize		Adjusted		Financial
Ledger →	Trial Balance	→	and Post Adjustments	→	Trial Balance	→	Statements

These final steps are needed to recognize the implicit transactions required by the accrual basis of accounting. The adjusted trial balance is needed to prove the equality of debits and credits, and to make preparation of the financial statements easier. (L. O. 5)

3. A classified balance sheet is needed to help readers quickly gain a perspective on the company's financial position. The classifications help to draw attention to certain amounts or groups of accounts. (L. O. 6)

4. A single-step income statement groups all revenues together and then lists and deducts all expenses together without drawing any intermediate subtotals.

    A multiple-step income statement contains one or more subtotals that highlight significant relationships. Examples of these subtotals are gross profit and operating income. (L. O. 7)

5. Profitability is the assessment of the likelihood that a company will provide investors with a particular rate of return on their investment. Profitability measures are also useful decision-making tools for company managers. Both external and internal users of financial statements use profitability comparisons through time, and within and among industries as a basis for predictions and decisions. (L. O. 7)

Exercises and Problems

1.

	Total Assets	Total Liabilities	Revenue	Expense	Net Income
A.	NE	D	I	NE	I
B.	D	NE	NE	I	D
C.	I	NE	I	NE	I
D.	NE	I	NE	I	D

2.

A.	Unearned ticket revenue	250,000	
	Ticket revenue		250,000
B.	Depreciation expense	6,000	
	Accumulated depreciation-equipment		6,000
C.	Accounts receivable	82,000	
	Service revenue		82,000
D.	Wages expense	23,000	
	Accrued wages payable		23,000

3.

MIT Computers, Inc.
Income Statement
For the year ended December 31, 19X9

Sales		$4,350,000
Cost of goods sold		1,838,000
Gross profit		$2,512,000
Operating expenses:		
Payroll expense	$1,000,000	
Rent expense	400,000	
Depreciation expense	100,000	
Other miscellaneous expenses	98,000	1,598,000
Operating income		$ 914,000
Other expense:		
Interest expense		(75,000)
Income before taxes		$ 839,000
Income taxes		334,000
Net income		$ 505,000

4.

MIT Computers, Inc.
Balance Sheet
December 31, 19X9

Assets

Current assets:
Cash $ 65,000
 Accounts receivable 110,000
 Inventory 320,000
 Prepaid rent 40,000
 Prepaid insurance 20,000
  Total current assets $ 555,000

Long-term assets:
 Land 410,000
 Equipment $ 350,000
 Accumulated depreciation-equipment (125,000) 225,000
 Building $1,435,000
 Accumulated depreciation-building (370,000) 1,065,000
  Total long-term assets $1,700,000

Total assets $2,255,000

Liabilities and Stockholders' Equity

Current liabilities:
 Accounts payable $ 90,000
 Notes payable 45,000
 Accrued income taxes payable 85,000
  Total current liabilities $ 220,000

Long-term liabilities:
 Long-term mortgage payable 655,000

Stockholders' equity:
 Paid-in capital $ 510,000
 Retained income 870,000* 1,380,000

Total liabilities and stockholders' equity $2,255,000

* Beginning retained income + Net income = Ending retained income
$365,000 + $505,000 = $870,000

5. Current ratio:

$$\frac{Current\ Assets}{Current\ Liabilities} = \frac{\$550,000}{\$220,000} = 2.5$$

Gross profit percentage:

$$\frac{Gross\ Profit}{Sales} = \frac{\$250,000*}{\$600,000} = 41.7\%\ (rounded)$$

* Sales   - Cost of goods sold = Gross profit
  $600,000 - $350,000   = $250,000

Return on sales:

$$\frac{Net\ Income}{Sales} = \frac{\$120,000}{\$600,000} = 20\%$$

Return on stockholders' equity:

$$\frac{Net\ Income}{Average\ Stockholders'\ Equity} = \frac{\$120,000}{.5(\$450,000 + \$570,000)} = 23.5\%\ (rounded)$$

Matching

1.	J	L. O. 1		7.	G	L. O. 8		13.	F	L. O. 7
2.	E	L. O. 1		8.	I	L. O. 8		14.	Q	L. O. 7
3.	N	L. O. 6		9.	C	L. O. 8		15.	H	L. O. 8
4.	K	L. O. 8		10.	P	L. O. 7		16.	A	L. O. 7
5.	O	L. O. 6		11.	M	L. O. 8		17.	L	L. O. 6
6.	D	L. O. 6		12.	R	L. O. 7		18.	B	L. O. 2

Multiple Choice

1.   c   A major adjustment classification is accrual of *unrecorded* expenses, *not* recorded expenses. (L. O. 1, 2, and 3)

2.   a   Adjustments are required for the accrual basis of accounting and are recorded prior to preparing financial statements. (L. O. 5)

3.   d   The final sequence of steps in the recording process are:

Ledger → Unadjusted Trial Balance → Journalize and Post Adjustments → Adjusted Trial Balance → Financial Statements   (L. O. 5)

4.   b   The multiple-step form is appropriate for the income statement, *not* the balance sheet. (L. O. 6)

5.   a   b, c, and d are all categories for assets that would provide future benefits beyond the next period. (L. O. 6)

6.   c   A single-step income statement does not present gross profit or other revenue and expenses; all expenses are presented in one group or category.

A multiple-step income statement presents cost of goods sold directly below sales to determine gross profit.
(L. O. 7)

7.   b   Interest income and interest expense are generally segregated from operations to highlight both the results from normal operations, and the existence and amount of additions and subtractions made to achieve net income. (L. O. 7)

8.   c   (L. O. 7)

9.   d   (L. O. 7)

10.   a   The International Accounting Standards Committee (IASC) seeks to eliminate differences in accounting principles between countries. Both b. and c. are true of GAAP. (L. O. 8)

Chapter 5

ACCOUNTING FOR SALES

I.   Learning Objectives

A thorough understanding of the interrelationships between sales revenue and related current assets is important to both managers and practitioners alike. Anyone involved in making financial decisions of any kind should have a clear understanding of the intertwined income statement and balance sheet effects. Use the following learning objectives as an aid in your study of Chapter 5.

1.   Recognize revenue items at the proper time on the income statement.

2.   Account for cash and credit sales.

3.   Record sales returns and allowances, sales discounts, and bank credit card sales.

4.   Manage cash and explain its importance to the company.

5.   Estimate and interpret uncollectible accounts receivable balances.

6.   Assess the level of accounts receivable.

7.   Develop and explain internal control procedures.

II. Pretest

SELECT THE BEST ANSWER AND ENTER THE IDENTIFYING LETTER IN THE SPACE PROVIDED.

_____ 1. The recording of expenses in the same time period as related revenues is known as:

    a. Operating cycle.
    b. Matching.
    c. Cost recovery.
    d. Cash basis.

_____ 2. Under accrual-basis accounting, recognition of revenue requires:

    a. Goods and services to be delivered to the customers.
    b. Cash or an asset virtually assured of being converted into cash to be received.
    c. Both a and b.
    d. None of the above are correct.

_____ 3. The amount of revenue to be recognized for a credit sale is:

    a. The present cash equivalent of the asset received.
    b. The gross realizable value.
    c. Always equal to the amount if it was a cash sale.
    d. All of the above are true.

_____ 4. Reductions of invoice prices awarded for prompt payment are:

    a. Trade discounts.
    b. Net sales discounts.
    c. Cash discounts.
    d. None of the above are correct.

_____ 5. Net sales is computed by:

    a. Subtracting from gross credit sales, sales returns and allowances, and cash discounts.
    b. Subtracting from gross sales, sales returns and allowances, and adding cash discounts.
    c. Subtracting from gross sales, cash discounts, and adding sales returns and allowances.
    d. Subtracting from gross sales, sales returns and allowances, and cash discounts.

_____ 6. Retailers accept bank credit cards:

    a. To attract credit customers who would otherwise shop elsewhere.
    b. To get cash immediately rather than wait for customers to pay.
    c. To avoid the cost of keeping track of many customers' accounts.
    d. All of the above are true.

_____ 7. Highly liquid short-term investments that can easily be converted into cash are known as:

    a. Compensating balances.
    b. Marketable equity securities.
    c. Cash equivalents.
    d. None of the above answers are correct.

_____ 8. The management of cash is important because:

    a.   The flow of cash can be enormous.
    b.   Cash is the most liquid asset.
    c.   Adequate cash is essential to the smooth functioning of operations.
    d.   All of the above are true of the management of cash.

_____ 9. The *cost* of granting credit that arises from accounts that some credit customers are either unable or unwilling to pay is known as:

    a.   uncollectible accounts.
    b.   bad debts expense.
    c.   trade receivables.
    d.   None of the above are correct.

_____ 10. The method of accounting for bad debt losses that makes use of an estimate of the amount of sales that will ultimately be uncollectible and the presence of a contra account is the:

    a.   Uncollectible accounts method.
    b.   Specific write-off method.
    c.   Allowance method.
    d.   Reserve method.

_____ 11. One measure of a firm's ability to generate sales without excessive growth in receivables is:

    a.   Days to collect accounts receivable.
    b.   Inventory turnover.
    c.   Accounts receivable turnover.
    d.   None of the above are correct.

_____ 12. Receivables can be assessed in terms of how long it takes to collect them. This is known as:

    a.   Days to collect accounts receivable.
    b.   Inventory turnover.
    c.   Accounts receivable turnover.
    d.   None of the above are correct.

_____ 13. Which of the following is *not* true of internal control?

    a.   It is a system of checks and balances.
    b.   It assures that all actions occurring within the company are in accord with organizational objectives.
    c.   It eliminates top management approving transactions.
    d.   All of the above are correct.

_____ 14. General objectives of internal control are:

    a.   Authorization, recording, safeguarding.
    b.   Authorization, safeguarding, reconciliation.
    c.   Recording, reconciliation, valuation.
    d.   All of the above are objectives of internal control.

III. Answers to Pretest

1. b   The *matching* of revenue and related expenses in the same period is the basis of accrual accounting. (L. O. 1)

2. c   Under accrual-basis accounting, recognition of revenue requires both goods and services to be delivered to the customers and cash or an asset virtually assured of being converted into cash to be received. (L. O. 1)

3. a   The amount of revenue to be recognized for a credit sale is the present cash equivalent of the asset received, which is the *net* realizable value, and may be *less* than the amount if it were a cash sale. (L. O. 2)

4. c   (L. O. 2)

5. d   Net sales is the *net* amount after sales returns and allowances and cash discounts are subtracted from *gross* sales (which includes both cash and credit sales). (L. O. 3)

6. d   (L. O. 3)

7. c   (L. O. 4)

8. d   (L. O. 4)

9. b   Bad debts expense is the *cost* of granting credit. Uncollectible accounts are the *accounts* or receivables that are determined to be uncollectible. (L. O. 5)

10. c   (L. O. 5)

11. c   (L. O. 6)

12. a   (L. O. 6)

13. b   Internal control does assure that all actions have the approval of top management. (L. O. 7)

14. d   a, b, and c all contain general objectives of internal control which are: authorization, recording, safeguarding, reconciliation, and valuation. (L. O. 7)

EVALUATION

The pretest contained two questions for each learning objective. If you did not answer both questions correctly for each learning objective, you should review the appropriate section of the textbook and study guide before you attempt the material after Part IV.

IV. Key Concept Review by Learning Objectives

L. O. 1: Recognize Revenue Items at the Proper Time on the Income Statement

A.   Recognition of Sales Revenue

    1.   The timing of revenue recognition is important because it is critical to the measurement of net income. Under the matching principle the cost of the items sold is reported in the same period in which revenue is recognized.

    2.   Under *cash-basis accounting*, revenue is recognized when cash is collected for sales of goods and services.

    3.   Under *accrual-basis accounting*, revenue is recognized when both:

        a.   Goods or services are delivered to the customers (revenue is earned).

        b.   Cash or an asset virtually assured of being converted into cash is received (revenue is realized).

B.   Most revenue is recognized at the point of sale. Sometimes the two revenue recognition tests are not met at the same time. In such cases, revenue is generally recognized only when both tests are met.

L. O. 2: Account for Cash and Credit Sales

Measurement of Sales Revenue

    1.   Revenue is measured in terms of the present cash equivalent value of the asset (either cash or accounts receivable) received, the *net realizable value*.

    2.   Revenue is recorded equal to the asset received. Both cash and credit sales transactions increase Sales Revenue, an income statement account and an asset account.

L. O. 3: Record Sales Returns and Allowances, Sales Discounts, and Bank Credit Card Sales

A.   Merchandise Returns and Allowances

    1.   Products returned by the customer are **sales returns** to the seller and **purchase returns** to the customer.

    2.   A reduction of the selling price (the price previously agreed upon) is called a **sales allowance** by the seller and a **purchase allowance** by the buyer (customer).

    3.   Sales allowances and returns are going to have an effect on **net sales**, but not on **gross sales**. Gross sales are equal to the initial revenues or asset inflows based on the sales price, and they must be decreased by the amount of the returns and allowances to give the net sales.

4. Both sales returns and sales allowances are combined into one account, Sales Returns and Allowances — a contra account that is subtracted from gross sales in determining net sales.

B. Discounts from Selling Prices

1. **Trade discounts** offer one or more reductions to the gross selling price for a particular class of customers to arrive at the actual selling or invoice price. Trade discounts are generally price concessions or purchase incentives, and are offered to be competitive or to encourage certain customer behavior.

2. **Cash discounts** are reductions of the *actual selling price* (*invoice price*) awarded for prompt payment. The terms of the cash discount may be quoted in various ways on the invoice. See the textbook illustration for this section.

STUDY TIP:
Cash discounts generally should be taken by purchasers, although the decision depends on the relative costs of interest.

C. Recording Charge Card Transactions

1. Retailers accept bank cards: to attract credit customers who would otherwise shop elsewhere, to get cash immediately, and to avoid the cost of keeping track of many customers' accounts.

2. Service charges for card sales are included in the calculation to determine net sales revenue on the income statement.

D. Accounting for Net Sales Revenue

Cash discounts and sales returns and allowances are deducted from gross sales to determine net sales on the income statement.

L. O. 4: Manage Cash and Explain Its Importance to the Company

A. Cash

1. Cash encompasses all the items that are accepted for deposit by a bank, notably paper money and coins, money orders, and checks.

2. Many companies combine cash and cash equivalents on their balance sheets. **Cash equivalents** are highly liquid short-term investments that can easily and quickly be converted into cash.

B. Compensating Balances

1. Banks frequently require companies to maintain **compensating balances**. The size of the compensating or minimum balance that is required often depends on either the amount borrowed, or the amount of credit available, or both.

2.   Compensating balances increase the effective interest rate paid by the borrower.

3.   To prevent any misleading information regarding cash, annual reports must disclose the state of any compensating balances. Without such a disclosure, financial statement readers might think that a company has more cash available than it really does have.

C.   Management of Cash

    1.   Managers spend much time managing cash because:

        a.   Even though the cash balance may be small at any one time, the flow of cash can be enormous.

        b.   Cash is the most liquid asset, which makes it enticing to thieves and embezzlers.

        c.   Adequate cash is essential to the smooth functioning of operations.

        d.   It is important not to hold *excess* cash, as cash itself does not earn income.

    2.   Most organizations have detailed, well-specified procedures for receiving, recording, and disbursing cash. Cash is usually placed in a bank account, and the company's books are periodically reconciled with the bank's records. To **reconcile a bank statement** means to verify that the bank balance and accounting records are consistent.

STUDY TIP:
The bank balance and the accounting book balance for cash are rarely identical. Various items impact either the bank or book balance and need to be used in the bank reconciliation to arrive at the true or correct cash balance.

    3.   In addition to reconciling the bank balance, other internal control procedures are set up to safeguard cash and ensure accurate accounting records. The major procedures are:

        a.   The individuals who receive cash do not also disburse cash.

        b.   The individuals who handle cash cannot access accounting records.

        c.   Cash receipts are immediately recorded and deposited and are not used directly to make payments.

        d.   Disbursements are made by serially numbered checks, only upon proper authorization by someone other than the person writing the check.

        e.   Bank accounts are reconciled monthly.

L. O. 5: Estimate and Interpret Uncollectible Accounts Receivable Balances

A.   Credit Sales and Accounts Receivable

       1.   **Accounts receivable**, which are amounts owed to the company by its customers as a result of delivering goods or services and extending credit for these goods or services, should be distinguished from deposits, accruals, notes, and other assets not arising out of everyday sales.

       2.   Accounts receivable is sometimes called **trade receivables** or simply **receivables**.

       3.   Credit sales on open account increase accounts receivable.

B.   Uncollectible Accounts

Granting credit entails cost and benefits.

       1.   Perhaps the most significant cost of granting credit is **uncollectible accounts** or **bad debts** — receivables that some credit customers are either unable or unwilling to pay. This cost is sometimes labeled **bad debt expense**. Another cost is administration and collection.

       2.   The benefit of granting credit is the boost in sales and profit that would otherwise be lost if credit was not extended.

C.   Deciding When and How To Grant Credit

Competition and industry practice affect whether and how companies offer credit. Companies offer credit only when the additional earnings on credit sales exceed the costs of offering credit.

D.   Measurement of Uncollectible Accounts

There are two basic ways to record uncollectibles:

       1.   By waiting to see which ones are unpaid — the specific write-off method.

       2.   By making estimates today of the portion that will not be collected — the allowance method.

E.   Specific Write-Off Method

       1.   A company that rarely experiences a bad debt might use the **specific write-off method**, which assumes that all sales are fully collectible until proven otherwise. At that point the bad debt is written off directly against accounts receivable.

       2.   The specific write-off method has been justifiably criticized because it fails to apply the matching principle of accrual accounting. If an accounts receivable becomes bad, it would be written off in that accounting period which may be different than the accounting period in which it was earned.

       3.   The principal arguments in favor of the specific write-off method are based on cost-benefit and materiality. Basically, the method is simple and extremely inexpensive to use. Also, no great error in measurement of income occurs if amounts of bad debts are small and similar from one year to the next.

F.   Allowance Method

1.   The **allowance method** for bad debt losses makes use of an estimate of uncollectible accounts that can be better matched to the related revenue.

2.   This method has two basic elements:

a.   An *estimate* of the amount of sales that will ultimately be uncollectible.

b.   A *contra account*, **allowance for uncollectible accounts** (or **allowance for doubtful accounts, allowance for bad debts,** or **reserve for doubtful accounts**), which records the estimate and is deducted from the accounts receivable.

STUDY TIP:
        The use of the allowance account enables us to record bad debt expense without identifying specific accounts that will be uncollectible.

3.   The various approaches to the allowance method are based on historical experience and assume the current year is similar to prior years in terms of economic circumstances and in terms of customer composition. Estimates are revised when conditions change.

STOP & REVIEW:

        Carefully review the **effects of the allowance method on the balance sheet equation** and **related journal entries** in the textbook.

G.   Applying the Allowance Method Using a Percentage of Sales

1.   One method used to estimate the *amount* recorded in the contra account, Allowance for Uncollectible Accounts, is the percentage of sales method.

a.   **Percentage of sales method** is based on the historical relationships between credit sales and uncollectible debt.

b.   Credit sales are for a specific period of time.

2.   The credit sales for the period are multiplied by the estimated percentage of uncollectible credit sales to arrive at the *bad debt expense* for the period. This bad debt expense figure is then *added to the existing balance in the allowance for uncollectible accounts* through the use of an adjusting entry.

3.   When actually writing-off an account receivable balance it is important to:

a.   Reduce (debit) the allowance for uncollectible accounts balance by the amount of the write-off.

b.   Reduce (credit) accounts receivable by the amount of the corresponding write-off. The specific customer's account should also be reduced (credited) by the amount of the write-off in the accounts receivable subsidiary ledger.

c.   *Do not write the account balance off against bad debt expense when using the allowance method.* This will result in overstating bad debt expense.

d. The write-off of an account balance *does not* have an effect on the net realizable value of accounts receivable.

 **& REVIEW:**

Carefully review the textbook **example for this method**.

B. Applying the Allowance Method Using a Percentage of Accounts Receivable

1. The **percentage of accounts receivable method** is based on the historical relationships of uncollectibles to year-end gross accounts receivable, not sales.

2. It differs from the percentage of sales method in the following ways:

   a. Ending accounts receivable is used in the calculation instead of credit sales.

   b. The amount calculated is the *desired ending balance* in the allowance for uncollectible account instead of bad debts expense.

   c. The adjusting entry for bad debt expense must be adjusted for the existing balance in the allowance account.

 **& REVIEW:**

Carefully review the textbook **example for this method**.

H. Applying the Allowance Method Using the Aging of Accounts Receivable

1. A refinement on the percentage of accounts receivable approach is the **aging of accounts receivable method**, which considers the composition of the end-of-year accounts receivable based on the age of the debt. The longer an account balance is outstanding the lesser the chances of collecting the entire balance.

2. Utilizing the aging method, the manager is able to analyze the composition of accounts receivable and, by applying a *bad debt percentage to each aging category*, arrive at the estimated dollar amount of the ending balance in the allowance for uncollectible accounts.

3. The adjusting entry is prepared in the same manner that is utilized when applying the percentage of ending accounts receivable method.

 **& REVIEW:**

Carefully review the textbook **example for this method**.

I. Bad Debt Recoveries

1. When **bad debt recoveries** occur, the write-off should be reversed, and the collection handled as a normal receipt on account. In this way, a company will be better able to keep track of the customer's true payment history.

 **& REVIEW:**

Carefully review the textbook **journal entries for bad debt recoveries**.

L. O. 6: Assess the Level of Accounts Receivable

Assessing the Level of Accounts Receivable

1. **Accounts receivable turnover** is one measure of the firm's ability to generate sales without excessive growth in receivables. It is computed:

$$Accounts\ Receivable\ Turnover = \frac{Credit\ Sales}{Average\ Accounts\ Receivable}$$

2. Receivables can also be assessed in terms of how long it takes to collect them, the **days to collect accounts receivable**, or **average collection period**. This computation is:

$$Days\ to\ Collect\ Accounts\ Receivable = \frac{365\ Days}{Accounts\ Receivable\ Turnover}$$

L. O. 7: Develop and Explain Internal Control Procedures

A. Overview of Internal Control

   1. The essence of internal control is the creation of a system of checks and balances that assures that all actions occurring within the company are in accord with organizational objectives and have the general approval of top management.

   2. In its broadest sense, **internal control** refers to both *administrative* control and *accounting* control.

      a. **Administrative controls** include the plan of organization and all methods and procedures that facilitate management planning and control of operations.

      b. **Accounting controls** include the methods and procedures for authorizing transactions, safeguarding assets, and ensuring the accuracy of the financial records.

   3. Internal accounting controls should provide reasonable assurance concerning:

      a. *Authorization* of transactions.

      b. *Recording* transactions.

      c. *Safeguarding* assets.

      d. *Reconciliation* of records.

      e. *Valuation* of assets.

   4. Management should recognize that an internal control system's purpose is as much a positive one (promoting efficiency) as a negative one (preventing errors and fraud).

B. The Accounting System

   1. The **accounting system** is integral to the internal control structure because it consists of a set of records, procedures, and equipment that routinely deals with the events affecting the financial performance and position of the entity.

2.   A major purpose of the accounting system is to help managers operate their entities more efficiently and effectively. Well-designed and well-run accounting systems are positive contributions to organizations and the economy.

C.   Management's Responsibility

1.   Management bears the primary responsibility for a company's financial statements and is responsible for all audited and unaudited information in the annual report.

2.   In the annual report there is a **management report** that states that management is responsible for all audited and unaudited information in the annual report. The management report also includes a statement on the adequacy of internal control, a description of the composition and duties of the audit committee as well as the duties of the independent auditor.

D.   The Audit Committee

1.   Most companies' boards of directors have an **audit committee** that oversees the internal accounting controls, financial statements, and financial affairs of the corporation.

2.   The committee provides contact and communication among the board, the external auditors, the internal auditors, the financial executives, and the operating executives.

E.   Checklist of Internal Control

All good systems of internal control have certain features in common which can be summarized in a *checklist of internal control*. This checklist is:

1.   Reliable Personnel with Clear Responsibilities

a.   The most important element of successful control is personnel: incompetent or dishonest individuals can undermine a system, no matter how well it is constructed.

b.   Assessing responsibility means tracking actions as far down in the organization as is feasible, so that results can be related to individuals. The psychological impact of fixing responsibility tends to promote care and efficiency.

2.   Separation of Duties

a.   The separation of duties not only helps ensure accurate compilation of data but also limits the chances for fraud that would require the collusion of two or more persons.

b.   Separation of duties may be subdivided into four parts:

1)   Separation of operational responsibility from record keeping responsibility.

2)   Separation of the custody of assets from accounting.

3)   Separation of the authorization of transactions from the custody of related assets.

4)   Separation of duties within the accounting function.

c. A main goal of separation of duties is to make sure that one person, acting alone, cannot defraud the company.

3. Proper Authorization

Authorization may be *general* or *specific*.

a. General authorization is usually found in writing and sets limits.

b. Specific authorization usually means that a superior manager must permit (usually in writing) any particular deviations from the limits set by general authorization.

4. Adequate Documents

Documents should be adequate to ensure immediate, complete, and tamper-proof recording.

5. Proper Procedures

a. Most organizations have *procedures manuals*, which specify the flow of documents and provide information and instructions to facilitate adequate record keeping.

b. Routine and automatic checks are major ways of attaining proper procedures.

6. Physical Safeguards

Losses of cash, inventories, and records are minimized by safes, locks, guards, and limited access.

7. Bonding, Vacations, and Rotation of Duties

a. Top executives, branch managers, and individuals that handle cash or inventories should have understudies and be required to take vacations.

b. These key employees should also be *bonded*: but bonding is not a substitute for vacations, rotation of duties, and similar precautions.

8. Independent Check

All phases of the system should be subjected to periodic review by outsiders (i.e., auditors) and by internal auditors and other checks such as the reconciliation of bank statements.

9. Cost-Benefit Analysis

Cost-benefit considerations are integral to all of the characteristics discussed to this point. If the value of the asset or information provided is overshadowed by the cost of acquiring the information or safeguarding the asset, prudent management dictates adjustments to the internal control structure relative to those areas.

STUDY TIP:
Study the "Summary Problems for Your Review" and solutions in the text.

 **& REVIEW:**

Before continuing, review the objectives for this chapter and make sure you have a good understanding of each one.

Appendix 5A: Bank Reconciliations

A.   The Bank Statement

 **& REVIEW:**

Before continuing, carefully review **Exhibit 5-1: An Actual Bank Statement** in the textbook.

The supporting documents for the detailed checks on the bank statement are canceled checks; for additional deposits, deposit slips.

B.   Bank Reconciliations

The depositor, to make sure that all cash receipts and disbursements are accounted for, does a monthly bank reconciliation. Bank reconciliations take many forms, but the objective is unchanged: to explain all differences in a cash balance at a given date.

 **& REVIEW:**

Before continuing, carefully review **Exhibit 6-2 and the bank reconciliation example** in the textbook.

V. Test Yourself

Questions

1. Discuss the proper time to recognize a revenue item on the income statement.

2. Define trade discounts and discuss the reasons it is used.

3. Explain why management of cash is important

4. Explain how uncollectible accounts affect the valuation of accounts receivable.

5. Discuss the specific write-off and allowance methods of accounting for uncollectible accounts.

Exercises and Problems

Data for use with #1 and #2

McCrann Associates had the following account balances on December 31, 19X9 (in thousands). All sales were on credit and all accounts receivable for 19X9 were collected in 19X9.

Sales (gross)	$8,000
Sales return and allowances	500
Cash discounts on sales	250
Cost of goods sold	5,200
Selling expenses	800
Administrative expenses	690
Income taxes	208

1. Prepare the revenue section of the 19X9 income statement.

2. Prepare journal entries for (a) initial revenue recognition for 19X9 sales, (b) sales returns and allowances, and (c) collection of accounts receivable.

3. The following information is available for the month ending October 31, 2001 for Mums' Nursery:

CUSTOMER	Amount	Remarks
Floral Cascade	$9,000	Current
Floral Elegance	4,000	61 - 90 days
Flower Basket	7,000	Current
The Greenhouse	3,200	1 - 30 days
Shade Tree Sales	1,000	over 90 days
Suffolk Floral	2,000	31 - 60 days

Experience indicates the following bad debt percentages:

Current	0.5%
1 -30 days	1.0%
31 - 60 days	3.0%
61 - 90 days	10.0%
over 91 days	90.0%

A. Prepare an aging schedule based upon the above information.

B. Prior to adjustment, the allowance for uncollectible accounts had a credit balance of $800. Prepare the journal entry to adjust the allowance account.

4. Gear Shoes sells on terms of 2/10, n/30. It sold shoes to Royal Retailers for $220,000 on open account on March 15. Payment (net of cash discount) was received on March 24. Prepare the appropriate journal entries.

5. Jones' Equipment has many accounts receivable. Jones' balance sheet on December 31, 19X9 showed: Accounts receivable, $295,000; and Allowance for uncollectible accounts, $5,000. In early 2000, write-offs of customer accounts of $2,000 were made. In late 2000, a customer, whose $500 debt had been written off earlier, remitted $500 to Jones'. Prepare the journal entries for the $2,000 write-off in early 2000 and the $500 receipt in late 2000.

Matching

MATCH EACH TERM WITH ITS DEFINITION BY WRITING THE APPROPRIATE LETTER IN THE SPACE PROVIDED.

Terms

_____ 1. Accounting controls

_____ 2. Accounts receivable

_____ 3. Accounts receivable turnover

_____ 4. Administrative controls

_____ 5. Aging of accounts receivable

_____ 6. Allowance for uncollectible accounts

_____ 7. Bad debt recoveries

_____ 8. Bad debts expense

_____ 9. Cash discounts

_____ 10. Cash equivalents

_____ 11. Compensating balances

_____ 12. Days to collect accounts receivables

_____ 13. Gross sales

_____ 14. Internal control

_____ 15. Net sales

_____ 16. Percentage of accounts receivable method

_____ 17. Percentage of sales method

_____ 18. Reconcile a bank statement

_____ 19. Sales allowance

_____ 20. Sales returns

_____ 21. Trade discounts

_____ 22. Uncollectible accounts

Definitions

A.   Accounts receivable that were written off as uncollectible but then were collected at a later date.

B.   Reduction of the selling price (the original price previously agreed upon).

C.   An approach to estimating bad debt expense and uncollectible accounts at year end using the historical relations of uncollectibles to accounts receivable.

D.   Highly liquid short-term investments that can easily be converted into cash.

E.   The cost of granting credit that arises from uncollectible accounts.

F.   A contra asset account that offsets total receivables by an estimated amount that will probably not be collected.

G.   On the income statement, total sales revenue reduced by sales returns and allowances and cash discounts.

H.   An approach to estimating bad debt expense and uncollectible accounts based on the historical relations between credit sales and uncollectibles.

I.   Receivables determined to be uncollectible because debtors are unable or unwilling to pay their debts.

J.   Credit sales divided by average accounts receivable.

K.   365 divided by accounts receivable turnover.

L.   Products returned by the customer.

M.   An analysis of the elements of individual accounts receivable according to the time elapsed after the dates of billing.

N.   Reductions of invoice prices awarded for prompt payment.

O.   Amounts owed to a company by customers as a result of delivering goods or services and extending credit in the ordinary course of business.

P.   Reductions to the gross selling price for a particular class of customers to arrive at the actual selling price.

Q.   Required minimum cash balances on deposit when money is borrowed from banks.

R.   Total sales revenue before deducting sales returns and allowances.

S.   To verify that the bank balance for cash is consistent with the accounting records.

T.   The plan of organization and all methods and procedures that facilitate management planning and control of operations.

U.   Refers to both administrative control and accounting control.

V.   The methods and procedures for authorizing transactions, safeguarding assets, and ensuring the accuracy of the financial records.

Multiple Choice

SELECT THE BEST ANSWER AND ENTER THE IDENTIFYING LETTER IN THE SPACE PROVIDED.

_____ 1.   Sales returns and allowances normally:

   a.   Carry a credit balance.
   b.   Carry a debit balance.
   c.   Are recorded as a liability of the period.
   d.   Are recorded as expenses of the period.

_____ 2.   Cash equivalents include:

   a.   Paper money and coins, checks, money orders, and post-dated checks.
   b.   Paper money and coins, money orders, and checks.
   c.   Checks, money orders, postage stamps, IOU's.
   d.   Post-dated checks, paper money and coins, IOU's.

_____ 3.   The allowance for uncollectible accounts is:

   a.   A contra asset account.
   b.   A contra liability account.
   c.   An expense.
   d.   None of the above are correct.

_____ 4.   Of the following methods utilized to determine bad debt expense, which would *not* utilize an allowance account?

   a.   Specific write-off.
   b.   Percentage of sales.
   c.   Percentage of ending accounts receivable.
   d.   Percentage of average accounts receivable.

_____ 5.   The allowance for uncollectible accounts:

   a.   Always has a credit balance.
   b.   Always has a debit balance.
   c.   Normally has a credit balance, but could have a debit balance.
   d.   Normally has a debit balance, but could have a credit balance.

_____ 6.   An approach to estimating bad debt expense and uncollectible accounts based on the historical relationship between credit sales and uncollectibles is the:

   a.   Percentage of sales method.
   b.   Percentage of accounts receivable method.
   c.   Aging of accounts receivable method.
   d.   None of the above are correct.

_____ 7. An approach to estimating bad debt expense and uncollectible accounts at year end, using the historical relationship of uncollectibles to accounts receivable is the:

      a.   Percentage of sales method.
      b.   Percentage of accounts receivable method.
      c.   Aging of accounts receivable method.
      d.   None of the above are correct.

_____ 8. Which of the following methods does *not* use the balance in the allowance for uncollectible accounts in its computation?

      a.   Aging of accounts receivable.
      b.   Percentage of sales.
      c.   Percentage of ending accounts receivable.
      d.   None of the above are correct.

_____ 9. Which of the following *cannot* be used to assess the firm's ability to control accounts receivable?

      a.   Days to collect accounts receivable.
      b.   Accounts receivable turnover.
      c.   Average collection period.
      d.   All of the above are correct.

_____10. When reviewing administrative controls within the internal control structure, a manager would be most interested in:

      a.   Procedures for the authorization of transactions.
      b.   Safeguarding of assets.
      c.   Accuracy of the financial statements.
      d.   Plan of organization.

VI. Solutions to Test Yourself

Questions

1. Under cash-basis accounting, revenue is recognized when cash is collected for sales of goods and services. Under accrual-basis accounting, however, recognition of revenue requires that goods or services must be delivered to the customers, and cash or an asset virtually assured of being converted into cash must be received. Accountants must sometimes exercise judgment in deciding when the recognition criteria are met. (L. O. 1)

2. Trade discounts are reductions to the gross selling price for a particular class of customers to arrive at the actual selling or invoice price. Companies set trade discounts to be competitive, and to encourage certain customer behavior. (L. O. 3)

3. The management of cash is important because, although the cash balance may be small at any one time, the flow of cash can be enormous. Cash is the most liquid asset making it enticing to thieves and embezzlers, and adequate cash is essential to the smooth functioning of operations. (L. O. 4)

4. Uncollectible accounts are receivables determined to be uncollectible because debtors are unable or unwilling to pay their debts. These uncollectible accounts give rise to bad debts expense, which is the cost of granting credit. The net realizable value is reduced by uncollectible accounts. (L. O. 5)

5. The specific write-off method of accounting for uncollectible accounts assumes all sales are fully collectible until proven otherwise, when the bad debt is written off directly against accounts receivable.

    The allowance method of accounting for bad debt losses makes use of estimates of the amount of sales that will ultimately be uncollectible and the presence of a contra asset account, allowance for doubtful or uncollectible accounts. This method uses an estimate of uncollectible accounts that can be better matched to the related revenue. (L. O. 5)

Exercises and Problems

1.

Gross sales		$8,000,000
Less:		
Sales returns and allowances	$500,000	
Cash discounts	250,000	(750,000)
Net sales		$ 7,250,000

2.

(a)

Accounts receivable	8,000,000	
Sales revenue		8,000,000

(b)

Sales returns and allowances	500,000	
Accounts receivable		500,000

(c)

Cash	8,000,000	
Cash discounts on sales	250,000	
Accounts receivable		7,750,000

3.A.

Mums' Nursery
Aging of Accounts Receivable
October 31, 2001

	Total	Current	1 - 30 Days	31 -60 Days	61 - 90 Days	Over 90 Days
Floral Cascade	$9,000	$9,000				
Floral Elegance	4,000				$4,000	
Flower Basket	7,000	7,000				
The Greenhouse	3,200		$3,200			
Shade Tree Sales	1,000					$1,000
Suffolk Floral	2,000			$2,000		
Total	$26,200	$16,000	$3,200	$2,000	$4,000	$1,000
Bad debt %		0.5%	1.0%	3.0%	10.0%	90.0%
Bad debt allowance to be provided	$1,472	$80	$32	$60	$400	$900

3.B.

Bad debt expense	672	
Allowance for uncollectible accounts		672

($1,472- $800 = $672)

	4.			
Mar. 15		Accounts receivable	220,000	
		Sales revenue		220,000
Mar. 27		Cash	215,600	
		Cash discount on sales	4,400	
		Accounts receivable		220,000
	5.			
		Allowance for uncollectible accounts	2,000	
		Accounts receivable		2,000
		Accounts receivable	500	
		Allowance for uncollectible accounts		500
		Cash	500	
		Accounts Receivable		500

Note: Although the last two entries could be summarized in a single entry debiting Cash for $500 and crediting the allowance account, two entries would usually be made. The debit and credit to Accounts Receivable would also be posted to the customer's account, which would then contain useful information for possible credit decisions in the future.

Matching

1.	V	L. O. 7	9.	N	L. O. 2	17.	H	L. O. 5
2.	O	L .O. 5	10.	D	L. O. 4	18.	S	L. O. 4
3.	J	L. O. 6	11.	Q	L. O. 4	19.	B	L. O. 2
4.	T	L. O. 7	12.	K	L. O. 6	20.	L	L. O. 2
5.	M	L. O. 5	13.	R	L. O. 2	21.	P	L. O. 2
6.	F	L. O. 5	14.	U	L. O. 7	22.	W	L. O. 5
7.	A	L. O. 5	15.	G	L. O. 2			
8.	E	L. O. 5	16.	C	L. O. 5			

Multiple Choice

1.   b   Sales returns and allowances is a contra account to sales revenue and, therefore, has a debit balance. (L. O. 2)

2.   b   Postage stamps, IOU's, and post-dated checks are not cash equivalents. (L. O. 4)

3.   a   Allowance for uncollectible accounts is a contra asset to accounts receivable. (L. O. 5)

4.   a   All the other methods are variations of the allowance method, and all include an allowance for uncollectible accounts. (L. O. 5)

5.   c   (L. O. 5)

6.   a   (L. O. 5)

7.   b   (L. O. 5)

8.   b   Percentage of sales method is based on sales, an income statement account, and does not include the allowance for uncollectible accounts balance, a balance sheet account, in its computation. (L. O. 5)

9.   d   Average collection period is another term for days to collect accounts receivable. (L. O. 6)

10.   d   The plan of organization refers to administrative controls. a, b, and c all refer to accounting controls. (L. O. 7)

Chapter 6

INVENTORIES AND COST OF GOODS SOLD

I. Learning Objectives

Understanding the theory and techniques associated with inventory valuation is important to financial statement users. The method of inventory valuation used not only affects the value reported on the balance sheet but, because of the interrelated nature of the balance sheet and income statement, it affects the reported gross profit and net income as well. It is important to attain an understanding of the issues and practices relating to: inventory valuation, cost of goods sold, and gross profit. Use the following learning objectives as an outline for your study of this material.

1. Link inventory valuation to gross profit.

2. Use both perpetual and periodic inventory systems.

3. Calculate the cost of merchandise acquired.

4. Choose one of the four principal inventory valuation methods.

5. Calculate the impact on net income of LIFO liquidations.

6. Use the lower-of-cost-or-market method to value inventories.

7. Show the effects of inventory errors on financial statements.

8. Evaluate the gross profit percentage and inventory turnover.

II. Pretest

_____ 1. The inventory system that helps managers control inventory levels and prepare interim financial statements is the:

     a.   Retail inventory system.
     b.   Periodic inventory system.
     c.   Perpetual inventory system.
     d.   None of the above are correct.

_____ 2. Under the periodic inventory system, cost of goods sold is computed:

     a.   On a day-to-day basis.
     b.   As a residual amount.
     c.   Is not computed.
     d.   None of the above are correct.

_____ 3. A physical count of inventory:

     a.   Must be taken when using both the periodic and perpetual inventory systems.
     b.   Reveals inventory shrinkage when compared to perpetual records.
     c.   Is a time-consuming and expensive process.
     d.   All of the above are true.

_____ 4. The perpetual inventory system:

     a.   Is more accurate than the periodic inventory system in providing timely information but is more costly.
     b.   Is more accurate than the periodic inventory system in providing timely information and is less costly.
     c.   Is less accurate than the periodic inventory system in providing timely information and is more costly.
     d.   Is less accurate than the periodic inventory system in providing timely information and is less costly.

_____ 5. The cost of merchandise includes:

     a.   The invoice price, directly identifiable transportation charges, and the cost of handling and storage.
     b.   The invoice price, directly identifiable transportation charges, less any offsetting discounts.
     c.   The invoice price, transportation charges, and the cost of the purchasing and receiving departments.
     d.   None of the above are correct.

_____ 6. The term for when the seller pays freight costs from the shipping point of the seller to the receiving point of the buyer is:

    a.   F.O.B. destination.
    b.   F.O.B. shipping point.
    c.   Freight in.
    d.   None of the above are correct.

_____ 7. This method of accounting for inventory assumes that the units acquired earliest are sold or used first:

    a.   Specific identification method.
    b.   First-in, first-out.
    c.   Last-in, first-out.
    d.   Weighted-average cost.

_____ 8. This method of accounting for inventory assumes that the units acquired most recently are sold or used first:

    a.   Specific identification method.
    b.   First-in, first-out.
    c.   Last-in, first-out.
    d.   Weighted average cost.

_____ 9. The cost at which an inventory item could be acquired today is the:

    a.   Retail market price.
    b.   Replacement cost.
    c.   Acquisition cost.
    d.   None of the above are correct.

_____ 10. The difference between a company's inventory valued at LIFO and what it would be under FIFO is the:

    a.   FIFO reserve.
    b.   LIFO reserve.
    c.   FIFO layer.
    d.   LIFO layer.

_____ 11. Selecting the methods of measurement that yield lower net income, lower assets, and lower stockholders' equity in the early years is:

    a.   Conservatism.
    b.   Lower-of-cost-or-market.
    c.   Holding gain.
    d.   None of the above are correct.

_____ 12. If a lower market price is indicative of lower ultimate sales prices:

    a.   Revenue should be adjusted.
    b.   No adjustment is required.
    c.   An inventory write-down is required.
    d.   None of the above are correct.

_____ 13.   An undiscovered inventory error usually affects:

   a.   Two reporting periods.
   b.   The balance sheet of the first period but not the balance sheet at the end of the second period.
   c.   The income statements of both periods.
   d.   All of the above are true.

_____ 14.   Which of the following is true?

   a.   If ending inventory is understated, retained income is understated. If ending inventory if overstated, retained income is overstated.
   b.   If ending inventory is understated, net income is understated. If ending inventory is overstated, net income is overstated.
   c.   If cost of goods sold is understated, retained income is overstated. If cost of goods sold is overstated, retained income is understated.
   d.   All of the above are true.

_____ 15.   The gross profit percentage is:

   a.   Used by auditors to help satisfy themselves about the accuracy of records.
   b.   Not important to management and investors.
   c.   Computed as a percentage of cost of goods sold.
   d.   None of the above are correct.

_____ 16.   Managers improve their inventory turnover by:

   a.   Raising prices and selling their inventory more quickly.
   b.   Lowering prices and selling their inventory more quickly.
   c.   Lowering prices and selling their inventory more slowly.
   d.   Raising prices and selling their inventory more slowly.

III. Answers to Pretest

1.   c   The perpetual inventory system tracks inventories and cost of goods sold on a day-to-day basis. (L. O. 1)

2.   b   Under the periodic inventory system, cost of goods sold and an updated inventory balance are computed only at the end of an accounting period, when a physical count is taken. (L. O. 1)

3.   d   (L. O. 2)

4.   a   (L. O. 2)

5.   b   The costs of handling, storage, and the purchasing and receiving departments are not part of the cost of merchandise. They are treated as period costs and appear on the income statement as they are incurred. (L. O. 3)

6.   a   (L. O. 3)

7.   b   (L. O. 4)

8.   c   (L. O. 4)

9.   c   (L. O. 5)

10.   b   (L. O. 5)

11.   a   (L. O. 6)

12.   c   Current revenue would not be adjusted because it is anticipated that the *future* sales price will decline. (L. O. 6)

13.   d   (L. O. 7)

14.   d   (L. O. 7)

15.   a   The gross profit percentage is very important to management and investors and is computed as a percentage of sales. (L. O. 8)

16.   b   By lowering prices, managers hope to increase gross profits by selling inventories more quickly. (L. O. 8)

EVALUATION

The pretest contained two questions for each learning objective. If you did not answer both questions correctly for each learning objective, you should review the appropriate section of the textbook and study guide before you attempt the material after Part IV.

IV. Key Concept Review by Learning Objectives

L. O. 1:   Link Inventory Valuation to Gross Profit

A.   Gross Profit and Cost of Goods Sold

1.   Sales revenue must cover the cost of goods sold and provide a gross profit sufficient to cover all other costs.

2.   The calculation for gross profit and cost of goods sold relies on the value of inventories.

STOP **& REVIEW:**

Review **Exhibit 6-1** in the textbook.

B.   The Basic Concept of Inventory Accounting

The key to calculating the cost of goods sold is accounting for inventory.

1.   To calculate the value of the inventory on hand, a *physical count* of inventory items is taken.

2.   A **cost valuation**, which assigns a specific value from the historical cost records to each item in ending inventory, is developed.

L. O. 2:   Use Both Perpetual and Periodic Inventory Systems

A.   Perpetual and Periodic Inventory Systems

1.   The **perpetual inventory system**:

a.   Keeps a running, continuous record that tracks inventories and cost of goods sold on a day-to-day basis. However, a **physical count** should be taken at least once a year to check on the accuracy of the continuous records.

b.   Helps managers control inventory levels and prepare interim financial statements. This system also provides managers with information that aids in pricing or ordering.

c.   When merchandise is purchased, the inventory account is increased, and when inventory is sold, the sale and the accompanying inventory reduction are recorded simultaneously.

2.   The **periodic inventory system**:

a.   Computes the cost of goods sold and an updated inventory balance only at the end of an accounting period, when a physical count of inventory is taken.

b.   The physical count allows management to delete from inventory goods that are damaged or obsolete and thus helps reveal **inventory shrinkage** (losses from theft, breakage, and loss).

c. Calculations for the cost of goods sold start with the **cost of the goods available for sale** — the sum of the opening inventory for the period plus purchases during the period.

STOP & REVIEW:

Before continuing, carefully review **Exhibit 6-2** in the textbook.

B. Comparison of Systems

1. For annual financial statements, the two methods produce the same cost of goods sold figure.

2. Historically, the perpetual system has been used for low-volume, high-value items. It is more accurate in providing timely information, but it is more costly.

3. The periodic system has been preferred for high-volume, low-value, and mixed-value inventory operations. It is less accurate, especially for interim statements, and it is less costly unless accumulation of obsolete merchandise is likely.

C. Physical Inventory

1. Good inventory control procedures require a physical count of each item being held in inventory at least annually in both periodic and perpetual inventory systems.

2. The physical count is a time-consuming and expensive process.

L. O. 3: Calculate the Cost of Merchandise Acquired

A. Cost of Merchandise Acquired

1. In practice, the cost of merchandise usually includes only the invoice price plus the directly identifiable transportation charges less any offsetting discounts.

2. The costs of the purchasing and receiving departments are treated as period costs and appear on the income statement as they are incurred.

B. Transportation Charges

1. The major cost of transporting merchandise is typically the freight charges from the shipping point of the seller to the receiving point of the buyer.

   a. When the seller bears this cost, the terms are stated on the sales invoice as **F.O.B. destination**.

   b. When the buyer bears this cost, the terms are stated as **F.O.B. shipping point**.

2. A separate transportation cost account, **freight in**, is often used instead of adding the cost to the inventory acquired.

   a. It is separate from inventory because it is easier to do, and management may want to compile freight costs separately to see how they compare to other periods' freight costs and other modes of transportation.

b. Freight in appears in the purchases section of an income statement as an additional cost of the goods acquired during the period. Freight in affects the gross profit section of the income statement for the buyer.

3. **Freight out** represents the costs borne by the *seller* and is shown as a shipping expense — a selling expense. It is shown below the gross profit line on the seller's income statement.

C. Discounts

Purchase returns, *purchase* allowances, and cash discounts on *purchases* are the opposite of their sales counterparts. They are deducted from purchases in calculating cost of goods sold.

STOP & REVIEW:

Before continuing, carefully review **Exhibit 6-3**, the **gross profit section** of the income statement, in the textbook.

D. Comparing Accounting Procedures for Periodic and Perpetual Inventory Systems

1. Note that in the perpetual system, the inventory and cost of goods sold account balances are always up to date at the end of the period. Under the periodic system, no balance appears in the cost of goods sold account until the company prepares financial statements and uses an adjusting journal entry to properly state inventory balances and cost of goods sold.

2. The perpetual system entails directly increasing the inventory account for purchases and decreasing it for returns and allowances and cost of goods sold. Under the periodic system, purchases and purchases returns and allowances are each accounted for in a separate account. Neither the cost of goods sold account nor the inventory account is computed on a daily basis.

STOP & REVIEW:

Carefully review the **detailed example** and **Exhibit 6-4** in the textbook before continuing.

L. O. 4: Choose One of the Four Principal Inventory Valuation Methods

A. Principal Inventory Valuation Methods

1. Each period, the cost of beginning inventory and merchandise acquired must be divided between cost of goods sold and the cost of items remaining in ending inventory. Regardless of the inventory system, costs of individual items must be determined by some inventory valuation method.

2. If unit prices and costs did not fluctuate, all inventory methods would show identical results. But prices do change, and these changes raise central issues regarding cost of goods sold (income measurement) and inventories (asset measurement).

3. A choice in method of inventory does *not* affect accounts payable. Each new inventory purchase is recorded at its cost and recognizes a liability in that amount in the same way under all of these methods.

B. Four Major Methods

1. **Specific identification method.**

    a. This method concentrates on the *physical* linking of the *particular* items sold.

    b. Because the cost of goods sold is determined by the specific item given to the customer, this method permits managers to manipulate income and inventory values by filling a sales order from a number of physically equivalent items with different historical costs.

    c. This method is easy to use, but works best for relatively expensive low-volume merchandise.

2. **First-in, first-out (FIFO).**

    a. This method assumes that the stock acquired earliest is sold first. It does not track the physical flow of individual items except by coincidence.

    b. This method, sometimes referred to as LISH (Last In, Still Here) tends to provide *inventory valuations* that closely approximate the actual market value of the inventory at the balance sheet date. This is because FIFO associates the most recent costs with inventories.

    c. In times of rising prices, FIFO usually shows the *largest* gross profit, which may favorably affect investor attitudes toward the company.

    d. Management cannot affect income by choosing to sell one identical item rather than another as FIFO specifies the order in which acquisition costs will become cost of goods sold.

3. **Last-in, first-out (LIFO).**

    a. This method assumes that the stock acquired most recently is sold first.

    b. In times of rising prices, LIFO generally shows the *lowest* gross profit and net income. This is important in the United States because LIFO is an acceptable inventory accounting method for income tax purposes: When lower net income is reported for tax purposes, lower taxes are paid.

    c. LIFO *does* permit management to influence reported income by the *timing of purchases* of inventory items.

4. **Weighted-average cost.**

    a. The **weighted-average method** computes a unit cost by dividing the total acquisition cost of all items available for sale by the number of units available for sale.

b. The weighted-average method usually produces a gross profit somewhere between that obtained under FIFO and that under LIFO.

c. The weighted average is also subject to minimal manipulation by management action.

STOP & REVIEW:

Before continuing, carefully review **Exhibit 6-5, Comparison of Inventory Methods**.

C. Cost Flow Assumptions

1. Under the matching principle, cost of goods sold is easy to link with the sales revenue generated when the product is delivered to a customer. It is harder to *measure* cost of goods sold.

2. Because the physical flow of products has little importance to the financial success of most businesses, companies may choose any of the four methods or *cost flow assumptions* to record cost of goods sold.

STUDY TIP:
Remember, no matter what cost flow assumptions are used, the cumulative gross profit over the life of a company remains the same.

3. LIFO is the most popular inventory method for large U.S. companies. FIFO is the second most popular, with weighted average third, and specific identification a distant fourth.

4. Some companies do not use LIFO because it yields lower net income and lower taxes only in a period of rising prices and constant or growing inventories. Some companies or industries do not face rising prices.

STOP & REVIEW:

Review **Exhibit 6-6 in the textbook** before continuing.

D. The Consistency Convention

1. Companies are expected to use the chosen cost flow assumption consistently over time. **Consistency** is conformity from period to period with unchanging policies and procedures.

2. Interpreting financial performance over time involves comparing the results of different periods. Meaningful comparisons over time would be impossible without consistency.

3. A company may, with justification and its auditor's approval, make a change in its inventory method. This change, however, will be noted in the auditor's opinion.

L. O. 5: Calculate the Impact on Net Income of LIFO Liquidations

A.   Characteristics and Consequences of LIFO

LIFO's dominant role in inventory accounting in the United States is more a result of an inflationary world and tax benefits than any theoretical dominance over other methods. Internationally, LIFO is not common.

B.   Holding Gains and Inventory Profits

    1.   **Replacement cost** is the cost at which an inventory item could be acquired today.

    2.   A **holding gain,** or an **inventory profit,** is the increase in the replacement cost or other measure of current value of the inventory held during the current period.

    3.   LIFO cost of goods sold typically offers a close approximation to replacement cost, and reported net income rarely contains significant holding gains because LIFO matches recent acquisition costs with sales revenue.

C.   LIFO Layers

    1.   The ending inventory under LIFO may contain prices from many different periods. As a company grows, the **LIFO layers** (also called **LIFO increments**) — an addition to inventory at an identifiable cost level — tend to pile on top of one another over the years.

    2.   Inventory for many LIFO companies include very old layers which results in reported values that may be far below what the true market value or current replacement value of the inventory might be.

    3.   From a balance sheet perspective, this means that the book values being reported will have little relevance to investors interested in assessing the assets of the company.

> **STUDY TIP:**
> While LIFO presents the economic reality on the income statement well, FIFO provides more up-to-date valuations on the balance sheet.

D.   LIFO Inventory Liquidations

    1.   The existence of old LIFO layers can cause problems in income measurement if inventory decreases.

        a.   In general, when the physical amount of inventory decreases, LIFO charges the cost of old LIFO layers as cost of good sold, beginning with the most recent layers.

        b.   This treatment can create a very low cost of goods sold, high gross profit, and high income tax expense in comparison with FIFO.

    2.   **LIFO reserve** is the cumulative difference between a company's inventory valued at LIFO and what it would be under FIFO. Many companies that report on LIFO explicitly measure and report this LIFO reserve on the front of the balance sheet or in the footnotes.

Review **Exhibits 6-7** and **6-8** in the textbook.

L. O. 6: Use the Lower-of-Cost-or-Market Method to Value Inventories

A. Lower-of-Cost-or-Market Method (LCM)

1. Under the **lower-of-cost-or-market method**, a market-price test is run on an inventory costing method — the *current market price* is compared with *historical cost* derived under one of the four primary methods of inventory valuation.

2. The lower of the two — current market value or historical cost — is conservatively selected as the basis for the valuation of goods at a specific inventory date.

3. When market value is lower and is used for valuing the ending inventory, the effect is to increase the amount reported as cost of goods sold.

4. LCM is an example of **conservatism**, which means selecting methods of measurement that yield lower net income, lower assets, and lower stockholders' equity.

B. Role of Replacement Cost

1. Implicit in LCM is the assumption that when replacement costs (market) decline in the wholesale market, so do retail selling prices.

2. If the lower market price is indicative of lower ultimate sales prices, an inventory **write-down** is required. A write-down is a reduction in carrying value to below cost in response to a decline in value.

3. If the market replacement cost falls but selling prices remain the same, items still have their original earnings power. No loss has occurred and no reduction in the book value of the inventory is necessary. Historical cost is the ceiling for valuation under generally accepted accounting principles.

C. Conservatism in Action

1. Compared with a pure cost method, the lower-of-cost-or-market method reports less net income in the period of decline in market value of the inventory and more net income in the period of sale.

STUDY TIP:
The lower-of-cost-or-market method affects how much income is reported in each year but not the total income over the company's life.

2. In practice, full use of LCM is rarely encountered because it is expensive to get the correct replacement costs of all the different inventory products in the market.

3. Auditors still feel that the cost of inventories should be fully recoverable from future revenue and will make market-price tests of a sample of the ending inventories.

Before continuing, carefully review **Exhibit 6-9** in the textbook.

L. O. 7: Show the Effects of Inventory Errors on Financial Statements

A.   Effects of Inventory Errors

     1.   Inventory errors can arise from many sources including wrong physical counts and clerical errors.

     2.   The effect of inventory errors on financial statements are as follows:

         a.   An undiscovered inventory error usually affects two reporting periods. Amounts will be misstated in the period in which the error occurred, but the effects will then be counterbalanced by identical offsetting amounts in the following period.

         b.   If ending inventory is understated, net income and retained income are understated.

         c.   If ending inventory is overstated, net income and retained income are overstated.

STUDY TIP:
It is important to remember that the ending inventory of one period is the beginning inventory of the following period.

 **& REVIEW:**

Before continuing, carefully review **Exhibit 6-10 in the textbook.**

L. O. 8: Evaluate the Gross Profit Percentage and Inventory Turnover

A.   The Importance of Gross Profits

Gross profit and changes in gross profit are important elements in the decision- making process.

B.   **Gross Profit Percentage**

$$Gross\ Profit\ Percentage = \frac{Gross\ Profit}{Sales}$$

C.   The nature of the business has a lot to do with wide variations in gross profit percentage.

    1.   **Wholesalers** — intermediaries that sell inventory to retailers — sell in larger quantity and incur fewer selling costs because they sell to other companies rather than to individuals. As a result of competition and high volumes, they have smaller gross profit percentages than do retailers.

    2.   **Retailers** (companies) that sell directly to the public — to individual buyers.

D.   Estimating Intraperiod Gross Profit and Inventory

When actual ending inventory is unavailable for monthly and quarterly financial statements, the gross profit percentage is often used to estimate the amount.

STOP & REVIEW:

Review the **example in the textbook** for this section.

D.   Gross Profit Percentage and Turnover

    1.   Retailers often attempt to increase total profits by increasing sales levels. They lower prices and hope to increase their gross profits by improving their **inventory turnover**.

    2.   Inventory turnover is computed:

$$Inventory\ Turnover = \frac{Cost\ of\ Goods\ Sold}{Average\ Inventory}$$

    3.   If a firm can increase inventory turnover while maintaining a constant gross profit percentage, it should do so. However, if the increased inventory turnover results from a decrease in sales price, the gross margin percentage may fall. The desirability of the change depends on whether the sales gain could offset the decreased margin.

    4.   The inventory turnover measure is especially effective for assessing companies in the same industry.

    5.   LIFO tends to decrease the gross profit percentage and to increase the inventory turnover relative to FIFO, because under LIFO, cost of goods sold is usually greater and inventory values are lower.

    6.   Auditors use the gross profit percentage to help satisfy themselves about the accuracy of records. The gross profit test is the comparing of gross profit percentages to detect any phenomenon worth investigating.

E.   Reports to Shareholders

Gross profits are important to investors.

F.   Internal Control of Inventories

The best deterrent to controlling inventory shrinkage is an alert employee at the point of sale.

G.   Shrinkage in Perpetual and Periodic Inventory Systems

    1.   In a perpetual inventory system, inventory shrinkage is simply the difference between the cost of inventory identified by a physical count and the clerical inventory balance.

2. In a periodic inventory system, there are no clerical balances of the inventory account so inventory shrinkage is automatically included in cost of goods sold. To assess shrinkage, we need some way to estimate what the ending inventory should be.

> **STUDY TIP:**
> Study the "Summary Problems for Your Review" and solutions in the text.

 **& REVIEW:**

Before continuing, review the objectives for this chapter and make sure you have a good understanding of each one.

Appendix 6: Inventory in a Manufacturing Environment

A. When a company manufactures products, the cost of inventory is a combination of the:

1. Acquisition cost of raw material.

2. The wages paid to workers who combine the raw materials into finished products.

3. An allocation of the costs of space, energy, and equipment used by the workers as they transform the various elements into a finished product.

B. In manufacturing there are three inventory accounts:

1. **Raw material inventory** includes the cost of items held for use in the manufacturing of a product.

2. **Work in process inventory** includes the cost incurred for partially completed items, including raw materials, labor, and other costs.

3. **Finished goods inventory** is the accumulated costs of manufacture for goods that are complete and ready for sale.

 **& REVIEW:**

Review **Exhibit 6-14 in the textbook** before continuing.

V. Test Yourself

Questions

1. Explain the importance of inventory in measuring profitability.

2. Discuss the differences between perpetual and periodic inventory systems.

3. Briefly explain the four major inventory valuation methods and their effect on measurement of assets and net income.

4. Discuss the effects of inventory errors on financial statements.

5. Explain the uses of the gross profit percentage and inventory turnover measures.

Exercises and Problems

1. Long Island Artwork has the following data available for 19X9:

Inventory, Jan. 1, 19X9	$150,000
Gross purchases	530,000
Purchase returns and allowances	10,000
Cost of goods sold	518,000
Inventory, Dec. 31, 19X9	152,000

   Using the data, prepare comparative journal entries for a perpetual and a periodic inventory system.

2. Given the following, prepare a detailed gross profit section for Ski Stop, Inc. for the year ended December 31, 20X1 (in thousands):

Cash discounts on purchases	$ 14
Sales returns and allowances	80
Gross purchases	1,300
Merchandise inventory, Dec. 31, 20X0	240
Gross sales	1,995
Cash discounts on sales	10
Purchases returns and allowances	52
Merchandise inventory, Dec. 31, 20X1	394
Freight in	100

3. The following data are from the 19X8 income statement of the Crew Sport Stores (in thousands):

Sales		$ 900
Deduct: Cost of goods sold:		
Beginning inventory	$220	
Purchases	390	
Cost of goods available for sale	$610	
Deduct: Ending inventory	230	
Cost of goods sold		380
Gross profit		$ 520
Other expenses		375
Income before income taxes		$ 145
Income tax expense at 40%		58
Net income		$ 87

The ending inventory was understated by $20,000 because of errors in the physical count. The income tax rate was 40% in 19X9 and 20X0.

A. Which items in the income statement are incorrect? By how much? Use O for overstated, U for understated, and N for no affect. Complete the following tabulation:

	19X9	20X0
Beginning inventory	N	O $40
Ending Inventory	?	?
Cost of goods sold	?	?
Gross margin	?	?
Income before income taxes	?	?
Income tax expense	?	?
Net income	?	?

B. What is the dollar effect of the inventory error on retained income at the end of 19X9? At the end of 20X0?

4. Harbor Trading Gift Shop had a fire on May 30, 19X9. Its last physical inventory had been on March 31, 19X9, the close of the fiscal year. For the past three years, Harbor Trading's gross profit percentage had been averaging 35%. The following data is available:

Purchases, April 1 - May 30, 19X9	$320,000
Inventory, March 31, 19X9	130,000
Sales, April 1 - May 30, 19X9	640,000

Estimate the cost of inventory on May 30, 19X9 for the insurance claim.

5. The inventory of the GemStone Company on March 31 shows 450 tons at $10 per ton. A physical inventory on April 30 shows a total of 700 tons on hand. Revenue from sales of stone for April totals $44,000. The following purchases were made during April:

April 10	2,000 tons @ $11 per ton
April 17	500 tons @ $12 per ton
April 30	650 tons @ $13 per ton

A. Compute the inventory cost as of April 30, using (1) LIFO and (2) FIFO.

B. Compute the gross profit, using each method.

Matching

Terms

_____ 1. Conservatism

_____ 2. Consistency

_____ 3. Cost of goods available for sale

_____ 4. Cost valuation

_____ 5. Finished goods inventory*

_____ 6. First-in, first-out (FIFO)

_____ 7. F.O.B. destination

_____ 8. F.O.B. shipping point

_____ 9. Freight in

_____ 10. Freight out

_____ 11. Holding gain

_____ 12. Inventory shrinkage

_____ 13. Inventory turnover

_____ 14. Last-in, first-out (LIFO)

_____ 15. LIFO layer

_____ 16. LIFO reserve

_____ 17. Lower-of-cost-or-market method

_____ 18. Periodic inventory system

_____ 19. Perpetual inventory system

_____ 20. Raw material inventory*

_____ 21. Replacement cost

_____ 22. Specific identification method

_____ 23. Weighted-average method

_____ 24. Work in process inventory*

_____ 25. Write-down

Definitions

A.   Buyer pays freight costs from the shipping point of the seller to the receiving point of the buyer.

B.   This inventory method concentrates on the physical tracing of the particular items sold.

C.   The transportation costs borne by the seller of merchandise.

D.   A system that keeps a running, continuous record that tracks inventories and the cost of goods sold on a day-to-day basis.

E.   The cost at which an inventory item could be acquired today.

F.   Selecting methods of measurement that yield lower net income, lower assets, and lower stockholders' equity in the early years.

G.   Seller pays freight costs from the shipping point of the seller to the receiving point of the buyer.

H.   This inventory method assumes that the units acquired most recently are used or sold first.

I.   Increase in the replacement cost of the inventory held during the current period.

J.   The difference between company's inventory valued at LIFO and what it would be under FIFO.

K.   The sum of beginning inventory plus current year purchases.

L. The difference between the value of inventory that would occur if there was no theft, breakage, or losses of inventory, and the value of inventory when it is physically counted.

M. This inventory method computes a unit cost by dividing the total acquisition cost of all items available for sale by the number of units available for sale.

N. An additional cost of the goods acquired during the period, which is often shown in the purchases section of an income statement.

O. A reduction in carrying value to below cost in response to a decline in value.

P. The system in which the cost of goods sold is computed at intervals by relying solely on physical counts without keeping day-to-day records of units sold or on hand.

Q. Includes the cost incurred for partially completed items.

R. The process of assigning specific historical costs to items counted in the physical inventory.

S. The superimposition of a market-price test on an inventory cost method.

T. Conformity from period to period with unchanging policies and procedures.

U. A separately identifiable additional segment of LIFO inventory.

V. The accumulated costs of manufacture for goods that are complete and ready for sale.

W. The cost of goods sold divided by the average inventory held during the period.

X. This method of accounting for inventory assumes that the units acquired earliest are used or sold first.

Y. Includes the cost of materials held for use in the manufacturing of a product.

Multiple Choice

_____ 1. Gross profit is the difference between sales and:

   a.   Cost of goods available for sale.
   b.   Cost of goods sold.
   c.   Net purchases.
   d.   None of the above are correct.

_____ 2. Inventory shrinkage may include items that are:

   a.   Lost.
   b.   Stolen.
   c.   Broken.
   d.   All of the above.

_____ 3. In calculating cost of goods sold which of the following should _not_ be included?

   a.   Freight out.
   b.   Purchase discounts.
   c.   Beginning inventory.
   d.   Freight in

_____ 4. If an invoice states F.O.B. shipping point, then the cost of shipping is borne by:

   a.   The seller.
   b.   The buyer.
   c.   The buyer and seller equally.
   d.   Whichever party is specified by the applicable state law.

_____ 5. During periods of rising prices, the inventory method that yields the lowest tax liability would be:

   a.   Weighted average.
   b.   FIFO.
   c.   LIFO.
   d.   LISH.

_____ 6. When the cumulative inventory profit from years of increasing prices is reflected in the income statement in one year it is a:

   a.   LIFO liquidation.
   b.   LIFO reserve.
   c.   LIFO layer.
   d.   None of the above are correct.

_____ 7. A write-down in inventory:

    a. Is only disclosed in a footnote to the financial statements.
    b. Results in a loss on the income statement.
    c. Can only be recorded once every five years.
    d. None of the above are correct.

_____ 8. During the physical inventory count at year end a $50,000 segment of inventory was missed and subsequently not included in the ending inventory balance. The effect of this error on the following would be:

	Net income	Cost of goods sold
a.	Understated	Understated
b.	Overstated	Understated
c.	Overstated	Overstated
d.	Understated	Overstated

_____ 9. Which of the following statements is true of inventory errors?

    a. If the error counterbalances, it does not have to be disclosed.
    b. A counterbalancing error impacts on two income statements, and one balance sheet.
    c. A counterbalancing error impacts on two balance sheets, and one income statement.
    d. None of the above statements are true.

_____ 10. Auditors, IRS agents, and managers may find items to investigate by using:

    a. Inventory turnover.
    b. Gross profit percentage.
    c. Gross profit test.
    d. None of the above.

VI. Solutions to Test Yourself

Questions

1. Inventory is important in measuring profitability because the calculation for gross profit and cost of goods sold rely on the value of inventories. If the value assigned to inventory is incorrect, cost of goods sold, gross profit, and net income for two periods will be misstated. Retained income will be misstated in the first period. (L. O. 1)

2. Perpetual inventory keeps a running, continuous record that tracks inventories and cost of goods sold on a day-to-day basis. As merchandise is purchased, the inventory account is increased, and when inventory is sold, the sale and the inventory reduction are recorded simultaneously. A physical inventory count must still be taken at least once a year to check on the accuracy of the accounting records. This inventory system helps managers control inventory levels and prepare interim financial statements.

    The periodic inventory system computes the cost of goods sold and an updated inventory balance only at the end of an accounting period, when a physical count of inventory is taken. The cost of goods purchased is accumulated by recording the individual purchase transactions throughout any given reporting period, such as a year. (L. O. 2)

3. The four major methods of inventory valuation are discussed below along with their effect on the measurement of assets and net income.

    1. **Specific identification method.** This method concentrates on the *physical* linking of the *particular* items sold.

    2. **First-in, first-out (FIFO).** This method assumes that the stock acquired earliest is sold first. It does not track the physical flow of individual items except by coincidence. In times of rising prices, FIFO usually shows the *largest* gross profit and tends to provide inventory valuations that closely approximate the actual market value of the inventory at the balance sheet date.

    3. **Last-in, first-out (LIFO).** This method assumes that the stock acquired most recently is sold first. In times of rising prices, LIFO generally shows the *lowest* gross profit and has inventory valuations on the balance sheet that are based on the oldest (lowest) costs.

    4. **Weighted-average cost.** This method computes a unit cost by dividing the total acquisition cost of all items available for sale by the number of units available for sale. The weighted-average method usually produces a gross profit and inventory valuation somewhere between that obtained under FIFO and that under LIFO. (L. O. 4)

4. Inventory errors can arise from many sources including wrong physical counts and clerical errors, and it is important to remember that the ending inventory of one period is the beginning inventory of the following period.

    The effects of inventory errors on financial statements are as follows:

    a. An undiscovered inventory error usually affects two reporting periods: It is counterbalanced by the ordinary accounting process in the next period.
    b. If ending inventory is understated, net income and retained income are understated.
    c. If ending inventory is overstated, net income and retained income are overstated. (L. O.7)

5.   Gross profit and changes in gross profit are important elements in the decision-making process. When actual ending inventory is unavailable for monthly and quarterly financial statements, the gross profit percentage is often used to estimate the amount. Retailers often lower prices and hope to increase their gross profits by improving their inventory turnover. (L. O. 8)

Exercises and Problems

1. <u>Perpetual Inventory Method:</u>

1. Gross purchases:	Inventory	530,000	
	Accounts payable		530,000
2. Returns and allowances:	Accounts payable	10,000	
	Inventory		10,000
3. As goods are sold:	Cost of goods sold	518,000	
	Inventory		518,000
4. End of period:	No entry		

<u>Periodic Inventory Method:</u>

1. Gross purchases:	Purchases	530,000	
	Accounts payable		530,000
2. Returns and allowances:	Accounts payable	10,000	
	Purchase returns and allowances		10,000
3. As goods are sold:	No entry		
4. End of period: a. Transfer to cost of goods sold:	Cost of goods sold	670,000	
	Purchase returns and allowances	10,000	
	Purchases		530,000
	Inventory		150,000
b. Recognize ending inventory:	Inventory	152,000	
	Cost of goods sold		152,000

2.

Ski Stop, Inc.
Statement of Gross Profit
For the year ended December 31, 20X1
(in thousands of dollars)

Gross sales			$1,990
Deduct: Sales returns and allowances		$ 80	
Cash discounts on sales		10	90
Net sales			$1,900
Cost of goods sold:			
Inventory, December 31, 20X0		$ 240	
Add: Gross purchases	$1,300		
Deduct: Purchase returns and allowances	$ 52		
Cash discounts on purchases	14	66	
Net purchases	$1,366		
Add: Freight in	100		
Cost of merchandise acquired		1,466	
Cost of goods available for sales		$1,574	
Deduct: Inventory, December 31, 20X1		394	
Cost of goods sold			1,180
Gross profit			$ 720

3.A.   (numbers are in thousands of dollars)

	19X9	20X0
Beginning inventory*	N	O $20
Ending inventory	U $20	N
Cost of goods sold	O $20	U $20
Gross margin	U $20	O $20
Income before income taxes	U $20	O $20
Income tax expense	U $ 8	O $ 8
Net income	U $12	O $12

* The ending inventory for 19X9 becomes the beginning inventory for 20X0.

B.   Retained income would be understated by $12,000 at the end of the first year. However, the error would be offset in the second year, assuming no change in the 40% income tax rate. Therefore, retained income would be correct at the end of the second year.

4.   <u>Using the Statement of Gross Profit</u> (numbers are in thousands of dollars)

Sales		$640
Deduct: Cost of goods sold:		
Inventory, March 31, 19X9	$ 130	
Purchases	320	
Cost of goods available for sale	$450	
Inventory, May 30, 19X9	34*	
Cost of goods sold		416
Gross profit (35%)		$224

* $450 - $416 = $34. The estimated amount of ending inventory on May 30, 19X9 is $17,000.

5.A.(1) <u>LIFO Method:</u>

Inventory shows:	700 tons on hand at April 30	
Costs:	450 tons @ $10.00	$ 4,500
	250 tons @ $11.00	2,750
April 30 inventory cost		$ 7,250

(2)<u>FIFO Method:</u>

Inventory shows:	700 tons on hand at April 30	
Costs:	650 tons @ $13.00	$ 8,450
	50 tons @ $12.00	600
April 30 inventory cost		$ 9,050

B.   Purchases:

2,000 tons @ $11.00	$22,000
500 tons @ $12.00	6,000
650 tons @ $13.00	8,450
Total purchases	$36,450
Beginning inventory:	
450 tons @ $10.00	9,500

		LIFO	FIFO
Cost available for sale	$40,950	$40,950	$40,950
Less: Ending inventory		7,250	9,050
Cost of goods sold		$33,700	$31,900
Sales		44,000	44,000
Gross profit		$10,300	$12,100

Matching

No.	Ans.	L.O.	No.	Ans.	L.O.	No.	Ans.	L.O.
1.	F	L. O. 7	10.	C	L. O. 3	19.	D	L. O. 1
2.	T	L. O. 4	11.	I	L. O. 6	20.	Y	*
3.	K	L. O. 1	12.	L	L. O. 2	21.	E	L. O. 6
4.	R	L. O. 1	13.	W	L. O. 9	22.	B	L. O. 4
5.	V	*	14.	H	L. O. 4	23.	M	L. O. 4
6.	X	L. O. 4	15.	U	L. O. 6	24.	Q	*
7.	G	L. O. 3	16.	J	L. O. 6	25.	O	L. O. 7
8.	A	L. O. 3	17.	S	L. O. 7			
9.	N	L. O. 3	18.	P	L. O. 1			

*Appendix 6

Multiple Choice

1.   b   Gross profit is the difference between sales and *cost of goods sold*. Cost of goods available is the beginning inventory plus net purchases for the current period. Net purchases are the purchases of the current period plus freight in, and is net of returns and cash discounts. (L. O. 1)

2.   d   Inventory shrinkage may include theft, breakage, and losses. (L. O. 2)

3.   a   Freight out is a shipping expense of the *seller* and is not part of cost of goods sold. (L. O. 3)

4.   b   (L. O. 3)

5.   c   During periods of rising prices, LIFO results in the lowest net income and, therefore, the lowest tax liability. (L. O. 4)

6.   a   LIFO liquidation results when the physical amount of inventory decreases. (L. O. 5)

7.   b   A write-down is recorded on the books and is done as often as necessary.   (L. O. 6)

8.   d   When ending inventory is understated (not included), then cost of goods sold is *over*stated, and net income is *under*stated. (L. O. 7)

9.   b   (L. O.7)

10.   c   Gross profit test helps point out unusual items when compared to similar companies. (L. O.8)

Chapter 7

LONG-LIVED ASSETS AND DEPRECIATION

I. Learning Objectives

Management invests in long-lived assets to generate revenue through the production of goods and services. Allocation of the cost of those long-lived assets can have a significant effect on reported income for a period. Understanding the theory and techniques associated with depreciation, depletion, and amortization can help in areas such as budgeting, statement analysis, and cash flow determination. Use the following learning objectives as stepping stones in completing your study of this chapter.

1.   Measure the acquisition cost of tangible assets such as land, buildings, and equipment.

2.   Compute depreciation for buildings and equipment using various depreciation methods.

3.   Differentiate financial statement depreciation from income tax depreciation.

4.   Explain depreciation's effects on cash flow.

5.   Distinguish expenses from expenditures that should be capitalized.

6.   Compute gains and losses on disposal of fixed assets.

7.   Interpret depletion of natural resources.

8.   Account for various intangible assets.

II. Pretest

____ 1.   Land, natural resources, buildings, and equipment are examples of:

        a.   Long-term investments.
        b.   Tangible assets.
        c.   Intangible assets.
        d.   None of the above are correct.

____ 2.   The systematic allocation of the acquisition cost of *long-lived assets* to the time periods of their use is known as:

        a.   Amortization.
        b.   Depreciation.
        c.   Depletion.
        d.   All of the above are correct.

____ 3.   The difference between the total acquisition cost and the predicted residual value is the:

        a.   Disposal value.
        b.   Depreciable value.
        c.   Terminal value.
        d.   None of the above are correct.

____ 4.   Which of the following is an accelerated depreciation method?

        a.   Straight-line.
        b.   Units of production.
        c.   Declining balance.
        d.   None of the above are correct.

____ 5.   Which depreciation method is used by most companies for reporting to shareholders?

        a.   Straight-line.
        b.   Units of production.
        c.   Declining balance.
        d.   None of the above are correct.

____ 6.   Reports to income tax authorities must abide by:

        a.   Generally accepted accounting principles (GAAP).
        b.   Income tax rules and regulations.
        c.   Both GAAP and income tax rules and regulations.
        d.   None of the above are correct.

_____ 7. The depreciation method that provides the *highest* before-tax ending cash balances is:

a. Straight-line.
b. Units of production.
c. Declining balance.
d. None of the above are correct.

_____ 8. For tax purposes, the higher the depreciation allowed to be deducted:

a. The higher the taxable income and the lower the cash disbursement for income taxes.
b. The lower the taxable income and the higher the cash disbursement for income taxes.
c. The lower the taxable income and the lower the cash disbursement for income taxes.
d. None of the above are correct.

_____ 9. Asset-related purchases that are expected to benefit more than the current accounting year and are added to an asset account are:

a. Repairs and maintenance.
b. Capital expenditures.
c. Expenses.
d. None of the above are correct.

_____ 10. An expenditure that is intended to add to the future benefits from an existing fixed asset by decreasing its operating cost, increasing its rate of output, or prolonging its useful life is:

a. A repair.
b. Maintenance.
c. An improvement.
d. None of the above are correct.

_____ 11. Gains and losses on the disposal of property, plant, and equipment are:

a. Unusual in nature, and are measured in a cash sale by the difference between the cash received and the cost of the asset given up.
b. Usual in nature, and are measured in a cash sale by the difference between the cash received and the net book value of the asset given up.
c. Not computed when an old asset is traded for a similar new asset.
d. None of the above are correct.

_____ 12. The disposal of equipment necessitates:

a. The removal of the original cost of the equipment.
b. The removal of the accompanying accumulated depreciation.
c. The recognition of a gain or loss, if any.
d. All of the above are correct.

_____ 13. An example of a wasting asset is:

a. Minerals.
b. Equipment.
c. Land.
d. Building.

_____ 14.   Depletion:

    a.   Focuses narrowly on a physical phenomenon.
    b.   Is the accounting measure of the gradual exhaustion of the original resources acquired.
    c.   Is measured on a units-of-production basis.
    d.   All of the above are true of depletion.

_____ 15.   Which of the following is *not* an example of an intangible asset?

    a.   Patent.
    b.   Franchise.
    c.   Oil.
    d.   Goodwill.

_____ 16.   Which of the following is true of intangible assets?

    a.   They are accounted for like plant and equipment.
    b.   The economic lives of intangible assets tend to be shorter than their legal lives.
    c.   They are shown on a company's balance sheet only if the rights to some benefit are purchased.
    d.   All of the above are true of intangible assets.

III. Answers to Pretest

1.   b   Land, natural resources, buildings, and equipment are examples of *tangible* assets because they are all physical items that can be seen and touched. (L. O. 1)

2.   d   All the terms are correct. For tangible assets such as buildings, machinery, and equipment, the allocation is called depreciation. For natural resources the allocation is called depletion. By convention, amortization is typically used to refer to the allocation of the costs of intangible assets to the periods that benefit from these assets. (L. O. 1)

3.   b   Disposal value and terminal value are other terms for residual value. (L. O. 2)

4.   c   (L. O. 2)

5.   a   Most companies use straight-line depreciation for reporting to shareholders because it is simple, convenient, and reports higher earnings in the early years than would be reported under accelerated depreciation. (L. O. 3)

6.   b   Although generally accepted accounting principles (GAAP) are often consistent with tax regulations, reports to tax authorities must abide only by tax rules and regulations. (L. O. 3)

7.   d   None of the answers are correct. Before taxes, any of the depreciation methods affect *only* the accumulated depreciation and retained earnings accounts. Before-tax cash balances are completely *un*affected and would be the same under all depreciation methods. (L. O. 4)

8.   c   The *higher* the depreciation expense deducted each year, the *lower* the taxable income, and, therefore, the *lower* the cash disbursement for income taxes. Thus, more cash is conserved and kept for use in the business. (L. O. 4)

9.   b   *Capital expenditures* are asset-related expenditures that are expected to benefit more than the current accounting year and are capitalized. Such capital expenditures generally add new fixed assets or increase the capacity, efficiency, or useful life of an existing fixed asset. (L. O.5)

10.   c   An improvement is an expenditure that is intended to add to the future benefits from an existing fixed asset by decreasing its operating cost, increasing its rate of output, or prolonging its useful life, and it is generally capitalized. (L. O.5)

11.   b   (L. O.6)

12.   d   (L. O.6)

13.   a   A wasting asset is another term for a natural resource, and minerals are natural resources. (L. O.7)

14.   d   (L. O.7)

15.   c   Oil is a natural resource, not an intangible asset. (L. O.8)

16.   d   (L. O.8)

EVALUATION

The pretest contained two questions for each learning objective. If you did not answer both questions correctly for each learning objective, you should review the appropriate section of the textbook and study guide before you attempt the material after Part IV.

IV. Key Concept Review by Learning Objectives

L. O. 1: Measure the Acquisition Cost of Tangible Assets Such as Land, Buildings, and Equipment

A. Overview of Long-Lived Assets

    1. Most businesses hold such major long-lived assets as land, buildings, equipment, natural resources, and patents.

    2. These **long-lived assets** help produce revenues over many periods by facilitating the production and sale of goods or services to customers. Because these assets are necessary in a company's day-to-day operations, companies do not sell them in the ordinary course of business.

    3. **Tangible assets** (also called **fixed assets** or **plant assets**) such as land, natural resources, buildings, and equipment are physical items that can be seen and touched.

    4. **Intangible assets** such as franchises, patents, trademarks, copyrights, and goodwill are rights or economic benefits that are not physical in nature.

    3. **Amortization** is the general term that means the systematic reduction of a lump-sum amount and it might be used to describe any allocation of the acquisition cost of long-lived assets to the time periods of their use.

        a. Tangible assets such as buildings, machinery and equipment are *depreciated*. Land is unique in that it does not wear out or become obsolete and, therefore, does not get depreciated for financial reporting purposes.

        b. For natural resources the allocation is called **depletion**.

        c. Although it has a broader meaning, *amortization* is typically used specifically to refer to the allocation of the costs of intangible assets.

B. Acquisition Cost of Tangible Assets

The acquisition cost of all long-lived assets is their cash-equivalent purchase price, including incidental costs required to complete the purchase, to transport the asset, and to prepare it for use.

C. Land

    1. The acquisition cost of land includes charges to the purchaser for the cost of land surveys, legal fees, title fees, realtors' commissions, transfer taxes, and even the demolition costs of old structures that might be torn down to get the land ready for its intended use.

    2. Under historical-cost accounting, land is carried indefinitely at its original cost, which is likely to be far below its current market value.

D.   Buildings and Equipment

The cost of buildings, plant, and equipment should include all costs of acquisition and preparation for use. These costs are **capitalized**, as distinguished from ordinary repair costs incurred after equipment is being used which are expensed.

L. O. 2:   Compute Depreciation for Buildings and Equipment Using Various Depreciation Methods

A.   Depreciation

1.   Depreciation is the key factor distinguishing accrual accounting from cash-basis accounting.

a.   If a long-lived asset is purchased for cash, cash-basis accounting would treat the entire cost of the asset as an expense immediately.

b.   In contrast, accrual accounting allocates the cost in the form of depreciation over the periods the asset is used — thereby matching expenses with the revenues produced.

2.   The amount of the acquisition cost to be allocated over the total useful life of the asset as depreciation is the **depreciable value**. It is the difference between the total acquisition cost and the predicted residual value. **Residual value,** also known as **terminal value**, **disposal value**, **salvage value**, and **scrap value**, is the amount predicted to be received from the sale or disposal of a long-lived asset at the end of its useful life.

3.   Depreciation allocates the depreciable value to the income statement during the useful life of the asset. The **useful** (or **economic**) **life** of an asset is determined as the shorter of the physical life of the asset before it wears out or the economic life of the asset before it is obsolete.

4.   A list of depreciation amounts for each year of an asset's useful life is called a **depreciation schedule**.

B.   Straight-Line Depreciation

1.   **Straight-line depreciation** spreads the depreciable value evenly over the useful life of an asset, and it by far the most popular method for corporate reporting to shareholders.

2.

$$Straight\text{-}line\ Depreciation = \frac{Acquisition\ Cost - Residual\ Value}{Years\ of\ Useful\ Life}$$

 **& REVIEW:**

Before continuing, carefully review **Exhibit 7-2** in the textbook.

C. Depreciation Based on Units

1. When physical wear and tear is the dominating influence on the useful life of the asset, depreciation based on units of service or production is used, which is called **unit depreciation**.

2.
$$\text{Unit Depreciation} = \frac{\text{Acquisition Cost - Residual Value}}{\text{Total Units of Service During Useful Life}}$$

3. This method is not widely used, probably for two major reasons:

a. Unit based depreciation frequently produces approximately the same yearly depreciation amounts as does straight-line depreciation.

b. Straight-line depreciation is easier because the entire depreciation schedule can be set at the time of acquisition. Under unit depreciation, detailed records of units of service must be kept to determine the amount depreciated each year.

D. Declining-Balance Depreciation

1. **Accelerated depreciation** is any pattern of depreciation that writes off depreciable costs more quickly than the ordinary straight-line method based on expected useful life.

2. The most popular form of accelerated depreciation is the **double-declining-balance (DDB)** method that is computed as follows:

a. Compute a rate by dividing 100% by the years of useful life. The result is the straight-line rate. Doubling the rate results in the DDB rate.

b.
$$\text{DDB Depreciation} = \text{DDB Rate x Beginning Book Value}$$

STUDY TIP:
Remember to *ignore* the residual value when computing DDB depreciation.

E. Comparing and Choosing Depreciation Methods

1. Companies do not necessarily use the same depreciation methods for all types of depreciable assets.

2. Reasons for selecting depreciation methods:

a. Tradition sometimes leads a company to select the method used by other companies in its industry to enhance comparability.

b. Sometimes one method provides far superior matching of expense and revenue.

c. Sometimes the method is chosen to present the life-cycle cost of the asset.

 **& REVIEW:**

Before continuing, carefully review **Exhibit 7-3** in the textbook.

L. O. 3: Differentiate Financial Statement Depreciation From Income Tax Depreciation

A. Income Tax Reporting and Shareholder Reporting

Reports to stockholders must abide by generally accepted accounting principles (GAAP). Reports to income tax authorities must abide by the income tax rules and regulations, which may or may not be consistent with GAAP.

B. Depreciation on Tax Reports

1. Since 1986 the tax authorities have required the *Modified Accelerated Cost Recovery System (MACRS)* for computing accelerated depreciation.

2. MACRS approximates double-declining-balance depreciation and is applied over *shorter lives* than previously allowed. This provides for greater acceleration of depreciation than was allowed before 1986.

C. Shareholder Reporting

1. Straight-line depreciation is generally used when reporting to shareholders even though MACRS is used for tax purposes.

2. Straight-line depreciation is used for shareholder reporting because it is simple, convenient, and reports higher earnings in early years than would be reported under accelerated depreciation.

L. O. 4: Explain Depreciation's Effects on Cash Flow

A. Depreciation and Cash Flow

1. Depreciation *does not* generate cash. Depreciation simply allocates the original cost of an asset to the periods in which the asset is used.

2. Accumulated depreciation is the portion of an asset's original cost that has already been written off to expense in prior periods. Thus, accumulated depreciation is *not* a pile of cash waiting to be used.

B. Effects of Depreciation on Cash

Before taxes, changes in the depreciation method affect only the accumulated depreciation and retained earnings accounts. The before-tax ending cash balances are completely *un*affected.

 **& REVIEW:**

Before continuing, carefully review **Exhibit 7-4** in the textbook.

C. Effects of Depreciation on Income Taxes

    1. Depreciation is a deductible noncash expense for income tax purposes. The higher the depreciation allowed to be deducted in any given year, the lower the taxable income, and, therefore, the lower the cash disbursement for income taxes.

    2. When compared with the straight-line depreciation method, the accelerated method results in a higher cash balance *after* income taxes but a lower reported net income.

    3. Straight-line depreciation may be used for reporting to shareholders while accelerated depreciation is used for income tax purposes.

> **STUDY TIP:**
> When depreciation expense is higher, taxes are lower, and more cash is conserved and kept for use in the business.

L. O. 5: Distinguish Expenses From Expenditures That Should Be Capitalized

A. Expenses Versus Expenditures

    1. **Expenditures** are purchases of goods or services, whether for cash or on credit. Asset-related expenditures that are expected to benefit more than the current accounting year are *capitalized* (added to an asset account) and are sometimes called *capital expenditures.*

    2. Generally, capital expenditures add new fixed assets or increase the capacity, efficiency, or useful life of an existing fixed asset.

    3. Expenditures benefiting the current period are matched with current revenues and, therefore, become expenses in the current period. Expenditures that are capitalized benefit future revenues, and they are charged as expenses over future periods.

B. The Decision to Capitalize

The decision whether to capitalize an expenditure is often subjective. Whenever doubt exists, there is a general tendency in practice to charge an expense rather than an asset account for repairs, parts, and similar items — usually because of cost-benefit.

C. Repairs and Maintenance Versus Capital Improvements

    1. Repairs and maintenance are usually regarded as expenses of the current period.

2. **Improvements** (sometimes called **betterments** or **capital improvements**) are expenditures that are intended to add to the future benefits from existing fixed assets by decreasing its operating cost, increasing its rate of output, or prolonging its useful life. Improvements are generally capitalized.

L. O. 6: Compute Gains and Losses on Disposal of Fixed Assets

A. Gains and Losses on Sales of Fixed Assets

Gains and losses for accounting purposes are the difference between the book value of an asset and the cash received or cash-equivalent given up.

B. Recording Gains and Losses

The disposal of the equipment requires the removal of its carrying amount or book value from the books.

1. The historical cost of the asset is removed from the books.

2. All accumulated depreciation related to that asset is removed from the accumulated depreciation account.

STOP & REVIEW:

Before continuing, carefully review **Exhibit 7-5** in the textbook.

C. Income Statement Presentation

1. In single-step income statements, gains or losses are shown at the top along with other revenue items.

2. In multiple-step income statements, gains or losses appear in some type of "other income or losses" section in the lower part of the income statement.

L. O. 7: Interpret Depletion of Natural Resources

Depletion of Natural Resources

1. Natural resources (wasting resources) such as minerals, oil, and timber are depleted. Depletion expense is the measure of that portion of the "long-term inventory" that is used up in a particular period.

2. Depletion is measured on a units-of-production basis, and the annual depletion may be accounted for as a direct reduction of the asset, or it may be accumulated in a separate contra account similar to accumulated depreciation.

L. O. 8: Account for Various Intangible Assets

A. Amortization of Intangible Assets

1. Intangible assets are a class of long-lived assets such as patents, copyrights, and franchises that are not physical in nature, and are rights to expected benefits that tend to be contractual in nature.

2. The acquisition costs of intangible assets are capitalized as assets and are then amortized over estimated useful lives. Because of obsolescence, the economic lives of intangible assets tend to be shorter than their legal lives.

3. An intangible asset is shown on a company's balance sheet *only* if the rights to some benefit are *purchased*. Internally developed intangibles are not assets and would be expensed in the period or periods over which they are developed.

B. Examples of Intangible Assets

1. **Patents** are granted to an inventor by the U.S. government for the exclusive right to produce and sell the invention in the United States for 17 years. Purchased patents are amortized over their expected useful lives.

2. **Copyrights** are the exclusive rights to reproduce and sell a book, musical composition, film, and similar items. In the U.S. these rights are issued by the federal government and provide protection to a company for 75 years. Copyrights are amortized over the useful life of the asset which is usually no longer than two or three years.

3. **Trademarks** are distinctive identifications of a manufactured product or of a service. For stockholder reporting purposes, trademarks are amortized over their useful lives but cannot exceed 40 years.

4. **Franchises** and **licenses** are legal contracts that grant the buyer the right to sell a product or service. The acquisition costs of franchises and licenses are amortized over their economic lives rather than their legal lives.

C. Amortization of Leaseholds and Leasehold Improvements

1. **Leaseholds** are the rights to use a fixed asset for the period stated in the lease. **Leasehold improvements** are any improvements made to the property by the lessee (tenant).

2. Both are technically intangible assets although they are usually classified with plant assets on the balance sheet. Both are amortized using the straight-line method over the life of the lease, even if the physical life of the leasehold improvement is longer.

D. Amortization of Deferred Charges

Deferred charges are similar to prepaid expenses but have longer-term benefits. Examples are costs of rearranging an assembly line and organization costs. These items are usually amortized over a three to five year period.

E. Basket Purchases

When companies acquire more than one type of long-lived asset for a single overall outlay, it is sometimes called a **basket purchase**. The cost should be allocated in proportion to some estimate of the relative sales values of the separate items. Allocating a basket purchase cost to the individual assets can significantly affect future reported income if the useful lives of various assets differ.

STUDY TIP:
Study the "Summary Problems for Your Review" and solutions in the text.

 **& REVIEW:**

Before continuing, review the objectives for this chapter and make sure you have a good understanding of each one.

V. Test Yourself

Questions

1. Distinguish between tangible and intangible assets, and explain how the costs of each are allocated.

2. Discuss the measurement of acquisition costs of tangible assets.

3. Explain how depreciation affects cash flow.

4. Differentiate financial statement depreciation from income tax depreciation.

5. Distinguish expenses from expenditures that should be capitalized.

Exercises and Problems

Data for use with #1 and #2

Gadue Computers purchased a machine, used in the production of computers, for $350,000 in 19X9. In addition to the price of the machine, Gadue paid insurance during shipment of $2,500; transportation costs of $3,500; installation costs of $10,000; and training costs of $7,000. Also, repair costs incurred prior to use of the machine were $2,000. The machine was expected to last five years and has a residual value of $25,000. Gadue uses double-declining-balance depreciation on all machines of this type. At the beginning of Year 3 the machine was sold for $175,000.

1. Record the journal entry for the acquisition of this machine.

2. A. Determine the gain or loss on the sale of the machine.

   B. Prepare the journal entry(s) to record the sale of the machine and to remove the machine from the books.

3. During 19X9 Sunset Equipment Company had the following results from operations:

Cash sales	$900,000
Cash operating expenses	$550,000
Depreciation expense:	
Accelerated	$150,000
Straight-line	$ 75,000
Income tax rate	40%

   Utilizing a schedule similar to Exhibit 7-4, determine:

   A. Net income before and after income taxes using straight-line and accelerated depreciation.

   B. Cash provided by operations after income taxes using straight-line and accelerated depreciation.

155

4.   A depreciable asset that was purchased by York Digital for $200,000 was expected to have a useful life of five years and a residual value of $10,000. New estimates at the beginning of Year 4 indicate the asset will last four more years. Using straight-line depreciation, compute depreciation expense for Year 4.

5.   The plant manager for Reiter Manufacturing purchased three different pieces of equipment for a total of $100,000. Fair market value of each machine was $49,500, $82,500, and $33,000, respectively. Compute the cost to be allocated to each of the three machines.

Matching

Terms

_____ 1. Accelerated depreciation

_____ 2. Amortization

_____ 3. Capital improvement

_____ 4. Capitalized

_____ 5. Copyrights

_____ 6. Deferred charges

_____ 7. Depletion

_____ 8. Depreciable value

_____ 9. Double-declining-balance depreciation

_____ 10. Expenditures

_____ 11. Franchises

_____ 12. Intangible assets

_____ 13. Leasehold

_____ 14. Leasehold improvement

_____ 15. Long-lived assets

_____ 16. Patents

_____ 17. Residual value

_____ 18. Straight-line depreciation

_____ 19. Tangible assets

_____ 20. Trademarks

_____ 21. Unit depreciation

_____ 22. Useful life

Definitions

A.   Grants by the federal government to the inventor, bestowing the exclusive right for 17 years to produce and sell the invention.

B.   Physical items that can be seen and touched.

C.   Similar to prepaid expenses, but they have longer-term benefits.

D.   The amount received from the disposal of a long-lived asset at the end of its useful life.

E.   Distinctive identification of a manufactured product or of a service taking the form of a name, a sign, a slogan, a logo, or an emblem.

F.   Investments by the lessee in items that are not permitted to be removed from the premises when a lease expires.

G.   The difference between the total acquisition cost and the estimated residual value.

H.   Resources that are held for an extended time.

I.   The process of allocating the cost of natural resources to the periods in which the resources are used.

J.   The most popular form of accelerated depreciation.

K.   An expenditure that is intended to add to the future benefits from an existing fixed asset.

L.   A method based on units of service when physical wear and tear is the dominating influence on the useful life of the asset.

M.   A cost that is added to an asset account, as distinguished from being expensed immediately.

N.   The time period over which an asset is depreciated.

O.   Privileges granted by a government, manufacturer, or distributor to sell a product or service in accordance with specified conditions.

P.   Any depreciation method that writes off depreciable costs more quickly than the ordinary straight-line method based on expected useful life.

Q.   The purchases of goods or services, whether for cash or on credit.

R.   When referring to long-lived assets, it usually means the allocation of the costs of intangible assets to the periods that benefit from these assets.

S.   Rights or economic benefits that are not physical in nature.

T.   The right to use a fixed asset for a specified period of time, typically beyond one year.

U.   A method that spreads the depreciable value evenly over the useful life of an asset.

V.   Exclusive rights to reproduce and sell a book, musical composition, film, and similar items.

Multiple Choice

_____ 1. Which of the following is *not* true of tangible assets?

    a. They are physical items that can be seen and touched.
    b. They are all amortized (depreciated).
    c. Their underlying purpose is to facilitate the production and sale of goods and services to customers.
    d. Ali of the above are true.

_____ 2. The acquisition cost of all long-lived assets includes:

    a. Their cash-equivalent purchase price.
    b. Costs required to obtain title.
    c. Costs to prepare the asset for use.
    d. All of the above.

_____ 3. Which of the following would *not* be included in the acquisition cost of land?

    a. Demolition costs of old structures that might be torn down to get the land ready for its intended use.
    b. Legal fees, title fees, and realtor's commissions.
    c. Old structures that will be refurbished for use by the company.
    d. All of the above would be included.

_____ 4. Which of the following is *not* true of useful life?

    a. It is the time period over which an asset is depreciated.
    b. It is the shorter of the physical life of the asset before it wears out or the economic life.
    c. It is sometimes measured directly in terms of the benefit it provides rather than the time periods.
    d. All of the above are true.

_____ 5. Which of the following is *not* true of depreciation methods?

    a. Once a depreciation method has been adopted, it must be used for both financial statement and tax reporting purposes.
    b. Generally accepted accounting principles and tax regulations for depreciation methods may differ.
    c. For tax purposes since 1986, either MACRS or straight-line depreciation must be used.
    d. All of the above are true.

_____ 6. Depreciation expense reduces net income and, therefore, income taxes. Which of the following statements is also true?

    a. This tax savings coupled with the depreciation expense serves to recover the cost of the asset.
    b. Accumulated depreciation is a reserve of cash for the replacement of the asset.
    c. Accelerated depreciation results in a lower net income than straight-line depreciation, lower taxes, and, therefore, less cash outlay for taxes.
    d. None of the above statements are true.

_____ 7. An example of a capital expenditure would be:

    a. Purchase of inventory.
    b. Purchase of a six-month certificate of deposit.
    c. Purchase of a used copier.
    d. None of the above are correct.

_____ 8. In most cases, gains or losses on disposition of plant assets:

    a. Are significant and are always listed separately on the income statement.
    b. Are usually listed as part of "other income" on the income statement.
    c. Are usually included in the computation of gross profit on a multiple step income statement.
    d. None of the above are correct.

_____ 9. The systematic allocation of organization costs to expense in the periods the organization costs provided benefit is termed:

    a. Depletion.
    b. Depreciation.
    c. Amortization.
    d. Transference.

_____ 10. When two or more types of assets are acquired for a lump-sum cost:

    a. The cost is allocated in proportion to some estimate of their relative sales values as separate items.
    b. The cost is allocated equally to each type of asset.
    c. The cost is allocated entirely to the asset type with the highest sales value.
    d. Assets cannot be acquired for a lump-sum cost.

VI. Solutions to Test Yourself

Questions

1. Tangible assets are physical items that can be seen and touched while intangible assets are rights or economic benefits that are not physical in nature. The acquisition costs of all long-lived assets except land are allocated to the time periods that benefit from the assets' use. For tangible assets such as buildings, machinery, and equipment, the allocation is called depreciation. For natural resources the allocation is called depletion, and amortization is, by convention, the term usually used to refer to the allocation of the costs of intangible assets. (L. O. 1)

2. The acquisition cost of all long-lived assets is their cash-equivalent purchase price, including incidental costs required to obtain title, to transport the asset, and to prepare it for use. For example, the cost of land would include the purchase price, land surveys, legal fees, title fees, realtor's commissions, transfer taxes, and the demolition cost of old structures that might be torn down to get the land ready for its intended use. (L. O. 1)

3. Depreciation is a vehicle for the transfer of acquisition cost of assets such as buildings and equipment from the balance sheet to the income statement. It is not a method used to recover the cost of an asset. Depreciation itself is not a savings account and it does not generate cash.

   Accelerated depreciation produces a higher depreciation deduction early in the asset's life. This in turn reduces taxable income and income tax outlays. Under straight-line depreciation, reported net income is higher but cash flow is lower after income taxes. Therefore, compared to straight-line depreciation, accelerated methods result in a higher cash balance after income taxes. (L. O. 4)

4. Reports to stockholders must abide by generally accepted accounting principles (GAAP). Reports to income tax authorities must abide by the income tax rules and regulations, which may or may not be consistent with GAAP.

   Since 1986 the tax authorities have required the *Modified Accelerated Cost Recovery System (MACRS)* for computing accelerated depreciation. MACRS approximates double-declining-balance depreciation and is applied over *shorter lives* than previously allowed. This provides for greater acceleration of depreciation than was allowed before 1986.

   Straight-line depreciation is generally used when reporting to shareholders even though MACRS is used for tax purposes. Straight-line depreciation is used for shareholder reporting because it is simple, convenient, and reports higher earnings in early years than would be reported under accelerated depreciation. (L. O. 3)

5. Expenditures are defined by accountants as the purchases of goods or services, whether for cash or on credit. Asset-related expenditures that are expected to benefit more than the current accounting year are added to an asset account or *capitalized*. Such capital expenditures generally add new fixed assets or increase the capacity, efficiency, or useful life, of an existing fixed asset. Expenditures deemed to have a life of one year or less are charged as *expenses* in the current year.

   All expenditures eventually become expenses. Expenditures benefiting the current period are matched with current revenues and, therefore, become expenses in the current period. Expenditures that are capitalized benefit *future* revenues, and they are charged as expenses over future periods. The problem is that the decision to capitalize is often subjective. (L. O. 5)

Exercises and Problems

1. Capitalized Costs:

Acquisition costs	$350,000
Insurance	2,500
Transportation costs	3,500
Installation costs	10,000
Repair costs	2,000
Training costs	7,000
Total capitalizable costs	$375,000

Journal Entry:

Equipment	375,000	
Cash		375,000

2. A. Depreciation schedule for double-declining-balance:

DDB Rate, 5 year life = 2(100% / 5) = 40%

Year	Rate	Beg. Book Value	Depre. Expense	End. Book Value
1	.40	$375,000	$150,000	$225,000
2	.40	225,000	90,000	135,000

Total accumulated depreciation end of Year 2 $240,000

Historical cost	$375,000		Sale price	$175,000
Accumulated depreciation	(240,000)		Book value	(135,000)
Book value	$135,000		Gain on sale	$ 40,000

B.

Cash	175,000	
Accumulated depreciation	240,000	
Equipment		375,000
Gain on sale		40,000

3.

	Before Taxes		After Taxes	
	S/L Depre.	Accel. Depre.	S/L Depre.	Accel. Depre.
A. Income Statement				
Sales	$900,000	$900,000	$900,000	$900,000
Operating expenses	550,000	550,000	550,000	550,000
Depreciation expense	75,000	150,000	75,000	150,000
Pretax income	$275,000	$200,000	$275,000	$200,000
Income tax expense	-	-	110,000	80,000
Net Income	$275,000	$200,00	$165,000	$120,000
B. Statement of Cash Flows				
Cash collections	$900,000	$900,000	$900,000	$900,000
Cash operating expenses	550,000	550,000	550,000	550,000
Cash tax payments	-	-	110,000	80,000
Cash provided by operations	$350,000	$350,000	$240,000	$270,000

4.   STEP 1: Determine book value at the date useful life is adjusted.

($200,000 - $10,000) / 5 years = $38,000 X 3 years = $114,000 accumulated
                                                        depreciation

$200,000 - $114,000 = $86,000 book value

STEP 2: Divide book value by the new estimate of remaining useful life.

$86,000 / 4 years = $21,500 depreciation per year

5.   Allocation of the basket purchase is based on the following:

Machine	Fair Market Value (FMV)	Ratio to Total FMV
1	$ 49,500	30%
2	82,500	50%
3	33,000	20%
Total	$165,000	100%

	Ratio	X	Total Basket Purchase Price	=	Cost Allocation
Machine 1	.30	X	$100,000	=	$30,000
Machine 2	.50	X	$100,000	=	$50,000
Machine 3	.20	X	$100,000	=	$20,000

Matching

1.	P	L. O. 2	9.	J	L. O. 2	17.	D	L. O. 2
2.	R	L. O. 1	10.	Q	L. O. 5	18.	U	L. O. 2
3.	K	L. O. 5	11.	O	L. O. 8	19.	B	L. O. 1
4.	M	L. O. 1	12.	S	L. O. 1	20.	E	L. O. 8
5.	V	L. O. 8	13.	T	L. O. 8	21.	L	L. O. 2
6.	C	L. O. 8	14.	F	L. O. 8	22.	N	L. O. 2
7.	I	L. O. 8	15.	H	L. O. 1			
8.	G	L. O. 2	16.	A	L. O. 8			

Multiple Choice

1.   b   Land is a tangible asset and it is *not* depreciated. (L. O. 1)

2.   d   (L. O. 1)

3.   c   Old structures that will be refurbished for use by a company are *not* part of the cost of the *land*. It would be part of the cost of the building. (L. O. 1)

4.   d   (L. O. 2)

5.   a   Different depreciation methods *may* be used for financial statements and tax reporting purposes. (L. O. 3)

6.   c   Depreciation expense does *not* serve to recover the cost of the asset, nor is accumulated depreciation a reserve of cash. Accumulated depreciation is simply the total of the amounts of the original cost already written off to expense in prior periods. (L. O. 4)

7.   c   A purchase of a used copier has future benefits that extend beyond the current period and, therefore, it *is* a capital expenditure. (L. O. 5)

8.   b   Gains or losses are usually *not* significant and, if listed separately, are part of "other income". They are also *ex*cluded from the computation of gross profit, not *in*cluded. (L. O. 6)

9.   c   Organization costs, an intangible asset, is amortized. (L. O. 8)

10.   a   The allocation of a *basket purchase* is in proportion to some estimate of the assets relative sales value as separate items. (L. O. 8)

Chapter 8

LIABILITIES AND INTEREST

I. Learning Objectives

A major element of generally accepted accounting principles (GAAP) in the United States is the careful definition of what constitutes a liability and how best to disclose the liability to readers of financial statements. This chapter considers the very broad categories of economic obligations that accountants classify as liabilities. Utilize the following learning objectives as an outline for your study of this chapter.

1. Account for current liabilities.

2. Design an internal control system for cash disbursements.

3. Explain simple long-term liabilities.

4. Understand restructurings and the liabilities they create.

5. Interpret deferred tax liabilities.

6. Locate and understand the contingent liabilities information in a company's financial statements.

7. Use ratio analysis to assess a company's debt levels.

II. Pretest

SELECT THE BEST ANSWER AND ENTER THE IDENTIFYING LETTER IN THE SPACE PROVIDED.

_____ 1. For which of the following decisions do investors, financial analysts, management, and creditors consider existing liabilities of the firm?

    a. Valuing of the firm's common stock.
    b. Evaluating a new loan to the company.
    c. Evaluating the reliability of warranties and product service.
    d. All of the above.

_____ 2. Depending on the type of obligation when a company cannot pay its debts, which of the following is *not* true? Creditors can legally:

    a. Force the company out of business.
    b. Force the board of directors to pay from personal assets.
    c. Force the sale of specific assets.
    d. All of the above are true.

_____ 3. Which of the following statements is *not* true?

    a. Most disbursement systems require that most payments be made by check.
    b. Checks should be prenumbered.
    c. All checks issued should be supported by source documents.
    d. All of the above statements are correct.

_____ 4. It is important to create internal controls over cash disbursements to:

    a. Ensure collusion cannot occur.
    b. Assure all payments involve approved and valid obligations of the company.
    c. Ensure excess cash is properly invested.
    d. All of the above statements are correct.

_____ 5. When money is borrowed from a few sources in a private placement, corporations issue:

    a. Bonds.
    b. Debentures.
    c. Notes.
    d. All of the above may be issued.

_____ 6. A mortgage bond:

    a. Is a form of long-term debt.
    b. Is secured by the pledge of specific property.
    c. Holder may have an additional unsecured claim on property in a default.
    d. All of the above statements are correct.

_____ 7.   A restructuring typically does *not* involve:

    a.   The closing of one or more plants.
    b.   Hiring of a significant number of employees.
    c.   Termination of various activities.
    d.   All of the above statements are correct.

_____ 8.   Restructuring costs may be charged to:

    a.   The current period.
    b.   Past and current periods.
    c.   The current and future periods.
    d.   Past, current, and future periods.

_____ 9.   A timing difference arises if a company:

    a.   Is allowed to deduct the full cost of a long-lived asset on its tax return in the year of acquisition while depreciating it over its useful life for financial reporting purposes.
    b.   Pays a fine for violating air pollution standards in a different year than the year the fine was recorded.
    c.   Amortizes goodwill over different lives for tax purposes and financial reporting purposes.
    d.   All of the above give rise to timing differences.

_____ 10.   When there are timing differences, generally accepted accounting principles require a tax expense number that is the tax that:

    a.   Is paid to the taxing authorities.
    b.   Meets the needs of the reader of financial statements.
    c.   Would have been paid if the pretax income used for shareholder reporting had also been reported to the tax authorities.
    d.   None of the above are correct.

_____ 11.   Which of the following is *not* true of a contingent liability?

    a.   It always has a definite amount
    b.   It is a potential liability.
    c.   It depends on a future event arising out of a past transaction.
    d.   All of the above are true.

_____ 12.   Contingent liabilities may be disclosed:

    a.   In footnotes to the financial statements.
    b.   On the balance sheet.
    c.   Both a and b.
    d.   No disclosure of contingent liabilities is required.

_____ 13.   Which of the following ratios does *not* show what part of the firm's resources is obtained by borrowing?

a.   Debt-to-equity ratio.
b.   Interest-coverage ratio.
c.   Debt-to-total-assets ratio.
d.   All of the above.

_____ 14.   When the interest-coverage ratio is:

a.   Low, this may be an indication there may be more risk for the bondholders.
b.   High, it indicates the firm's ability to meet its interest obligation.
c.   Low, this may imply the company has less ability to meet bond obligations.
d.   All of the above are correct.

III. Answers to Pretest

1.   d   (L. O. 1)

2.   b   Creditors may *take over* a board of directors of a company that does not pay its debts, but creditors cannot force the board of directors to pay debts from personal assets. (L. O. 1)

3.   a   Most disbursement systems require *all* payments to be made by check. (L. O. 2)

4.   b   Internal controls cannot prevent collusion (although the controls can make collusion more difficult). Internal controls also cannot ensure cash is invested properly. (L. O. 2)

5.   c   (L. O. 3)

6.   d   (L. O. 3)

7.   b   A restructuring involves the *firing*, not hiring, of a significant number of employees.

8.   c   Restructuring costs can*not* be charged to past periods. (L. O. 4)

9.   a   Any type of fine creates a permanent difference. Goodwill also gives rise to a permanent difference, as it is not an allowable expense for tax purposes. (L. O. 5)

10.   c   The difference between the tax paid and the required tax expense number based on pretax income for financial statement purposes gives rise to deferred taxes. (L. O. 5)

11.   a   Contingent liabilities *sometimes* have a definite amount but not always. (L. O. 6)

12.   c   (L. O. 6)

13.   b   (L. O. 7)

14.   d   (L. O. 7)

EVALUATION

The pretest contained two questions for each learning objective. If you did not answer both questions correctly for each learning objective, you should review the appropriate section of the textbook and study guide before you attempt the material after Part IV.

IV. Key Concept Review by Learning Objectives

L. O. 1: Account for Current Liabilities

A.   Liabilities in Perspective

    1.   Investors, financial analysts, management, and creditors consider existing liabilities of the firm when valuing the firm's common stock, when evaluating a new loan to the company, and in numerous other decisions.

    2.   When a debt problem gets so bad that the company cannot pay, the creditors can take legal action to collect the debt. Depending on the type of obligation, creditors may be able to:

        a.   Force the sale of specific assets.

        b.   Take over the board of directors.

        c.   Force the company out of business.

    3.   Common practice classifies liabilities as either current or long-term, which helps financial statement readers interpret the immediacy of the company's obligations.

        a.   **Long-term liabilities** are obligations that fall due more than one year beyond the balance sheet date.

        b.   *Current liabilities* are obligations that fall due within the coming year or within the normal operating cycle if longer than a year.

    4.   Conceptually, a liability is best measured as the amount of cash needed to meet or pay off an obligation.

B.   Accounting for Current Liabilities

Some current liabilities are recorded automatically as result of a transaction with an outside entity, such as a lender or supplier. Other liabilities are recorded with an adjusting journal entry to acknowledge an obligation arising over time, such as interest and wages.

C.   Accounts Payable

    1.   *Accounts payable* (or *trade accounts payable*) are obligations resulting from purchasing goods or services on credit and are owed to creditors.

    2.   Most companies show accounts payable as a separate line under current liabilities.

D.   Notes Payable

    1.   A **promissory note** is a written promise to repay the loan principal plus interest at specific future dates. Most promissory notes are payable to banks and are called *notes payable*.

    2.   Only notes that are payable within the next year are shown as current liabilities; others are long-term liabilities.

3. Notes payable often result from **lines of credit**, which are agreements with a bank or other lender to automatically provide short-term loans up to some predetermined maximum.

4. Companies sometimes use commercial paper to meet short-term needs for credit. **Commercial paper** is a debt contract issued by prominent companies that borrow directly from investors, which always falls due in nine months or less, usually in sixty days after issuance.

E. Accrued Employee Compensation

1. Expenses that have been incurred and recognized on the income statement but not yet paid are *accrued liabilities*. Employee related liabilities account for a large part of most companies' accrued liabilities.

2. This classification also includes amounts withheld from employees' paychecks and outstanding employer liabilities for taxes such as matching FICA tax and federal unemployment taxes.

STOP **& REVIEW:**

Review the **example and journal entries** in the textbook.

F. Income Taxes Payable

The accrued liability for income taxes at year end is generally much smaller than the annual income tax expense as corporations make periodic installment payments based on their estimated tax for the year.

STOP **& REVIEW:**

Review the **example** in the textbook.

G. Current Portion of Long-Term Debt

A company's long-term debt often includes some payments due within a year that should be reclassified from a noncurrent liability to current liabilities.

H. Sales Tax

1. Retailers collect sales tax from customers on behalf of the local and state governments.

2. The sales tax payable appears on the balance sheet as a liability until the taxes are paid to the government. The sales tax *never* affects the income statement.

STOP **& REVIEW:**

Review the **example and journal entries** in the textbook.

I. Product Warranties

1. If warranty obligations are material, they must be accrued when products are sold because the obligation arises then, not when the actual services are performed. Therefore, a liability is established to offset the estimated expense that is recorded. Subsequent actual claims are used to reduce the product liability balance.

2.   Differences between the estimated and actual results are usually added to or subtracted from the current warranty expense account as additional information unfolds.

 **& REVIEW:**

Review the **example and journal entries** in the textbook.

J.   Returnable Deposits

1.   Returnable deposits are current liabilities of the company receiving the deposit.

2.   Deposits may include money deposits such as savings or checking deposits; deposits for returnable containers such as soft-drink bottles, oil drums, or beer kegs; and damage deposits from lessees (tenants).

K.   Unearned Revenue

1.   Revenues that are collected before services or goods are delivered are called unearned revenue under accrual accounting.

2.   Unearned revenues are usually considered current liabilities. The seller must deliver the product or service, or is obligated to make a full refund.

STOP & REVIEW:

Review the **example and journal entries** in the textbook.

L. O. 2:   Design an Internal Control System for Cash Disbursements

A.   It is important to create internal controls over cash disbursements to assure that all payments involve properly approved and valid obligations of the company.

B.   Most disbursement systems require that all payments be made by check.

1.   Checks should be prenumbered because this makes record keeping easy, and companies can trace exactly how much of their money is going where.

2.   All checks issued must be supported by source documents.

3.   Checks in excess of a specified amount typically require additional authorization and must be signed by two people.

C.   This process leaves a paper trail that is easy to follow in case anything should go wrong and that permits periodic, systematic reviews to assure that nothing does go wrong.

L. O. 3: Explain Simple Long-Term Liabilities

A.   Long-Term Liabilities

Some long-term liabilities are very similar to short-term liabilities except for the time frame. The accounting for these liabilities involves reporting them on the balance sheet and recording interest expense in the income statement.

 **& REVIEW:**

Review **Exhibit 8-2** in the textbook.

B.   Bonds and Notes

1.   Two of the most common forms of long-term liabilities are bonds and notes. They are common financial contracts that businesses use to raise money and are legal contracts that specify how much is to be borrowed as well as the dates and amounts for repayment by the borrower

2.   Notes are issued when money is borrowed from a few sources in a **private placement**. Notes issued in private placements are not traded among the general public.

3.   Corporations often borrow from the general public by issuing **bonds** which are formal certificates of indebtedness that typically represent:

  a.   A promise to pay interest in cash at a specified annual rate (the **nominal interest rate**, **contractual rate**, **coupon rate**, or **stated rate**).

  b.   A promise to pay the principal (often called the **face amount** or **par value**) of the loan amount at a specific maturity date.

4.   Fundamentally, bonds are individual promissory notes issued to many lenders.

5.   The **interest rate** on the bond represents the return the lender earns for loaning the money.

> **STUDY TIP:**
> A basic principle about interest is that lenders charge higher interest rates for riskier loans.

C.   Bond Accounting

 **& REVIEW:**

Review **Exhibit 8-3** in the textbook.

D.   Mortgage Bonds and Debentures

1.   Different lenders have different priority claims in collecting their money.

2.   A **mortgage bond** is a form of long-term debt that is secured by the pledge of specific property. In case of default, these bondholders can sell the pledged property to satisfy their claims. If the proceeds from the pledged property are insufficient, mortgage bondholders have an additional unsecured claim on the corporation.

3.   A **debenture** is a debt secured only by a general claim against the total assets of a company. If there is a *liquidation*, a debenture bondholder shares the available assets with other general creditors.

4.   **Subordinated debentures** are debt securities whose holders have claims against only the assets that remain after the claims of general creditors are satisfied.

5.   **Unsubordinated debentures** are debt securities whose holders have general claims on the assets with a priority like an accounts payable.

E.   Bond Provisions

A **trust indenture** is designed primarily to protect the safety of the bondholders. It outlines the **protective covenants** or simply **covenants** pertaining to payments of principal and interest, sales of pledged property, restrictions on dividends, etc.

STUDY TIP:
In general, the more covenants there are, the more restricted the borrower is, and the more attractive the security is to the lender.

F.   Callable, Sinking Fund, and Convertible Bonds

1.   Some bonds are **callable**, which means that they are subject to redemption before maturity at the option of the issuer. Typically the call is at a redemption price in excess of par. This excess is a call premium.

2.   **Sinking fund bonds** require the issuer to make annual payments into a **sinking fund**, which is an asset that is a pool of cash or securities set aside solely for meeting certain obligations. This helps assure the bondholder that sufficient cash will be accumulated to repay the principal at maturity.

3.   **Convertible bonds** are those bonds that may, at the *holder's* option, be exchanged for other securities, usually for a predetermined number of common shares of the issuing company. Because of the conversion feature, convertible bondholders are willing to accept a lower interest rate than on a similar bond without the conversion privilege.

L. O. 4: Understand Restructurings and the Liabilities They Create

A **restructuring** is a significant makeover of part of the company. It typically involves the closing of one or more plants, firing of a significant number of employees, and the termination or relocation of various activities.

L. O. 5: Interpret Deferred Tax Liabilities

A. Deferred Taxes

   1. Sometimes the difference between GAAP reporting and tax laws forces some income tax expense to be recorded long before it is paid and thus creates a deferred income tax liability.

   2. The differences arise because GAAP is designed to provide useful information to investors, while the tax code is written to generate revenue for the government. Revenue recognition and expense recognition rules for tax purposes can differ from GAAP rules on two dimensions:

      a. *Whether* an item is recognized (*permanent differences*).

      b. *When* an item is recognized (*temporary differences*).

   3. To save their companies money, good managers struggle to pay the least amount of income tax at the latest possible moment permitted within the law. They delay the reporting of taxable revenue as long as possible while deducting tax-deductible expense items as quickly as possible.

   4. Although the company tries to minimize taxable income to minimize taxes, it does not have the same incentive for financial reporting purposes. Reporting higher net income may often be desirable for financial reporting purposes — to increase bonuses or to make the company appear more profitable.

B. Permanent Differences

   Permanent differences involve revenue and expense items that are:

   1. Recognized for tax purposes but not recognized under GAAP.

   2. Not recognized for tax purposes but recognized under GAAP. Examples are interest on municipal bonds and fines levied against a company.

C. Temporary Differences

   1. Items recognized for both tax purposes and GAAP may not be recognized at the same time. This is a **temporary** or **timing difference**: the same lifetime expense or revenue is recorded, but items are recognized in one period for tax purposes and in another for shareholder reporting.

   2. A common temporary difference arises when *expenses* are deducted in determining taxable income *earlier* than they are deducted in determining pretax income for shareholder-reporting purposes. The major example is depreciation.

   3. When timing differences arise, GAAP requires the tax expense number to be the tax that would have been paid if the pretax income used for shareholder reporting had also been reported to the tax authorities. This requirement correctly matches the income tax expense with the income to which it relates.

   4. The tax expense would be recorded as indicated above, and there would be a payable for taxes as computed for tax purposes. The difference between these numbers is a deferred tax liability because it will be paid only when a future tax return is filed.

5.   The deferred tax liability account will appear in the liability section of the balance sheet, often just above stockholders' equity.

STUDY TIP:
Remember that differences between reported income and taxable income result in *deferral* of taxes, not *cancellation* of taxes.

---

6.   Not all temporary differences result in early deduction for tax purposes, and later deduction for financial reporting. In such cases like warranty costs, a deferred tax asset is recorded to acknowledge that the taxes being paid now are higher than the tax expense provided, based on pretax income reported for financial purposes.

L. O. 6: Locate and Understand the Contingent Liabilities Information in a Company's Financial Statements

Contingent Liabilities

1.   A **contingent liability** is a *potential* (possible) liability that depends on a *future* event arising out of a *past* transaction. Sometimes it has a definite amount (a guarantee of a related company's note), and sometimes it does not (a lawsuit).

2.   Most contingent liabilities are disclosed in the footnotes to the financial statements and are not accrued with an amount on the face of the statements.

L. O. 7: Use Ratio Analysis to Assess a Company's Debt Levels

Debt Ratios and Interest-Coverage Ratios

1.   The following three ratios are alternate ways of expressing the same thing: what part of the firm's resources is obtained by borrowing and what part is invested by the owners.

a.
$$Debt\text{-}to\text{-}equity\ ratio = \frac{Total\ liabilities}{Total\ shareholders'\ equity}$$

b.
$$Long\text{-}term\text{-}debt\text{-}to\text{-}capital\ ratio = \frac{Total\ long\text{-}term\ debt}{Total\ shareholders'\ equity + Long\text{-}term\ debt}$$

c.
$$Debt\text{-}to\text{-}total\text{-}assets\ ratio = \frac{Total\ liabilities}{Total\ assets}$$

2. The interest-coverage ratio measures the firm's ability to meet its interest obligation:

$$\text{Interest-coverage ratio} = \frac{\text{Pretax income} + \text{Interest expense}}{\text{Interest expense}}$$

3. While the level of debt is relative to the industry, it still remains a good indicator of risk. Generally, the higher the level of debt used by the company, the higher the level of risk associated with that company. This, in turn, leads to potentially higher interest rates for the company in the debt and equity markets.

STUDY TIP:
Study the "Summary Problems for Your Review" and solutions in the text.

STOP **& REVIEW:**

Before continuing, review the objectives for this chapter and make sure you have a good understanding of each one.

V. Test Yourself

Questions

1. Discuss why information about liabilities is important to readers of financial statements.

2. Explain how to account for current liabilities.

3. Distinguish between callable, sinking fund, and convertible bonds.

4. Explain how timing differences create deferred taxes.

5. Discuss contingent liabilities.

Exercises and Problems

1. In-the-Pocket Manufacturing produces billiard tables. Total sales for 19X9 were $4,500,000. Experience has indicated that .5% of sales will be refunded due to product warranties.

    A. Prepare the journal entry necessary to record product warranty expense for 19X9.

    B. Assume that during the first month of the next year $5,000 in refunds are given in cash. What is the entry to record this event?

2. New England Power sold 1000, 15 year, $5,000 par value bonds on January 2 at par value. The bonds had a stated interest rate of 10% and paid interest semiannually on January 1 and July 1. New England Power's year end is December 31. Prepare the journal entries for the:

    A. Issuance of the bond.
    B. The cash interest payments each six-month period.
    C. Retirement at maturity.

3. Atlantic Furniture had the following items on its September 30, 19X8 balance sheet.

Cash and cash equivalents	$325,000
Additional paid-in capital	827,000
Inventories	439.000
Accounts payable	248,000
Short-term debt	563,000
Long-term debt	772,000
Accrued liabilities and expenses	964,000
Payments due within one year on long-term debt	209,000

    Prepare the current liabilities section of Atlantic Furniture's balance sheet. Compute the total for the current liabilities section.

4. Nugent Manufacturing purchased a new piece of equipment for $350,000 on January 2, 19X8. Nugent makes a $50,000 down payment and borrows $300,000 at 10% interest for five years, agreeing to pay $79,140 each December 31.

    A. Prepare an analysis on the loan similar to Exhibit 8-2 in the textbook.

    B. Prepare the journal entry for the December 31, 20X0 payment.

5.   During 19X9 the Ed Sullivan Theater sold season tickets for 20X0 for $200,000 cash in advance. During the first quarter of 20X0, 25% of the performances were held.

    A.   What is the appropriate entry for the sale of the tickets? What is the effect on the December 31, 19X9 balance sheet and income statement?

    B.   What is the related entry for the quarter ended March 31, 20X0? What is the effect on the March 31, 20X0 balance sheet and income statement?

Matching

MATCH EACH TERM WITH ITS DEFINITION BY WRITING THE APPROPRIATE LETTER IN THE SPACE PROVIDED.

Terms

_____ 1. Bonds

_____ 2. Callable bonds

_____ 3. Commercial paper

_____ 4. Contingent liability

_____ 5. Covenant

_____ 6. Debenture

_____ 7. Nominal interest rate

_____ 8. Par value

_____ 9. Permanent difference

_____ 10. Restructuring

_____ 11. Temporary difference

Definition

A. A provision stated in a bond, usually to protect the bondholders' interests.

B. A debt security with a general claim against all assets rather than a specific claim against particular assets.

C. A significant makeover of part of the company.

D. A potential liability that depends on a future event arising out of a past transaction.

E. A contractual rate of interest paid on bonds.

F. Involve either revenue and expense items that are recognized for tax purposes but not recognized under GAAP, or items that are not recognized for tax purposes but are recognized under GAAP.

G. Arise because some items are recognized at different times for tax purposes than for financial reporting purposes.

H. Bonds subject to redemption before maturity at the option of the issuer.

I. A debt contract issued by prominent companies that borrow directly from investors.

J. The principal as indicated on the certificates of bonds or other debt instruments.

K. Formal certificates of indebtedness that are typically accompanied by a promise to pay interest at a specified annual rate plus a promise to pay the principal at a specific maturity date.

Multiple Choice

_____ 1. Which of the following is *not* a current liability?

    a.   Wages payable.
    b.   Mortgage payable.
    c.   Employer's contribution to FICA.
    d.   Returnable deposit held on one year lease.

_____ 2. A sinking fund:

    a.   Is required of the issuer of sinking fund bonds.
    b.   Helps assure bondholders that sufficient cash will be accumulated to repay the principal at maturity.
    c.   Is an asset that is usually classified as part of "Investments" or "Other assets."
    d.   All of the above are true of sinking funds.

_____ 3. Which of the following are *not* examples of current liabilities?

    a.   Accounts payable, accrued employee compensation, income taxes payable.
    b.   Accounts payable, sales tax, product warranties.
    c.   Accounts payable, income taxes payable, earned revenue.
    d.   All of the above are examples of current liabilities.

_____ 4. When a company's long-term debt includes some payments due within a year, these payments should be presented on the financial statements as:

    a.   A current liability.
    b.   A separate portion of long-term debt.
    c.   A net reduction of the current or long-term assets designated for payment.
    d.   None of the above.

_____ 5. Bonds that can be exchanged at the holder's option for other securities of the issuing company are:

    a.   Callable bonds.
    b.   Convertible bonds.
    c.   Sinking fund bonds.
    d.   Subordinated bonds.

_____ 6. Bonds that require the issuer to make annual payments into an asset account set aside solely for meeting certain obligations are:

    a.   Callable bonds.
    b.   Convertible bonds.
    c.   Sinking fund bonds.
    d.   Subordinated bonds.

_____ 7. Bonds that are subject to redemption before maturity at the option of the issuer are:

      a.   Callable bonds.
      b.   Convertible bonds.
      c.   Sinking fund bonds.
      d.   Subordinated bonds.

_____ 8. Income tax expense for financial statement purposes is generally composed of:

      a.   Income tax payable and the addition/subtraction to deferred taxes.
      b.   Income tax payable and the balance in the deferred tax liability account.
      c.   Income tax payable.
      d.   Additions to the deferred tax liability account.

_____ 9. When there is a timing difference, the difference between income taxes paid and income tax expense as computed per GAAP is known as:

      a.   Prepaid taxes.
      b.   Deferred taxes.
      c.   Taxes payable.
      d.   None of the above are correct.

_____ 10. The law firm of Weiss and Wise has a malpractice suit outstanding at the end of the period. Their counsel, Best and Better, feels there is a good chance the suit will be settled in the next period and that Weiss and Wise will have to pay $500,000. This is an example of a:

      a.   Current liability.
      b.   Deferred liability.
      c.   Contingent liability.
      d.   Long-term liability.

VI. Solutions to Test Yourself

Questions

1. Investors, financial analysts, management, and creditors consider existing liabilities of the firm when valuing the firm's common stock, when evaluating a new loan to the company, and in numerous other decisions. When companies show signs of excessive debt or of an inability to meet existing obligations, problems arise. As problems multiply, conditions can worsen quickly.

   When the debt burden is so heavy that the company cannot pay, the creditors can pursue legal channels to collect the debt. Depending on the type of obligation, creditors may be able to: force the sale of specific assets, take over the board of directors, or force the company out of business. (L. O. 1)

2. Some current liabilities are recorded automatically as result of a transaction with an outside entity, such as a lender or supplier. Other liabilities are recorded with an adjusting journal entry to acknowledge an obligation arising over time, such as interest and wages. (L. O. 1)

3. Callable bonds are subject to redemption before maturity at the option of the issuer. Typically the call is at a redemption price in excess of par. This excess is a call premium.

   Sinking fund bonds require the issuer to make annual payments into a sinking fund, which is an asset, that is a pool of cash or securities set aside solely for meeting certain obligations. This helps assure the bondholder that sufficient cash will be accumulated to repay the principal at maturity.

   Convertible bonds are those bonds that may, at the *holder's* option, be exchanged for other securities, usually for a predetermined number of common shares of the issuing company. Because of the conversion feature, convertible bondholders are willing to accept a lower interest rate than on a similar bond without the conversion privilege. (L. O. 3)

4. When timing differences arise, GAAP requires the tax expense number to be the tax that would have been paid if the pretax income used for shareholder reporting had also been reported to the tax authorities.

   The tax expense would be recorded as indicated above, and there would be a payable for taxes as computed for tax purposes. The difference between these numbers is a deferred tax liability because it will be paid only when a future tax return is filed. The deferred tax liability account will appear in the liability section of the balance sheet, often just above stockholders' equity. (L. O.5)

5. A contingent liability is a *potential* (possible) liability that depends on a *future* event arising out of a *past* transaction. Sometimes it has a definite amount (a guarantee of a related company's note), and sometimes it does not (a lawsuit).

   Most contingent liabilities are disclosed in the footnotes to the financial statements and are not accrued with an amount on the face of the statements. (L. O. 6)

Exercises and Problems

1. An estimate of the potential returns associated with the sales must be made in the period of the sales.

   A. Warranty expense ($4,500,000 X .005)   22,500

        Liability for warranties   22,500

   B. When the refund is made, the warranty liability account is reduced.

       Liability for warranties   5,000

          Cash   5,000

2. A. Cash   5,000,000

        Bonds payable   5,000,000

   B. Interest expense   500,000

        Cash   500,000

   C. Bonds payable   5,000,000

        Cash   5,000,000

3.

Atlantic Furniture
Partial Balance Sheet
September 30, 19X9

Current liabilities:

Accounts payable	$ 248,000
Accrued liabilities and expenses	772,000
Short-term debt	563,000
Current portion of long-term debt	209,000
Total current liabilities	$1,792,000

4.

	(1)	(2)	(3)	(4)	(5)
		Interest	December 31	Reduction of	Ending
	Beginning	10%	Cash	Principal	Liability
Year	Liability	(1) X 0.10	Payment	(3) – (2)	(1) – (4)
19X8	$300,000	$30,000	$79,140	$49,140	$250,860
19X9	250,860	25,086	79,140	54,054	196,806
20X0	196,806	19,681	79,140	59,459	137,347
20X1	137,347	13,735	79,140	65,405	71,942
20X2	71,942	7,198*	79,140	71,942	– 0 –

*Due to rounding

   B. Interest expense   13,735

       Loan payable (principal)   65,405

          Cash   79,140

5. A. Cash   200,000

        Unearned sales revenue   200,000

At December 31, 19X9 the balance sheet will include a current liability for the entire unearned revenue amount, $200,000. The December 31, 19X9 income statement is not affected by these transactions as none of the revenue was earned in 19X9.

B.	Unearned sales revenue	50,000	
	Sales		50,000
	($200,000 X .25)		

The March 31, 20X0 balance sheet will include only $150,000 as a current liability, as $50,000 was earned during this quarter and will be included on the March 31 income statement.

Matching

1.	K	L. O. 3	5.	A	L. O. 3	9.	F	L. O. 5
2.	H	L. O. 3	6.	B	L. O. 3	10.	C	L. O. 4
3.	I	L. O. 1	7.	E	L. O. 3	11.	G	L. O. 5
4.	D	L. O. 6	8.	J	L. O. 3			

Multiple Choice

1. b Mortgage payable is generally a long-term liability. All of the others would, by their nature, be short-term liabilities. (L. O. 1)

2. d (L. O. 3)

3. c Earned revenue is *not* any type of liability. *Un*earned revenue would usually be classified as a current liability. (L. O. 1)

4. a When a company's long-term debt includes some payments due within a year, the payments are reclassified as a current liability, "current portion of long-term obligations." (L. O. 1)

5. b Convertible bonds may be exchanged at the *holder's* option. (L. O.3)

6. c (L. O. 3)

7. a Callable bonds are subject to redemption before maturity at the option of the *issuer*. (L. O. 3)

8. a Income tax expense for financial statement purposes is composed of two elements: income tax payable for the current period and the addition/subtraction to the deferred tax liability account. (L. O. 5)

9. b Deferred taxes are recorded when there is a difference between income taxes paid per the tax return and income tax expense computed on pretax income for financial statements. (L. O. 5)

10. c Contingent liabilities are potential liabilities dependent on a future event arising out of a past transaction. Contingent liabilities of this type are referenced in the footnotes. (L. O. 6)

Chapter 9

VALUING AND ACCOUNTING FOR BONDS AND LEASES

I. Learning Objectives

Measuring and reporting long-term liabilities uses fundamental concepts of compound interest, especially present value techniques. This chapter will use present value techniques to value and account for bond issues, and for leases, and to interpret disclosures about pensions and other postretirement employee benefits. Use the following learning objectives as stepping stones in completing your study of this chapter.

1. Compute and interpret present and future values.

2. Use present value techniques in valuing long-term liabilities.

3. Account for bond issues over their entire life.

4. Value and account for long-term lease transactions.

5. Evaluate pensions and other postretirement benefits.

II. Pretest

_____ 1. The amount accumulated, including principal and interest is the:

    a. Present value.
    b. Future value.
    c. Annuity value.
    d. None of the above.

_____ 2. The value today of a future cash inflow or outflow is the:

    a. Present value.
    b. Future value.
    c. Annuity value.
    d. None of the above.

_____ 3. Discounts and premiums:

    a. Are determined by market forces that fluctuate from day to day and by the choice of the nominal rate of interest.
    b. Mean that the credit worthiness of the issuer is especially bad or good.
    c. Are not usual in bond issues.
    d. All of the above are true.

_____ 4. The nominal or stated rate of interest on a bond issue is determined by the:

    a. Underwriters.
    b. Board of directors.
    c. Market forces.
    d. None of the above.

_____ 5. Discount on bonds payable is:

    a. A contra account.
    b. Deducted from bonds payable.
    c. Amortized over the life of the bonds.
    d. All of the above.

_____ 6. Which of the following is _not_ true of effective-interest amortization?

    a. It uses a constant interest rate.
    b. It is required by the FASB for bond discounts and amortizations.
    c. It produces a constant amount of interest expense each period.
    d. All of the above are true.

_____ 7.   A lease that should be accounted for by the lessee as ordinary rent expense is a:

a.   Capital lease.
b.   Financing lease.
c.   Operating lease.
d.   None of the above.

_____8.   Which of the following is *not* one of the test conditions for a capital lease

a.   Title is transferred to the lessee by the end of the lease term.
b.   An expensive purchase option is available to the lessee at the end of the lease.
c.   The lease term equals or exceeds 75% of the estimated economic life of the property.
d.   All of the above are test conditions for a capital lease.

_____ 9.   Accounting for postretirement benefits requires:

a.   A liability to be recorded as the benefit is earned.
b.   The use of present value to compute a dollar amount.
c.   The expense of pensions, life insurance, health insurance, etc. to be paid to retirees be considered in the liability computation.
d.   All of the above.

_____ 10.   Postretirement benefits:

a.   Are mandated by the U.S. government for all employees and companies.
b.   Requires estimates of life expectancy, future work lives, ages at retirement, and levels of future payments to retirees.
c.   Are optional but payments must be made to an independent trustee.
d.   None of the above are correct.

II. Answers to Pretest

1. b   (L. O. 1)

2. a   (L. O. 1)

3. a   Discounts and premiums *are* usual in bond issues and have little relationship to the credit worthiness of a company. (L. O. 2)

4. b   The underwriters are investment bankers who sell bond issues, and market forces determine discounts or premiums — *not* the nominal or stated rate of interest.
(L. O. 2)

5. d   (L. O. 3)

6. c   Effective-interest amortization, which is required by the FASB, uses a constant *rate* of interest but does *not* yield a *constant* dollar amount of interest expense.
(L. O. 3)

7. c   Capital lease and financing lease are both terms that refer to a lease that transfers substantially all of the risks and benefits of ownership to the lessee. (L. O. 4)

8. b   A test condition of a capital lease is an *in*expensive purchase option to the lessee at the end of the lease, not an expensive purchase option. (L. O. 4)

9. d   (L. O. 5)

10. b   Postretirement benefits are not mandated, and payments are not required to be made to an independent trustee, although this is preferred. (L. O. 5)

EVALUATION

The pretest contained two questions for each learning objective. If you did not answer both questions correctly for each learning objective, you should review the appropriate section of the textbook and study guide before you attempt the material after Part IV.

IV. Key Concept Review by Learning Objectives

L. O. 1: Compute and Interpret Present and Future Values

A. Compound Interest, Future Value, and Present Value

    1. The amount borrowed is known as the loan principal. For the borrower, interest is the cost of using money. For the investor, interest is the return on investment or the fee for lending money.

    2. Calculation of the amount of interest depends on the interest rate and the interest period.

    3. **Simple interest** is calculated by multiplying an interest rate by an unchanging principal amount. **Compound interest** is calculated by multiplying an interest rate by a principal amount that is changed each interest period by the previously accumulated (unpaid) interest. The accumulated interest is added to the principal to become the principal for the new period.

B. Future Value

    1. The amount accumulated from a deposit made today, including principal and interest, is called the **future value**. Compound interest provides interest on interest; therefore, principal changes from period to period.

    2. Future value can be calculated in one of two ways:

        a. Future value $= S(1 + I)^n$ where S stands for the value today of a single lump sum, I represents interest, and n represents the number of periods.

        b. From a future value table, find the factor corresponding to the time period necessary and the relevant interest rate. Multiply that factor by the present value of the single lump sum to arrive at the future value of the single lump sum.

C. Present Value

    1. The **present value** is the value today of a future cash inflow or outflow. Accountants generally use present values rather than future values to record long-term liabilities.

    2. Present value may be calculated as follows:

        a. Since the present value is the reciprocal of the future value formula, future value is calculated as:
$$PV = FV / (1 + I)^n$$

        b. The present value may also be found using the appropriate present value factor in a present value of a single lump sum table, then multiplying that factor by the future value amount to arrive at the present, discounted value of the future amount. Again, the factor depends on the appropriate time period and interest rate (**discount rate**).

        c. The **rate of return** refers to the amount earned by the investor expressed as a percentage of the amount invested.

D.   Present Value of an Ordinary Annuity

   1.   An ordinary **annuity** is a series of equal cash flows to take place at the end of successive periods of equal length.

   2.   The easiest method of computation involves the use of a present value of an ordinary annuity table. The factor corresponding to the appropriate interest rate and time period is multiplied by the value for one of the payments to arrive at the present value of the future cash flow annuity payments.

> **STUDY TIP:**
> Note that the higher the interest rate, the lower the present value. At a higher interest rate, you would need to invest less now to obtain the same future value.

L. O. 2:   Use Present Value Techniques in Valuing Long-Term Liabilities

Valuing Bonds

Prices on the bond market vary from the par value of the bond due to fluctuations in the effective or market interest rate. This fluctuation or difference between the stated or nominal interest rate and the effective or market interest rate causes the bonds to sell at:

   1.   Par or face value of the bond if the effective interest rate equals the stated interest rate.

   2.   A **discount** when the effective interest rate is *higher* than the stated interest rate.

   3.   A **premium** when the effective interest rate is *lower* than the stated interest rate.

 **& REVIEW:**

   Before continuing, carefully review **Exhibit 9-2** in the textbook.

L. O. 3:   Account for Bond Issues Over Their Entire Life

A.   Issuing and Trading Bonds

   1.   Bonds are typically sold through a syndicate or special group of investment bankers called **underwriters** who buy the entire issue from the corporation thus guaranteeing that the company will obtain all of its desired funds. The syndicate then sells the bonds to the general investing public.

   2.   The company sets the terms of the bond contract, which include the time to maturity, interest payment dates, interest amounts, and the size of the bond issue.

   3.   The rate of interest to be paid by the bond (coupon rate, nominal rate) is usually set as close to the current market rate as possible. The **market rate** is the rate available on investments in similar bonds at a moment in time.

a. Many factors affect the market rate including general economic conditions, industry conditions, risks of the use of the proceeds, and specific features of the bonds.

b. When the **yield to maturity** (market rate, **effective interest rate**) — the rate of interest demanded by investors in a bond — differs from the nominal rate of interest the bond sells at a discount (below par) or at a premium (above par).

STUDY TIP:
The yield to maturity is the interest rate at which all contractual cash flows for interest and principal have a present value equal to the proceeds of the issue.

---

4. The **current yield** is calculated as the annual interest divided by the current price.

B. Assessing the Riskiness of Bonds

1. The higher the risk, the higher the interest rate investors will require before making the investment.

2. Bonds are rated according to their credit worthiness. Higher ratings are safer and therefore companies with better ratings pay lower interest rates.

C. Bonds Issued at a Discount

1. When the effective or market rate of interest is higher than the stated rate of interest, the present value of the bonds is *lower* than par value and the bonds will be sold at a discount.

2. The bonds are recorded in a long-term liability account at par or face value. The discount is recorded in a *contra account*, which is deducted from bonds payable on the balance sheet. This net carrying value is equal to the present value of the bond obligation.

3. The FASB requires **discount amortization** — bond discounts to be amortized over the life of the bond — using the **effective-interest amortization method** (or **compound interest method**):

Interest expense = Carrying value of liability x Effective interest rate at the date of issue

---

STUDY TIP:
The difference between the effective-interest amount, which is the interest expense, and the cash interest payment is the amount of the discount amortized for the period.

STOP **& REVIEW:**

Review **the example and Exhibits 9-3** and **9-4** in the textbook.

D. Bonds Issued at a Premium

    1. The differences for accounting for bonds issued at a premium from accounting for bonds issued at a discount are:

        a. The cash proceeds *exceed* the face amount.

        b. The amount of the account Premium on Bonds Payable is *added* to the face amount to determine the net liability reported in the balance sheet.

        c. The amortization of bond premium *decreases* the interest expense.

STOP & REVIEW:

    Review **the example and Exhibits 9-5** and **9-6** in the textbook.

E. Early Extinguishment

    1. Bonds may be redeemed by the issuing company through purchases on the open market or by exercising its call options.

    2. Gains or losses on these early extinguishments of debt are computed as the difference between the cash paid and the net carrying amount of the bonds (face, less unamortized discount or plus unamortized premium).

STOP & REVIEW:

    Review **the example and Exhibit 9-7** in the textbook.

F. Bonds Sold Between Interest Dates

The sale price of bonds sold between interest dates is the market price *plus accrued interest*. The market quotations for bonds *always* mean that the investor must pay an extra amount for any *unearned* interest to be received at the next interest payment date.

STOP & REVIEW:

    Review **the example and Exhibit 9-8** in the textbook.

G. Non-Interest-Bearing Notes and Bonds

    1. Some notes and bonds do not provided interest payments. Instead they contain a promise to pay a lump sum at a specified date, such as **zero coupon** bonds. To say that these bonds are non-interest-bearing is misleading as the investor gets interest revenue by paying less than the face value.

    2. Discounting the maturity value, using the market rate of interest for notes having similar terms and risks (the **implicit** or **imputed interest**) does this. This discount is amortized, or systematically reduced, as interest over the life of the note or bond.

    3. The imputed interest amount is based on an **imputed interest rate**, which is the market rate that equates the future amount of the loan repayment with the present value of the amount loaned.

STOP & REVIEW:

    Review **the example and Exhibit 9-9** in the textbook.

L. O. 4:   Value and Account for Long-Term Lease Transactions

A. Accounting for Leases

    1. A **lease** is a contract whereby an owner (**lessor**) grants the use of property to a second party (**lessee**) in exchange for rental payments.

    2. Leasing is important from an accounting perspective because lease contracts create both property rights and financial obligations for the lessee. Sometimes it becomes difficult to distinguish the economic characteristics of a lease contract from the rights conveyed by ownership of the property.

B. Operating and Capital Leases

    1. **Capital leases** (or **financing leases**) transfer substantially all the risks and benefits of ownership. They are equivalent to installment sale and purchase transactions. The asset must be recorded essentially as having been sold by the lessor and having been purchased by the lessee.

    2. All other leases are **operating leases**. Operating lease payments are expenses of the period. No leased asset or its accompanying liability account are recorded.

STOP & REVIEW:

    Before continuing, carefully review the **examples** and **computations for leases** including **Exhibit 9-10** in the textbook.

C. Differences in Income Statements

    1. In comparison with the operating lease approach, the capital lease approach tends to bunch heavier charges in the early years. The longer the lease, the more pronounced the differences will be in the early years. Immediate reported income is reduced more under the capital lease approach.

    2. An operating lease affects the income statement as rent expense, which is the amount of the lease payment. A capital lease affects the income statement as amortization (of the asset) plus interest expense (on the liability).

STOP & REVIEW:

    Review **Exhibit 9-11** in the textbook.

D. Tests for Capital Leases

    Under GAAP, a *capital lease* exists if *one* or more of the following conditions are met:

    1. Title is transferred to the lessee by the end of the lease term.

    2. An inexpensive purchase option is available to the lessee at the end of the lease.

    3. The lease term equals or exceeds 75% of the estimated economic life of the property.

    4. At the start of the lease term, the present value of minimum lease payments is at least 90% of the property's fair value.

L. O. 5:   Evaluate Pensions and Other Postretirement Benefits

Pensions and Other Postretirement Benefits

1. Most U.S. companies provide retired employees with **pensions** (reduced wages) after they stop working. Retirees may also continue to receive health insurance, life insurance, or other employee benefits, which are commonly called **other postretirement benefits**.

2. Since the worker "earns" the right to postretirement payments during the working years, accrual accounting requires recognition of the growing liability for future payments (at present value) as the years pass, and a matching of expense with appropriate periods.

3. The expense of life insurance, health insurance, and similar benefits paid for retirees is conceptually similar to pensions. Therefore, a liability equal to the present value of expected payments should be recorded under GAAP rules. Increases in the liability will be recognized as a current expense.

STUDY TIP:
Study the "Summary Problems for Your Review" and solutions in the text.

STOP & REVIEW:

Before continuing, review the objectives for this chapter and make sure you have a good understanding of each one.

V. Test Yourself

Questions

1. Discuss future value and present value.

2. Discuss why present value techniques are used in valuing long-term liabilities.

3. Explain the differences between accounting for bonds issued at a premium or issued at a discount.

4. Briefly discuss capital and operating leases.

5. Explain the nature of postretirement benefits.

Exercises and Problems

1. You are the agent for Tiger Woods. A sports equipment company has just offered him a contract with either a lump sum payment of $10,000,000 today, or $15,000,000 payable at the end of three years. The current market rate of interest is 12%, and Tiger Woods does not need the money to live on during the next three years. Which deal should he take, and why should he take it?

   Data for use in #2 and #3

   In order to finance the purchase of new equipment, RainGear Manufacturing issued $10,000,000 in new bonds. The bonds had a par value of $10,000 each, a nominal rate of 8%, and paid interest semiannually. The bonds had a maturity of 10 years and sold for $7,776 each.

2. A. Calculate the effective rate of interest at the date of sale.

   B. Prepare the journal entry for the sale of the bonds.

3. A. What is the book value of bonds payable immediately after the first semiannual interest payment and adjustment for amortization?

   B. What is the journal entry to retire the bonds at maturity assuming the last interest payment and amortization adjustment have been made?

4. Scott Rehn purchased 10, Con Edison Utility, 15 year, $1,000 par value bonds on May 1. The bonds had a stated interest rate of 10% and paid interest semiannually on January 1 and July 1. On the date of the purchase the effective interest rate was 12%. How much did Scott write his check for?

5.   Indicate which of the following leases are a capital lease (C), and which are an operating lease (O).

_____ A.   Rental of a computer for $500 per month, renewable annually.

_____ B.   Rental of a warehouse for $10,000 per month on a 5-year lease, with an option to buy for $10,000 at the end of the 5 years.

_____ C.   Rental of equipment for $1,000 per month on a 6-year lease. At the end of 6 years the equipment is expected to have a fair market value of $2,000.

_____ D.   Rental of a van on a 2-year lease for $800 per month. The van will be returned to the dealer after the 2 years.

_____ E.   Rental of 10 printing presses for $2,000 per month on a 6-year lease. The value of the printing presses at the end of 6 years is uncertain, but the total economic life is not expected to be more than 7 years.

Matching

MATCH EACH TERM WITH ITS DEFINITION BY WRITING THE APPROPRIATE LETTER IN THE SPACE PROVIDED.

Terms

_____ 1. Annuity

_____ 2. Capital lease

_____ 3. Compound interest

_____ 4. Current yield

_____ 5. Discount amortization

_____ 6. Discount on bonds

_____ 7. Effective interest rate

_____ 8. Future value

_____ 9. Lessor

_____ 10. Operating lease

_____ 11. Premium on bonds

_____ 12. Present value

Definition

A. The excess of face amount over the proceeds upon issuance of a bond.

B. A lease that should be accounted for by the lessee as ordinary rent expense.

C. The excess of the proceeds over the face amount of a bond.

D. The interest rate that equates market price at issue to the present value of principal and interest.

E. The owner of property who grants usage rights to someone else.

F. The spreading of a bond discount over the life of the bonds as expense.

G. For any period, the interest rate multiplied by a changing principal amount. The unpaid interest is added to the principal to become the principal for the new period.

H. Annual interest payments divided by the current price of a bond.

I. The value today of a future cash inflow or outflow.

J. A lease that transfers substantially all the risks and benefits of ownership.

K. Equal cash flows to take place during successive periods of equal length.

L. The amount accumulated, including principal and interest.

Multiple Choice

_____ 1. An amount that is calculated by multiplying an interest rate by a principal amount that is changed each interest period by the previously accumulated (unpaid) interest is known as:

    a. Simple interest.
    b. Compound interest.
    c. Interest.
    d. None of the above are correct.

_____ 2. A series of equal cash flows to take place at the end of successive periods of equal length is:

    a. An ordinary annuity.
    b. A deferred annuity.
    c. A serial note.
    d. None of the above are correct.

_____ 3. Long-term liabilities are generally recorded at:

    a. The face value of the obligation.
    b. Present value of all future payments discounted at the coupon rate of interest.
    c. Present value of all future payments discounted at the market interest rate in effect at the date of the original transaction.
    d. Future value of the bond obligation plus the interest payments.

_____ 4. As the effective rate of interest rises above the nominal or stated interest rate for a bond, the market price of the bond will:

    a. Rise.
    b. Fall.
    c. Stay the same.
    d. Cannot be determined without more information.

_____ 5. Which of the following statements is _not_ true? Premiums on bonds payable:

    a. Increase the interest expense.
    b. Are added to the face amount of bonds payable on the balance sheet.
    c. Means the cash proceeds exceed the face amount of the bond.
    d. All of the above statements are correct.

_____ 6. Which of the following are considered when recording long-term liabilities?

    a. The present value of all future payments.
    b. The market interest rate in effect when the liability was incurred.
    c. The time value of money.
    d. All of the above are considered.

_____ 7.   Which of the following long-term liabilities is *not* discounted?

     a.   Bonds.
     b.   Notes.
     c.   Deferred income taxes.
     d.   All of the above are discounted.

_____ 8.   Which of the following is *not* true of bonds issued at a premium?

     a.   The cash proceeds exceed the face amount of the bonds.
     b.   The amount of the Premium on Bonds Payable account is subtracted from the face amount to determine the net liability reported in the balance sheet.
     c.   The amortization of bond premium decreases the interest expense.
     d.   All of the above are true.

_____ 9.   A capital lease:

     a.   Will record an asset and liability related to the lease on the balance sheet.
     b.   Is the equivalent of a sale by the lessor and a purchase by the lessee.
     c.   Payment consists of interest expense plus an amount that reduces the outstanding liability.
     d.   All of the above are true of a capital lease.

_____ 10.   Which one of the following is *never* considered a postretirement benefit?

     a.   Life insurance.
     b.   Health insurance.
     c.   Matching of FICA.
     d.   All of the above are postretirement benefits.

VI. Solutions Test Yourself

Questions

1. Future value is the amount accumulated from a deposit made today, including principal and interest. Compound interest provides interest on interest; therefore, principal changes from period to period.

    The present value is the value today of a future cash inflow or outflow. Accountants generally use present values rather than future values to record long-term liabilities. (L. O. 1)

2. Prices on the bond market vary from the par value of the bond due to fluctuations in the effective or market interest rate. This fluctuation or difference between the stated or nominal interest rate and the effective or market interest rate, causes the bonds to sell at:

    a. Par or face value of the bond if the effective interest rate equals the stated interest rate.
    b. A *discount* when the effective interest rate is *higher* than the stated interest rate.
    c. A *premium* when the effective interest rate is *lower* than the stated interest rate.

    Both the interest and principal related to a bond have to be calculated at present value in order to record the appropriate liability amount. (L. O. 2)

3. The differences for accounting for bonds issued at a premium from accounting for bonds issued at a discount are:

    a. The cash proceeds *exceed* the face amount.
    b. The amount of the account Premium on Bonds Payable is *added* to the face amount to determine the net liability reported in the balance sheet.
    c. The amortization of bond premium *decreases* the interest expense. (L. O. 3)

4. Capital leases (or financing leases) transfer substantially all the risks and benefits of ownership. They are equivalent to installment sale and purchase transactions. The asset must be recorded essentially as having been sold by the lessor and having been purchased by the lessee.

    All other leases are operating leases. Operating lease payments are expenses of the period. No leased asset or its accompanying liability account is recorded.

    In comparison with the operating lease approach, the capital lease approach tends to bunch heavier charges in the early years. The longer the lease, the more pronounced the differences will be in the early years. Immediate reported income is reduced more under the capital lease approach.

    An operating lease affects the income statement as rent expense, which is the amount of the lease payment. A capital lease affects the income statement as amortization (of the asset) plus interest expense (on the liability). (L. O. 4)

5. Since the worker "earns" the right to postretirement payments during the working years, accrual accounting requires recognition of the growing liability for future payments (at present value) as the years pass, and a matching of expense with appropriate periods. (L. O. 5)

Exercises and Problems

1. This problem may be solved two ways: as a present value problem or a future value problem.

    Future Value:

    Future value = Present value X (FV factor, table 1, 12%, 3 years)
    FV   = $10,000,000   X   (1.4049)
    FV   = $14,049,000

    According to this calculation, if the group invests the $10,000,000 at 12%, the best they could do is to earn $14,049,000. This is less than the $15,000,000 so they should take the $15,000,000, assuming there are no other unknown factors.

    Present Value:

    Present value = Future value X (PV factor, table 2, 12%, 3 years)
    PV   = $15,000,000   X   (.7118)
    PV   = $10,677,000

    This confirms the FV calculation. In order for Tiger Woods to have $15,000,000 available in three years he would have to invest $10,677,000 today at 12%. This is obviously an amount greater than the $10,000,000 that was offered. He should take the $15,000,000, assuming there are no other unknown factors.

2. A.   To find the effective rate of interest you must calculate the yield to maturity on the bond.

        (per bond)
        $7,776   = $400* X (unknown PV annuity factor, 20 periods)   +
                    $10,000 X (unknown PV factor, 20 periods)

        *$400 = $10,000 X .04 per interest period

        Let (I) equal the unknown interest factor.
        $7,776   = $400 (I) + $10,000 (I)

        Knowing that the bonds were issued at a discount and using trial-and-error, let (I) equal the factor at a 6% semiannual rate of interest.

                            table 3   table 2
        $7,776   = $400 (11.4699) + $10,000 (.3118)
        $7,776   = $4,588   + $3,188

        With a semiannual interest rate of 6%, the annual effective interest rate is 12%.

    B.   Cash (1,000 X $7,776)   7,776,000
          Discount on bonds payable   2,224,000
                Bonds payable   10,000,000

3. A.   Interest expense = Effective semiannual rate X beginning book value

Beginning Book Value	Effctv. Rate	Interest Exp.	Cash Interest Payments	Amortize Bond Disc.	Ending Book Value
$7,776,000	.06	$466,560	$400,000	$66,560	$7,842,560

    B.   Bonds payable   10,000,000
                Cash   10,000,000

4. Since Scott bought his bonds between interest periods he will pay *both* the market price of the bond and the accrued interest since the last payment.

Bond:

Bond value = Semiannual interest payment X (PV factor, 6%, 30 periods, table 3)
             + principal X (PV factor, 6%, 30 periods, table 2)

Bond value = $50* (13.7648) + $1,000 (.1741)
  $862.34 = $688.24 + $174.10

        *$50 = $1,000 X .05 per interest period

Interest:

Accrued interest = Principal X % of period outstanding X stated interest rate
        $33.33   = $1,000 X 4/12 X .10

Total:

Market value of bond $862.34
Accrued interest   33.33
     Total price paid $895.67   X 10 bonds = $8,956.70

5.   A.   O   D.   O
     B.   C   E.   C
     C.   C

          O = operating lease
          C = capital lease

Matching

1.	K	L. O. 1	6.	A	L. O. 2	10.	B	L. O. 4
2.	J	L. O. 4	7.	D	L. O. 3	11.	C	L. O. 2
3.	G	L. O. 1	8.	L	L. O. 1	12.	I	L. O. 1
4.	H	L. O. 2	9.	E	L. O. 4			
5.	F	L. O. 3						

Multiple Choice

1.   b   (L. O. 1)

2.   a   A deferred annuity takes place at the *beginning* of successive periods of equal length and a serial note may be either an ordinary annuity or a deferred annuity. (L. O. 1)

3.   c   (L. O. 2)

4.   b   As market interest rates rise, bond prices fall. As market interest rates fall, bond prices rise. (L. O. 2)

5.   a   Premiums on bonds payable *decrease* interest expense when amortized. (L. O. 2)

6.   d   (L. O. 2)

7.   c   Deferred income taxes are measured by the total tax payments that have been deferred, not the present value of the payments. (L. O. 2)

8.   b   The amount of premium on bonds payable is *added* (not subtracted) to the face amount to determine the net liability reported in the balance sheet.   (L. O. 3)

9.   d   (L. O. 4)

10.   c   Matching of FICA is a current expense of each period that the person works — it is not a postretirement benefit. (L. O. 5)

Chapter 10

STATEMENT OF CASH FLOWS

I.   Learning Objectives

While many users of financial statement information are interested in the results of operations as reflected in the income statement, the ability to generate sufficient cash to satisfy maturing obligations may mean the difference between survival and closing the doors to the business. Recognizing the potential disparity between net income and cash flows from operations, the FASB has mandated that a statement of cash flows be included with the other required financial statements. Use the following learning objectives as a guide for your study of this interesting and informative financial statement.

1.   Explain the concept of the statement of cash flows.

2.   Classify activities affecting cash as operating, investing, or financing activities.

3.   Use the direct method to measure cash flows.

4.   Determine cash flows from income statement and balance sheet accounts.

5.   Use the indirect method to calculate cash flows from operations.

6.   Relate depreciation to cash flows provided by operating activities.

7.   Reconcile net income to cash provided by operating activities.

8.   Adjust for gains and losses from fixed asset sales and debt extinguishments in the statement of cash flows. (Appendix 10A)

9.   Use the T-account approach to prepare the cash flow statement. (Appendix 10B)

II. Pretest

_____ 1.   A statement of cash flows:

   a.   Reports the cash receipts and cash payments of an entity during a period.
   b.   Explains the causes for the changes in cash by providing information about operating, financing, and investing activities.
   c.   Is a basic financial statement required by the FASB in all corporate annual reports.
   d.   All of the above are true of the statement of cash flows.

_____ 2.   A statement of cash flows shows the:

   a.   Performance of a company over a period of time.
   b.   Performance of a company at a single point in time.
   c.   Status of a company over a period of time.
   d.   Status of a company at a single point in time.

_____ 3.   Operating management activities in a company are largely concerned with:

   a.   Where to get cash.
   b.   How to use cash.
   c.   Generating revenues and expenses.
   d.   All of the above are correct.

_____ 4.   Which of the following is _not_ an operating activity?

   a.   Interest paid.
   b.   Payment of dividends.
   c.   Collections from customers.
   d.   All of the above are operating activities.

_____ 5.   The _direct method_:

   a.   Calculates net cash provided by operating activities as collections minus operating disbursements.
   b.   Adjusts the accrual net income to reflect only cash receipts and outlays.
   c.   Adds depreciation to the computation.
   d.   None of the above is correct.

_____ 6.   Which of the following is _true_? The statement of cash flows requires:

   a.   The beginning cash balance to be shown.
   b.   The ending cash balance to be shown.
   c.   The net change in cash during the period to be shown.
   d.   All of the above are required.

_____ 7.   Cash may be expressed as:

      a.   Cash = Liabilities – Stockholders' equity + Noncash assets
      b.   Cash = Liabilities + Stockholders' equity + Noncash assets
      c.   Cash = Liabilities + Stockholders' equity - Noncash assets
      d.   None of the above is correct.

_____ 8.   Major investment and financing activities that do not affect cash:

      a.   Are not required to be reported with the statement of cash flows.
      b.   Must be reported in a schedule that accompanies the statement of cash flows.
      c.   Must be integrated into the statement of cash flows.
      d.   None of the above are correct.

_____ 9.   The *indirect method*:

      a.   Begins the net cash provided by operations with net income.
      b.   Adds back depreciation.
      c.   Adds or deducts changes in related current asset and current liability accounts.
      d.   All of the above are true of the indirect method.

_____ 10.   Which of the following is *not* true for the indirect method?

      a.   Increases in noncash current assets result in less cash flow from operations.
      b.   Decreases in noncash current assets result in more cash flow from operations.
      c.   Increases in current liabilities result in less cash flow from operations.
      d.   All of the above are true.

_____ 11.   When using the indirect method, depreciation:

      a.   Cancels its deduction in calculating net income.
      b.   Is a source of cash.
      c.   Is not considered.
      d.   None of the above are correct.

_____ 12.   If depreciation is to be considered when preparing a statement of cash flows, it is listed under:

      a.   Financing activities.
      b.   Operating activities.
      c.   Investing activities.
      d.   It is never listed on the statement of cash flows.

_____ 13.   Which of the following is *not added* to net income to reconcile it to net cash provided by operating activities?

      a.   Amortization of long-lived assets.
      b.   Extraordinary losses.
      c.   Amortization of premium on bonds payable.
      d.   All of the above are added.

_____ 14.   Which of the following is *deducted* from net income to reconcile it to net cash provided by operating activities?

   a.   Income tax expense arising from deferred income taxes.
   b.   Nonoperating gains.
   c.   Depletion.
   d.   All of the above are deducted.

_____ 15.*   Which of the following is *not* true of gains or losses on disposal of fixed assets in the statement of cash flows?

   a.   Under the direct method, these gains or losses would not be included in the cash flows from operating activities section.
   b.   Under the indirect method, these gains or losses would be included in the cash flows from operating activities section.
   c.   These gains or losses are always included in the cash flows from operating activities no matter what method is used.
   d.   Under both the direct and indirect methods, the entire proceeds from the sale of the fixed assets would be included as an investing activity.

_____ 16.*   Which of the following statements is *true*?

   a.   Issuing and retiring debt are financing activities.
   b.   The entire payment for debt retirement would be listed.
   c.   Gains or losses from the extinguishment of debt are only included under the indirect method.
   d.   All of the above are true.

_____ 17.*   The T-account approach:

   a.   Is a methodical procedure for being sure all increases and decreases to cash are identified.
   b.   Is the only recommended method for preparing the statement of cash flows.
   c.   Can only be used with the direct method.
   d.   All of the above are true.

_____ 18.*   When using the T-account approach with the direct method:

   a.   Reasonably complete re-creations of the summary journal entries for the year are required.
   b.   Every entry for the year needs to be entered in the T-accounts.
   c.   All the T-accounts are broken down into operating, investing, and financing activities.
   d.   None of the above are true.

III. Answers to Pretest

1. d (L. O. 1)

2. a The statement of cash flows and also the income statement show the *performance* of a company *over a period* of time. The balance sheet shows the *status* of a company at a *single point* in time. (L. O. 1)

3. c Where to get cash and how to use cash are *financial management* activities. (L. O. 2)

4. b Payment of dividends is a financing activity, *not* an operating activity. (L. O. 2)

5. a b and c are part of the *in*direct method. (L. O. 3)

6. c The statement of cash flows requires only the net change in cash during the period to be shown. (L. O. 3)

7. c (L. O. 4)

8. b (L. O. 4)

9. d (L. O. 5)

10. c Increases in current liabilities result in *more* cash flow from operations. *Decreases* in current liabilities result in *less* cash flow. (L. O. 5)

11. a Depreciation must be considered when using the indirect method and it cancels its deduction in calculating net income. It is *never* a source of cash under any method or system. (L. O. 6)

12. b When using the indirect method, depreciation is added back to net income in the net cash provided by *operating* activities section. (L. O. 6)

13. c Amortization of *discounts* on bonds payable is added to net income. Amortization of *premiums* is *deducted* in the reconciliation. (L. O. 7)

14. b Of those items listed, only nonoperating gains are deducted. Both income tax expense arising from deferred income taxes and depletion are added to net income in the reconciliation. (L. O. 7)

15.* c Gains or losses on disposal of fixed assets would only be included under the *in*direct method. (L. O. 8)

16.* d (L. O. 8)

17.* a There is no one recommended preparation method as there are several methods that may be used to prepare the statement of cash flows under both the direct and indirect methods. (L. O. 9)

18.* a (L. O. 9)

EVALUATION

The pretest contained two questions for each learning objective. If you did not answer both questions correctly for each learning objective, you should review the appropriate section of the textbook and study guide before you attempt the material after Part IV.

IV. Key Concept Review by Learning Objectives

L. O. 1: Explain the Concept of the Statement of Cash Flows

Purposes of Cash Flow Statements

1. A *statement of cash flows* reports the cash receipts and cash payments of an entity *during* a given period.

2. It shows the relationship of net income to changes in cash balances. Cash balances can decline despite positive net income and vice versa.

3. It reports past cash flows as an aid to:

   a. Predicting future cash flows.

   b. Evaluating the way management generates and uses cash.

   c. Determining a company's ability to pay interest and dividends and to pay debts when they are due.

4. It identifies changes in the mix of productive assets.

5. The statement of cash flows explains where cash and cash equivalents — highly liquid short-term investments that can easily be converted into cash with little delay — came from during a period and where it went.

> **STUDY TIP:**
> Balance sheets show the *status* of a company at a single point in time. In contrast, statements of cash flows and income statements show the *performance* of a company over a period of time.

L. O. 2: Classify Activities Affecting Cash As Operating, Investing, or Financing Activities

A. Activities Affecting Cash

1. Cash affects and is affected by two primary areas of a firm:

   a. **Operating management,** which is largely concerned with the major day-to-day activities that generate revenues and expenses.

   b. **Financial management,** which is largely concerned with where to get cash (financing activities) and how to use cash (investing activities).

2. **Operating activities** are generally activities or transactions that affect the income statement. For example, sales are linked to collections from customers, and wage expenses are closely tied to cash payments to employees.

3. **Investing activities** involve providing and collecting cash as a lender or as an owner of securities, and acquiring and disposing of plant, property, and equipment, and other long-term productive assets.

4.   **Financing activities** involve obtaining resources as a borrower or issuer of securities and repaying creditors and owners.

 **& REVIEW:**

Before continuing, review the **examples of typical statement of cash flows activities and Exhibit 10-1** in the textbook.

B.   Approaches to Calculating the Cash Flow from Operating Activities

1.   The **direct method** computes **cash flow from operating activities** as collections less operating disbursements. This means that only the cash part of each item in the income statement is identified.

2.   The **indirect method** computes cash flow from operating activities by adjusting the accrual net income to reflect only cash receipts and outlays.

3.   The FASB prefers the direct method because it shows operating cash receipts and payments in a way that is easier for investors to understand. However, the indirect method is more common.

C.   Activities Affecting Cash

Cash flow emphasizes the flow of cash to and from customers and suppliers; accrual accounting emphasizes the flow of goods and services.

& REVIEW:

Before continuing, carefully review **Exhibit 10-2** in the textbook.

D.   Cash Flow and Earnings

1.   A focal point of the statement of cash flows is the net cash flow from operating activities, or simply, cash flow.

2.   Both cash flow and income convey useful information about an entity.

L. O. 3:   Use the Direct Method To Measure Cash Flows

The Eco-Bag Company — A More Detailed Example of the Direct Method for Preparing the Statement of Cash Flows

& REVIEW:

Carefully review the **Eco-Bag Company example** and **Exhibit 10-3** in the textbook.

L. O. 4: Determine Cash Flows From Income Statement and Balance Sheet Accounts

A. Changes in the Balance Sheet Equation

    1. The balance sheet equation provides the conceptual framework underlying all financial statements, including the statement of cash flows.

    2. The equation can be rearranged as:

Cash = Liabilities + Stockholders' equity - Noncash assets

Therefore,

Change in cash = Change in all noncash accounts

    3. The statement of cash flows focuses on the changes in the noncash accounts as a way of explaining how and why the level of cash has gone up or down during a given period.

        a. Thus, the major changes in the accounts on the right side of the equation appear in the statement of cash flows as *causes* of the change in cash.

        b. The left side of the equation measures the net *effect* of the change in cash.

 **& REVIEW:**

Review **Exhibit 10-4** in the textbook.

B. Computing Cash Flows from Operating Activities

    1. Cash collections from sales to customers are almost always the major operating activity that increases cash. Disbursements for purchases of goods to be sold and operating expenses are almost always the major operating cash outflows.

    2. By analyzing changes in the noncash current accounts on the balance sheet (noncash current assets and current liabilities) and their effect on cash receipts and disbursements, it is possible to derive cash flows from operations.

> **STUDY TIP:**
> The amount of inflows (collections) minus the amount of outflows (disbursements) is the net cash provided by — or used up by — operating activities.

C. Working From Income Statement Amounts to Cash Amounts

    1. Many accountants build the statement of cash flows from the *changes* in balance sheet items, a few additional facts, and a familiarity with the typical causes of changes in cash.

    2. Most accounting systems do not provide such additional facts. Therefore, accountants often compute the collections and other cash flow items from figures on the income statement.

Carefully review the **examples for Eco-Bag Company** in this section of the textbook.

D. Comparison of Income Statement and Cash Flow Statement

1. Accrual-based measures of revenue and expense are reported in the income statement. Most of these are naturally linked to asset or liability accounts and the cash effects of the revenue and expense transactions are moderated by changes in their related asset or liability accounts.

2. The balance sheet approach relies on adjusting accrual-based income statement values for changes in asset and liability account balances.

STUDY TIP:
Liability changes have the *opposite* effects from asset changes, and each revenue or expense account has a related asset and/or liability account.

STOP **& REVIEW:**

Review **Exhibit 10-5** in the textbook for the **comparison of net income and net cash provided by operating activities**.

E. Computing Cash Flows from Investing and Financing Activities

1. Determining cash flows from investing and financing activities are identical under either the direct or indirect method of constructing the statement of cash flows.

2. **Cash flows from investing activities** deal primarily with changes in long-term asset accounts and their effect on cash.

3. **Cash flows from financing activities** shows cash flows to and from providers of capital, which would include related long-term liabilities and stockholders' equity accounts.

STUDY TIP:
Increases in cash (cash inflows) stem from:
    Increases in liabilities or stockholders' equity or
    Decreases in noncash assets.
Decreases in cash (cash outflows) stem from:
    Decreases in liabilities or stockholders' equity or
    Increases in noncash assets.

4. Tracing the cash flow from investing activities requires some knowledge of the year's activity. Sometimes there is incomplete information and you need to solve for the unknown values.

F. Noncash Investing and Financing Activities

Major investment and financing activities that *do not* affect cash must be reported in a schedule that accompanies the statement of cash flows.

G. The Crisis of Negative Cash Flow

L. O. 5: Use the Indirect Method to Calculate Cash Flows From Operations

A. Preparing a Statement of Cash Flows -- The Indirect Method

1. The *indirect method* of computing cash flows from operating activities shows the link between the income statement and the statement of cash flows.

2. The indirect method considers the same changes in related asset and liability accounts as the direct method but shows their effects directly on the net income number, rather than on the individual revenue and expense items that comprise net income.

B. Reconciliation of Net Income to Net Cash Provided by Operations

1. In the indirect method, the statement of cash flows begins with net income. Then additions or deductions are made for changes in related asset or liability accounts (for items that affect net income and net cash flow differently).

2. The general rules for additions and deductions to adjust net income using the indirect method are identical to those for adjusting the line items of the income statement under the direct method.

3. A final step is to reconcile for gains and losses that are included in net income but arise from investing or financing activities (in contrast to operating activities). See Appendix 10A for more information.

 **& REVIEW:**

Review **Exhibit 10-6** in the textbook before continuing.

L. O. 6: Relate Depreciation to Cash Flows Provided by Operating Activities

Role of Depreciation

1. The most crucial aspect of a statement of cash flows prepared by the indirect method is how depreciation and other expenses that do not require cash relate to the flow of cash.

2. Depreciation is an allocation of historical cost to expense and *does not* entail a current outflow of cash. Therefore, depreciation is added to net income to compute cash flow simply to cancel its original deduction in calculating net income in the income statement.

3. Depreciation is *not* a source of cash under any method or system of accounting.

L. O. 7: Reconcile Net Income to Cash Provided by Operating Activities

A.   Reconciling Items

Net income rarely coincides with net cash provide by operating activities. Consequently, many necessary additions or deductions are commonly shown to reconcile net income to net cash provided by operating activities, such as depreciation and changes in noncash current assets and current liabilities.

STOP & REVIEW:

Study **Exhibit 10-7** of **other additions and deductions** in the textbook.

B.   Liz Claiborne's Cash Flow Statement

> **STUDY TIP**:
> Study the "Summary Problems for Your Review" and solutions including Exhibits 10-9 through 10-11 in the text.

Appendix 10A: More on the Statement of Cash Flows

L. O. 8: Adjust For Gains and Losses From Fixed Asset Sales and Debt Extinguishments in the Statement of Cash Flows

A.   Gain or Loss on Disposal of Fixed Assets

   1.   The body of the statement of cash flows under the direct method, in the section "Cash flows from operating activities," would *not* include any gains (*or* losses) from the disposal of fixed assets.

   2.   Under the indirect method, in order to avoid double counting gains or losses on disposals of fixed assets, the gains or losses must be deducted from, or added to net income, respectively.

   3.   In both the direct and indirect methods, the amount of the proceeds from the sale of fixed assets would be listed in investing activities.

B.   Gain or Loss on Extinguishment of Debt

   1.   Issuing and retiring debt are financing activities. Any gain or loss on extinguishment of debt must be removed from net income in a reconciliation schedule.

   2.   The entire *payment* for debt retirement would be listed among the financing activities.

Appendix 10B: T-Account Approach to Statement of Cash Flows

L. O. 8: Use the T-Account Approach to Prepare the Cash Flow Statement

A.   T-Account Approach

When constructing any cash flow statement, the increases and decreases of cash due to various activities must add up to the overall change in the cash during the year. The T-account approach is simply an easier way of ensuring that all the appropriate activities are identified and treated properly.

B.   T-Accounts and the Direct Method

      1.   For this method, reasonably complete re-creations of the summary journal entries for the year are required.

      2.   The focus is on the *changes* in the noncash accounts to explain why cash *changed*.

      3.   The summarized transactions entered in the Cash account are the basis for the preparation of the formal statement of cash flows.

STOP & REVIEW:

Review **Exhibit 10-12** in the textbook.

STOP & REVIEW:

Before continuing, review the objectives for this chapter and make sure you have a good understanding of each one.

V. Test Yourself

Questions

1. Explain the concept of the statement of cash flows.

2. Discuss operating, investing, and financing activities that affect cash.

3. Discuss the direct and indirect approaches to the statement of cash flows.

4. Explain how depreciation affects cash flows provided by operating activities.

5. Discuss reconciling items between net income and cash provided by operating activities.

Exercises and Problems

1. For each item, indicate which section of the statement should contain the item —the operating, investing, or financing section — and indicate the effect of each item on the cash balance. Use + for increase, — for decrease, 0 for no change.

		Activity	Cash Impact
a.	Sale of goods for cash	_____	_____
b.	Sale of common stock	_____	_____
c.	Sale of a fixed asset at book value for cash	_____	_____
d.	Depreciation expense	_____	_____
e.	Payment of accounts payable	_____	_____
f.	Purchase of a long-term security	_____	_____
g.	Payment of dividends	_____	_____
h.	Purchase of inventory on credit	_____	_____

Data for use in #2 - #5

TSI Manufacturing Co.
Balance Sheet
December 31

Assets:	19X9	19X8
Cash	$ 88,000	$ 58,000
Accounts receivable	136,000	76,000
Inventory	128,000	108,000
Prepaid expense	8,000	-0-
Net fixed assets	720,000	440,000
Total assets	$1,080,000	$682,000

Liabilities and Stockholders' Equity:		
Accounts payable	$ 60,000	$ 38,000
Wages payable	6,000	8,000
Long-term debt	250,000	52,000
Capital stock	354,000	254,000
Retained earnings	410,000	330,000
Total liabilities & stockholders' equity	$1,080,000	$682,000

TSI Manufacturing Co.
Income Statement and Statement of Retained Earnings
For the period ended December 31, 19X9

Sales		$916,000
Less cost of goods sold:		
Inventory, January 1, 19X9	$108,000	
Purchases	396,000	
Cost of goods available	$504,000	
Inventory, December 31, 19X9	128,000	376,000
Gross profit		$540,000
Operating expenses:		
Selling and administrative expense	$212,000	
Depreciation expense	40,000	
Property taxes	22,000	
Interest expense	12,500	
Wages expense	143,500	
Total operating expenses		430,000
Net income		$110,000
Retained earnings, December 31, 19X8		330,000
Dividends		(30,000)
Retained earnings, December 31, 19X9		$410,000

During the period TSI Manufacturing purchased machinery for $320,000. A portion of the purchase was financed through the sale of $100,000 in new stock and the acquisition of $198,000 in new long-term debt.

2. Calculate the cash flow from operations for 19X9 using the *direct* method.

3. Calculate the cash flow from operations for 19X9 using the *indirect* method.

4. A. Calculate the cash flows from investing activities for 19X9.

    B. Calculate the cash flows from financing activities for 19X9.

5. Using your answers from #2 - #4, show a reconciliation of the change in the cash account.

Matching

MATCH EACH TERM WITH ITS DEFINITION BY WRITING THE APPROPRIATE LETTER IN THE SPACE PROVIDED.

Terms

_____ 1. Cash flows from financing activities

_____ 2. Cash flows from investing activities

_____ 3. Cash flows from operating activities

_____ 4. Direct method

_____ 5. Financial management

_____ 6. Financing activities

_____ 7. Indirect method

_____ 8. Investing activities

_____ 9. Operating activities

_____ 10. Operating management

Definitions

A. Transactions that affect the income statement.

B. In a statement of cash flows, the method that adjusts the accrual net income to reflect only cash receipts and cash outlays.

C. Mainly concerned with the major day-to-day activities that generate revenues and expenses.

D. The second major section of the statement of cash flows, describing purchase or sale of plant, property, equipment, and other long-lived assets.

E. In the statement of cash flows, obtaining resources as a borrower or issuer of securities and repaying creditors and owners.

F. In a statement of cash flows, the method that calculates net cash provided by operating activities as collections minus operating disbursements.

G. The third major section of the statement of cash flows, describing flows to and from providers of capital.

H. Mainly concerned with where to get cash and how to use cash for the benefit of the entity.

I. Activities that involve providing and collecting cash as a lender or as an owner of securities, and acquiring and disposing of plant, property, equipment, and other long-term productive assets.

J. The first major section of the statement of cash flows. It shows the cash effects of transactions that affect the income statement.

Multiple Choice

_____ 1.   The FASB requires a statement of cash flows because:

    a.   It shows the relationship of net income to changes in cash balances.
    b.   It identifies changes in the mix of productive assets.
    c.   It reports past cash flows as an aid to predicting future cash flows.
    d.   All of the above are true.

_____ 2.   Which of the following is _not_ an investing activity?

    a.   Issuing equity securities.
    b.   Purchase of long-term securities.
    c.   Sale of securities that are not cash equivalents.
    d.   All of the above are investing activities.

_____ 3.   Which of the following is _not_ a financing activity?

    a.   Borrowing cash.
    b.   Purchase of treasury stock.
    c.   Dividends collected.
    d.   All of the above are financing activities.

_____ 4.   Which of the following is _not_ an operating activity?

    a.   Collections from customers.
    b.   Cash payments to suppliers.
    c.   Taxes paid.
    d.   All of the above are operating activities.

_____ 5.   The _indirect method_:

    a.   Shows collections less operating disbursements as cash from operations.
    b.   Adjusts the accrual net income to reflect only cash receipts and outlays.
    c.   Subtracts depreciation in the computation.
    d.   All of the above are correct.

_____ 6.   Accountants often compute cash collections by:

    a.   Beginning with the sales revenue shown on the income statement.
    b.   Adding the ending accounts receivable balance.
    c.   Subtracting the beginning accounts receivable balance.
    d.   All of the above are correct.

_____ 7.   Depreciation:

a.   Is not considered in the direct method.
b.   Is added back in the indirect method.
c.   Is a noncash transaction that is used to adjust the accrual net income to reflect cash receipts and outlays.
d.   All of the above are true of depreciation.

_____ 8.   Which of the following is *not* a reconciling item of accrual net income to net cash provided by operating activities?

a.   Sale of fixed assets.
b.   Gains or losses on the sale of fixed assets.
c.   Equity in earnings of affiliated companies.
d.   Amortization of goodwill.

_____ 9.*   Under the *direct* method, gains and losses on disposal of an asset would be classified as:

a.   An operating activity.
b.   An investing activity.
c.   A financing activity.
d.   Not classified.

_____ 10.*   Gains or losses on extinguishment of debt:

a.   Are never considered when preparing the statement of cash flows.
b.   Are listed as a financing activity under the indirect method.
c.   Are added or deducted in the operating activity section under the direct method.
d.   None of the above are correct.

VI. Solutions to Test Yourself

Questions

1.   A *statement of cash flows* reports the cash receipts and cash payments of an entity during a period. It shows the relationship of net income to changes in cash balances and it reports past cash flows as an aid to :

        a.   Predicting future cash flows.
        b.   Evaluating management's generation and use of cash.
        c.   Determining a company's ability to pay interest and dividends and to pay debts when they are due.

It also identifies changes in the mix of productive assets. (L. O. 1)

2.   Operating activities are generally the effects of transactions that affect the income statement. For example, sales are linked to collections from customers, and wage expenses are closely tied to cash payments to employees.

Investing activities involve providing and collecting cash as a lender or as an owner of securities, and acquiring and disposing of plant, property, and equipment, and other long-term productive assets.

Financing activities involve obtaining resources as a borrower or issuer of securities and repaying creditors and owners. (L. O. 2)

3.   The direct method computes cash flow from operating activities as collections less operating disbursements. This means that only the cash part of each item in the income statement is identified.

The indirect method computes cash flow from operating activities by adjusting the accrual net income to reflect only cash receipts and outlays.

The FASB prefers the direct method because it shows operating cash receipts and payments in a way that is easier for investors to understand. However, the indirect method is more common. (L. O. 2)

4.   The most crucial aspect of a statement of cash flows prepared by the indirect method is how depreciation and other expenses that do not require cash relate to the flow of cash.

Depreciation is an allocation of historical cost to expense and *does not* entail a current outflow of cash. Therefore, depreciation is added to net income to compute cash flow simply to cancel its original deduction in calculating net income in the income statement.

Depreciation is *not* a source of cash under any method or system of accounting. (L. O. 6)

5.   Net income rarely coincides with net cash provided by operating activities. Consequently, many necessary additions or deductions are commonly shown to reconcile net income to net cash provided by operating activities.

Some other additions and deductions in this section are: depletion, amortization of long-lived assets such as patents, copyrights, etc., extraordinary and nonoperating gains and losses, income tax expense arising from deferred income taxes, amortization of bond premiums and discounts, and equity in earnings of affiliated companies. (L. O. 7)

Exercises and Problems

1.
a.	operating	+	e.	operating	—
b.	financing	+	f.	investing	—
c.	investing	+	g.	financing	—
d.	operating	0	h.	operating	0

2. <u>Cash flows from operations - direct method:</u>

Cash collections from customers (a)			$856,000
Cash payments:			
To suppliers (b)	$374,000		
To employees (c)	145,500		
For taxes	22,000		
For interest	12,500		
For misc. selling & administrative (d)	220,000		
Total cash payments		774,000	
Cash flows from operations			$ 82,000

(a)	Sales	$916,000
	+ Beginning accounts receivable	76,000
	- Ending accounts receivable	136,000
	Cash collected from customers	$856,000

(b)	Beginning accounts payable	$ 38,000
	+ Purchases	396,000
	- Ending accounts payable	60,000
	Cash payments to suppliers	$374,000

(c)	Beginning balance wages payable	$ 8,000
	+ Wages expense	143,500
	- Ending balance wages payable	6,000
	Cash payments to employees	$ 145,500

(d)	Ending balance prepaid expense	$ 8,000
	+ Selling and administrative expense	212,000
	- Beginning balance prepaid expense	-0-
	Cash paid selling & admin. Expense	$220,000

3. <u>Cash flows from operations - indirect method:</u>

Net income	$110,000
(Increase) in accounts receivable	(60,000)
(Increase) in inventory	(20,000)
(Increase) in prepaid expenses	(8,000)
Increase in accounts payable	22,000
(Decrease) in wages payable	(2,000)
Depreciation expense	40,000
Cash flows from operations	$82,000

4. A. <u>Cash flows from investing activities:</u>

Purchase of machinery	$320,000	
Cash flows from investing activities		$(320,000)

B.   Cash flow from financing activities:

Sale of new stock	$ 100,000	
Addition to long-term debt	198,000	
Dividends paid	(30,000)	
Cash flows from financing activities		$ 268,000

5.   Reconciliation of the change in the cash account:

Cash flows from operations	$ 82,000
Cash flows from investing activities	(320,000)
Cash flows from financing activities	268,000
Increase in cash	$ 30,000
Beginning cash	58,000
Ending cash	$ 88,000

Matching

1.	G	L. O. 4		5.	H	L. O. 2		8.	I	L. O. 2
2.	D	L. O. 4		6.	E	L. O. 2		9.	A	L. O. 2
3.	J	L. O. 2		7.	B	L. O. 2		10.	C	L. O. 2
4.	F	L. O. 2								

Multiple Choice

1.   d   (L. O. 1)

2.   a   Issuing equity securities is a *financing* activity. (L. O. 2)

3.   c   Dividends *collected* is an operating activity. (L. O. 2)

4.   d   (L. O. 2)

5.   b   The indirect method adjusts accrual net income to reflect only cash receipts and outlays, and *adds* back depreciation in the computation. Choice "a" is the definition of the direct method. (L. O. 2)

6.   a   Choices b and c are incorrect because the *beginning* accounts receivable balance should be *added* and the *ending* accounts receivable balance should be *subtracted*. (L. O. 4)

7.   d   (L. O. 6)

8.   a   Sale of fixed assets is an investing activity, not a reconciling item. (L. O. 7)

9.*   d   Under the direct method, gains and losses are not classified as each operating activity is computed on the cash basis and, therefore, there is no need to adjust for noncash transactions such as gains or losses. The entire proceeds from the sale of an asset are classified as an investing activity. (L. O. 8)

10.*   d   (L. O. 8)

Chapter 11

STOCKHOLDERS' EQUITY

I. Learning Objectives

Stockholders' equity represents the investment made by the shareholders or owners of the corporation and provides significant information concerning equity investment in the firm. Any user of financial statements should have a complete understanding of stockholders' equity and its composition. The following objectives will help you in studying this important section of the balance sheet.

1. Describe the rights of the shareholders.

2. Differentiate among authorized, issued, and outstanding shares.

3. Contrast bonds, preferred stock, and common stock.

4. Identify the economic characteristics of stock splits and dividends.

5. Account for stock splits and both large-percentage and small-percentage stock dividends.

6. Interpret treasury stock transactions.

7. Record conversions of debt for equity or of preferred stock into common stock.

8. Use the rate of return on common equity and book value per share.

II. Pretest

_____ 1.   Shareholders are entitled to:

        a.   Vote.
        b.   Share in corporate profits.
        c.   Share residually in corporation assets upon liquidation.
        d.   All of the above.

_____ 2.   When creditors of a corporation have claims only on the assets owned by the corporation, and not on the assets of the owners of the corporation it is called:

        a.   Unlimited liability.
        b.   Limited liability.
        c.   Preemptive right.
        d.   None of the above are correct.

_____ 3.   Shares in the hands of shareholders are:

        a.   Treasury stock.
        b.   Issued shares.
        c.   Outstanding shares.
        d.   None of the above are correct.

_____ 4.   A corporation's issued stock that has been repurchased by the corporation and not retired is:

        a.   Treasury stock.
        b.   Outstanding stock.
        c.   Corporate proxies.
        d.   None of the above are correct.

_____ 5.   Accumulated unpaid dividends on preferred stock are:

        a.   Cumulative dividends.
        b.   Dividend arrearages.
        c.   Liquidation dividends.
        d.   Participating dividends.

_____ 6.   Preferred stock and bonds:

        a.   Each pay a specific return to the investor.
        b.   Are accounted for in the same manner.
        c.   Both have specific maturity dates.
        d.   None of the above are correct.

_____ 7.   When additional shares of stock are issued to existing shareholders without any additional cash payment to the firm, and there is a corresponding adjustment to the par value this is called a:

a.   Stock distribution.
b.   Stock dividend.
c.   Stock split.
d.   None of the above are correct.

_____ 8.   The purpose of a stock split is to:

a.   Allow the company to maintain the stock price in a trading range accessible to small investors and company employees.
b.   Allow the company to increase the stock price on the open market when it drops due to economic conditions.
c.   Create an immediate return to investors.
d.   None of the above are correct.

_____ 9.   When accounting for a stock split:

a.   The number of shares increases.
b.   The par value is reduced.
c.   No accounting entry is made.
d.   All of the above are correct.

_____ 10.   Which of the following is true?

a.   Small-percentage stock dividends are less than 20%.
b.   Large-percentage stock dividends are accounted for at par value.
c.   Small-percentage stock dividends are accounted for at market value.
d.   All of the above are true.

_____ 11.   Which of the following is *not* true? Companies repurchase their own shares:

a.   To manipulate the market price of the stock.
b.   To permanently reduce shareholder claims.
c.   To temporarily hold shares for later use.
d.   All of the above are true.

_____ 12.   Which of the following is true of treasury stock? Treasury stock:

a.   Decreases stockholders' equity.
b.   Is a contra account.
c.   Does not affect common stock at par value, additional paid-in capital, and retained income.
d.   All of the above are true.

_____ 13. When a company issues its stock in a noncash exchange, the value of the transaction is the:

   a. Lower of the market value of either the securities or the exchanged assets.
   b. Higher of the market value of either the securities or the exchanged assets.
   c. Fair value of either the securities or the exchanged assets, whichever is more objectively determinable.
   d. Cannot be determined without more specific information.

_____ 14. When companies issue convertible preferred stock, the conversion feature:

   a. Makes the securities more attractive to investors.
   b. Decreases the price the issuer receives.
   c. Increases the dividend the issuer must pay.
   d. All of the above are true.

_____ 15. One ratio that aids in evaluating how effectively the company uses resources provided by the shareholders is:

   a. Book value per share of common stock.
   b. Rate of return on common equity.
   c. Rate of return on assets.
   d. All of the above.

_____ 16. If the book value per share of common stock is lower than market value:

   a. It is an indication that the company may be in trouble.
   b. Suggests the company has many unrecorded assets.
   c. The shareholders are paying for future earning power rather than for the historical cost of assets.
   d. None of the above are correct.

III. Answers to Pretest

1. d (L. O. 1)

2. b (L. O. 1)

3. c (L. O. 2)

4. a (L. O. 2)

5. b (L. O. 3)

6. a Bonds are accounted for as long-term liabilities and do have a specific maturity date. Preferred stock, however, is accounted for in the same manner as common stock, and usually has an unlimited life. (L. O. 3)

7. c Both stock dividends and stock splits are stock distributions. However, stock splits usually have an adjustment to par value. (L. O. 4)

8. a (L. O. 4)

9. d Although no accounting entry is made for a stock split, the number of shares is increased and the par value is decreased. Stock splits may be accounted for "as a stock dividend" if the corporation does not want to physically exchange the old stock certificates for certificates with the new par value. This would entail a journal entry to reallocate the dollars in different stockholder equity accounts. (L. O. 5)

10. d (L. O. 5)

11. a Choices b and c are true. Choice a is not true because companies are not legally allowed to repurchase their own stock with the intent of market price manipulation. (L. O. 6)

12. d (L. O. 6)

13. c (L. O. 7)

14. a The convertible feature on a preferred stock does make the security more attractive to investors. It also *increases* the price the issuer receives, or equivalently, *reduces* the dividend it must pay. (L. O. 7)

15. b (L. O. 8)

16. c (L. O. 8)

EVALUATION

The pretest contained two questions for each learning objective. If you did not answer both questions correctly for each learning objective, you should review the appropriate section of the textbook and study guide before you attempt the material after Part IV.

IV. Key Concept Review by Learning Objectives

L. O. 1: Describe the Rights of Shareholders

A. Background on Stockholders' Equity

    1. The owners of a business have a *residual interest* in the assets of the firm after both current and long-term liabilities have been deducted.

    2. Corporations are perpetual entities created in accordance with state laws.

    3. The corporate charter specifies the rights of stockholders (or shareholders) that generally includes the right to:

        a. Vote on important matters at shareholders meetings. Stockholders may also grant in writing — by **corporate proxy** — to a third party (usually members of corporate management) the authority to cast the shareholders' votes.

        b. Share in corporate profits.

        c. Share in any assets left upon liquidation.

        d. Acquire more shares of subsequent issues of stock to maintain their percentage of ownership. This is known as **preemptive rights**.

    4. Perhaps the most important right of common shareholders is *limited liability*, which means that creditors of the corporation have claims only on the assets owned by the corporation, not on the assets of the owners of the corporation.

L. O. 2: Differentiate Among Authorized, Issued, and Outstanding Shares

A. Authorized, Issued, and Outstanding Stock

The state approves the articles of incorporation, which includes authorization of the number and types of capital stock that can be issued.

    1. The total number of shares that may be issued is known as **authorized shares**.

    2. When the company receives cash in exchange for stock certificates, the shares become **issued shares**.

    3. Shares that are issued and held by the stockholders are called **outstanding shares**.

    4. Shares that are issued but no longer outstanding because the company reacquired the shares by purchasing them from its own shareholders are called **treasury stock**.

B. Accounting for Stock Issuance

    1. To account for a stock issuance the receipt of cash is recorded and a common stock account is created to represent the ownership interest.

2. Many companies separate their common stock recognition into two categories, par value (the minimum capital required of the stockholder) and additional paid-in capital. In some cases the minimum capital is called stated value rather than par value.

L. O. 3: Contrast Bonds, Preferred Stock, and Common Stock

A. Preferred Stock

1. **Preferred stock** offers owners different rights and preferential treatment than those listed above.

2. Preferred stock owners do not usually have voting rights, but they do have a preferred claim on assets upon liquidation.

3. Preferred stock is stock that has some priority over other shares regarding dividends. Preferred stock generally also has a specified dividend rate, which does not change over time.

4. Preferred stock usually appears in the top part of the stockholders' equity section of the balance sheet.

B. Cumulative Dividends

1. The **cumulative** characteristic of preferred stock requires that undeclared dividends accumulate and be paid in the future before common dividends.

2. The holders of cumulative preferred stock would receive all accumulated unpaid dividends (called **dividend arrearages**) before the holders of common shares receive anything. The amount of dividends in arrears is *not* a liability, because no dividends are owed until declared. However, dividends in arrears must be disclosed in a footnote to the balance sheet.

C. Preference in Liquidation

1. In addition to the cumulative dividend feature, preferred stock usually has a **liquidating value**, which is the preference to receive assets in the event of corporate liquidation. The exact liquidating value is stated on the stock certificate, and is often the same as par value.

2. In a liquidation when cash available exceeds the claims of creditors and preferred shareholders, the excess goes to the common shareholders as residual claimholders. When cash is insufficient to pay other claims, the common shareholders receive nothing.

D. Other Features of Preferred Stock

Each of the following characteristics affects the attractiveness of the security to potential investors. The issuing company chooses the mix of features that best meets its needs given the market conditions at the time the preferred stock is being offered.

1. A **participating** preferred stock ordinarily receives a minimum dividend but also receives higher dividends when the company has a very good year and pays substantial dividends on common shares. This might be an attractive feature that a company with strong growth opportunities might use to make its preferred stock more attractive and, thereby, lower the required dividend.

2. A **callable** preferred stock gives the issuing company the right to purchase the stock back from the owner upon payment of the **call price**, or **redemption price**. This call price is typically set 5% to 10% above the par value or issuance price of the stock to compensate investors for the fact that the stock can be automatically bought back at any time.

3. A **convertible** preferred stock gives the owner the option to exchange the preferred for common. Convertible securities typically carry a lower dividend rate because the investor can convert when it benefits him or her to do so.

E. Comparing Bonds and Preferred Stock

1. Preferred stock, like a bond, is a contract between an investor and an issuer that spells out each party's rights and responsibilities.

2. As companies may have many different bonds outstanding at any particular time, some companies issue a variety of preferred stock. Each issue is called a **series** and has distinct characteristics from other preferred stock issued by the company.

3. Preferred stock and bonds are similar securities in the sense that each pays a specific return to the investor.

    a. The specific return to bondholders is called interest and appears on the income statement as an expense.
    b. The specific return to preferred shareholders is a dividend and represents a distribution of profits, which reduces the retained income account directly.

4. Preferred stock and bonds differ:

    a. In that dividends only become a liability of the company when they are declared, while interest due to a bondholder becomes a liability as it becomes due.

    b. Also because bonds have specific maturity dates, at which time they must be repaid, but preferred stock typically has an unlimited life.

5. From the investor's perspective, preferred stock is riskier than bonds because it never matures and the company does not have to declare dividends.

B. Cash Dividends

1. *Dividends* are proportional distributions of assets to shareholders to satisfy their claims arising from the generation of net income.

2. The following dates are related to dividends:

    a. The **declaration date** is the date on which the board formally announces that it will pay a dividend. The declaration will specify the amount of the dividend, and it becomes a liability on that date.

    b. The board specifies a **date of record,** which is a future date that determines which stockholders will receive the dividend. No entry is required on the date of record, although the company's stock transfer agent must identify all parties to whom dividends will be paid as of that date.

    c. The actual **payment date** is the day the checks are mailed and follows the date of record by a few days or weeks.

3.   The amount of cash dividends declared by the board of directors depends on many factors including the stock market's expectations, current and predicted earnings, and the corporation's current cash position and financial plans regarding spending on plant assets and repayment of debt.

> **STUDY TIP:**
> Remember that payment of cash dividends requires cash. Thus the single biggest factor affecting the size of dividends is the availability of cash that is not otherwise committed. The least important factor in the dividend decision is the amount of retained income.

L. O. 4: Identify the Economic Characteristics of Stock Splits and Dividends

A.   Additional Stock Issuance

After the company is formed, companies occasionally issue additional shares to investors, to executives or to current shareholders. There are several motivations and several procedures for additional stock issues. Such minor differences in the distribution lead to the use of a different term for the transaction and to somewhat different accounting.

B.   Stock Options

1.   **Stock options** are rights often granted to executives to purchase a corporation's capital stock. Although options have assorted conditions, a typical option grants the holder the right to purchase shares during some specified time in the *future* at *today's* market price (the exercise price, which is set at the date of grant).

2.   Options are frequently given to corporate officers as a form of incentive compensation. Executive options may not be sold to others.

3.   The FASB has considered the reporting issue related to stock options and has chosen to require extensive disclosure of options, but not to require expense recognition.

C.   Stock Splits and Stock Dividends

Several procedures exist for the company to issue additional shares of stock to its investors without receiving any money. In practice, such distributions of new shares take a variety of forms, specifically: the stock split and the stock dividend.

L. O. 5: Account for Stock Splits and Both Large-Percentage and Small-Percentage Stock Dividends

A.   Accounting for Stock Splits

1.   A **stock split** refers to the issuance of additional shares to existing shareholders without any additional cash payment to the firm.

a.   Shareholders are as well off as they were before because they have paid no additional money and they still have the same proportional ownership interest in the company.

b. Stock is often split because it causes the stock price to fall on a per share basis.

2. In a stock split, usually no accounting entry occurs because the number of shares increases and the par value is reduced. Thus, the total par value in the common stock account is unchanged.

3. Although less common, a company that did not want to bother physically exchanging the old par value stock certificates for new par value certificates, could simply issue more of the old par value shares. This would mean an accounting entry would be required to increase the par value of the common stock account and reduce additional paid-in capital.

4. Finally, a stock split could be accounted for as a stock dividend: this would mean issuing additional shares of the new par stock, and recording an accounting entry that would decrease retained earnings and increase the par value of the common stock account.

D. Accounting for Stock Dividends

Stock dividends are also issuances of additional shares to existing shareholders without additional cash payment, but the number of new shares issued is usually smaller than in a split, and there is no change in par value.

E. Large-Percentage Stock Dividends

1. Large-percentage stock dividends (typically those 20% or higher) are accounted for at par or stated value. As in the case of stock splits, the market value of the outstanding shares tends to adjust completely when additional shares are issued.

2. An accounting entry is made to transfer the par or stated value of the new shares from the retained income account to the common stock account within stockholders' equity.

3. In substance, there is absolutely no difference between a 100% stock dividend and a two-for-one stock split. In form, the shareholder receiving a dividend has different par value shares.

F. Small-Percentage Stock Dividends

1. When a stock dividend of less than 20% is issued, accountants require that the dividend be accounted for at market value, *not* at par value. This is partly the result of tradition and partly because small-percentage stock dividends often accompany increases in the total dividend payments or other changes in the company's financial policies.

2. The individual shareholder receives no assets from the corporation, and the corporation receives no cash from the shareholder. Also, because the overall number of shares and the number of shares held by each investor have both increased, the shareholders' fractional interest is unchanged.

3. The company records the small-percentage dividend transaction by transferring the market value of the additional shares from retained income to common stock and additional paid-in capital.

G. Why Use Stock Splits and Dividends?

1. Splits allow the company to maintain the stock price in a trading range accessible to small investors and company employees.

2. Often a stock split or stock dividend accompanies other announcements, such as new corporate investment strategies or changes in cash dividend levels.

H. Relation of Dividends and Splits

Companies typically use large-percentage stock dividends to accomplish exactly the same purpose as a stock split: the companies want a material reduction in the market price of their shares and simultaneously they want to signal an increase in total dividend payments to shareholders.

I. Fractional Shares

When shareholders are entitled to stock dividends in amounts equal to fractional units corporations issue additional shares for whole units plus cash equal to the market value of the fractional amount.

J. The Investor's Accounting for Dividends and Splits

 **& REVIEW:**

Review the **journal entries for the investor's accounting of dividends and splits** in the textbook.

L. O. 6: Interpret Treasury Stock Transactions

A. Repurchase of Outstanding Shares

1. Companies repurchase their own shares for two main purposes:

   a. To permanently reduce shareholder claims, called *retiring stock*.

   b. To temporarily hold shares for later use, most often to be granted as part of employee bonus or stock purchase plans. These temporarily held shares are called *treasury stock*.

2. The purpose of the repurchase determines which stockholders' equity accounts are affected.

B. Retirement of Shares

1. A retirement of stock reduces the total stockholders' equity, the stock certificates are canceled, and the shares are no longer issued and outstanding.

2. Sometimes when stock is retired **dilution** occurs. Dilution is usually defined as a reduction in stockholders' equity per share or earnings per share that arises from some changes among shareholders' proportionate interests.

 **& REVIEW:**

Review the **example and journal entry** in the textbook.

C.   Treasury Stock

    1.   Treasury stock is a decrease in stockholders' equity; it is *not* an asset as it does not generate revenue. Cash dividends are not paid on shares held in the treasury because treasury stock is not considered outstanding.

    2.   The treasury stock account is a contra account to stockholders' equity. A separate treasury stock account is a deduction from total stockholders' equity on the balance sheet.

    3.   The common stock at par value, additional paid-in capital, and retained income accounts remain untouched by treasury stock purchases.

STOP & REVIEW:

    Review **Exhibit 11-7** in the textbook.

D.   Disposition of Treasury Stock

    1.   If treasury shares are resold below their cost, accountants tend to debit (decrease) additional paid-in capital for the difference.

    2.   Although the specific accounting for transactions in a company's own stock may vary from company to company, one rule is constant: any differences between the acquisition costs and the resale proceeds of treasury stock must never be reported as losses, expenses, revenues, or gains in the income statement. Changes in a corporation's capitalization should produce no gain or loss but should merely require direct adjustments to the owners' equity.

E.   Effect of Repurchases on Earnings Per Share

    1.   When shares are repurchased for any reason, the number of shares outstanding is reduced which will tend to increase earnings per share.

    2.   The only time a repurchase lowers earnings per share is when using cash to repurchase shares leads to lower earnings.

L. O. 7:   Record Conversions of Debt For Equity Or of Preferred Stock Into Common Stock

A.   Noncash Exchanges

The proper dollar value of a noncash transaction is the "fair value" of either the securities or the exchanged assets, whichever is more objectively determinable. Both companies should use that amount.

STOP & REVIEW:

    Review the **example and journal entries** in the textbook.

B.   Conversion of Securities

    1.   When companies issue *convertible* bonds or preferred stock, the conversion feature makes the securities more attractive to investors and increases the price the issuer receives (or, equivalently, reduces the interest or dividend it must pay).

    2.   Since the conversion is a transaction of form rather than substance, the accounts are simply adjusted as if the common stock had been issued initially.

 **& REVIEW:**

    Review the **example and journal entries** in the textbook.

C.   Retained Income Restrictions

    1.   To protect creditors, dividend-declaring power is restricted by either state laws or contractual obligations or both. Boards of directors can also voluntarily restrict their declarations of dividends.

    2.   States typically do not permit dividends if stockholders' equity is less than total paid-in capital. Therefore, retained income must exceed the cost of treasury stock. If there is no treasury stock, retained income must be positive.

    3.   Most of the time, restrictions of retained income are disclosed by footnotes.

        a.   Occasionally, restrictions appear as a line item on the balance sheet called **restricted retained income**, **appropriated retained income**, or **reserve**. The term reserve can be misleading as it has three broad meanings in accounting. In the United States the use of retained earnings reserves is limited.

L. O. 8:   Use the Rate of Return on Common Equity and Book Value Per Share

Financial Ratios Related to Stockholders' Equity

    1.   The **rate of return on common equity (ROE)** is defined as:

$$\frac{Net\ income\ \text{-}\ Preferred\ dividends}{Average\ common\ equity}$$

    2.   The **book value per share of common stock** is calculated as:

$$\frac{Total\ stockholders'\ equity\ \text{-}\ Book\ value\ of\ preferred\ stock}{Number\ of\ common\ shares\ outstanding}$$

STUDY TIP:
Study the "Summary Problems for Your Review" and solutions in the text.

 **& REVIEW:**

    Before continuing, review the objectives for this chapter and make sure you have a good understanding of each one.

V. Test Yourself

Questions

1. Discuss the rights of shareholders.

2. Differentiate among authorized, issued, and outstanding shares.

3. Explain the characteristics of preferred stock.

4. Discuss treasury stock and how it is accounted for.

5. Describe the motivation for and importance of restrictions on retained earnings.

Exercises and Problems

1. The following information is available for Greenlawn Corporation in 19X8:

8%, cumulative, preferred stock, $50 par, 25,000 shares authorized, 10,000 shares issued and outstanding	$500,000
Common stock, $1 par value, 100,000 shares authorized, issued and outstanding	100,000
Paid-in capital - common stock	495,000
Retained earnings	200,000
Total stockholders' equity	$1,295,000

Earnings 19X9 through 20X4:

Year	Net income
19X9	$ (100,000)
20X0	(50,000)
20X1	-0-
20X2	200,000
20X3	300,000
20X4	450,000

The board of directors declared total dividend distributions of $100,000 in 20X2, $180,000 in 20X3, and $270,000 in 20X4.

A. What was the total amount the company was in arrears in 20X1?

B. What was the total amount of common stock dividends paid through 20X4?

C. What is the balance in retained earnings at the end of year 20X4?

Data for use with #2 - #4

On October 1, 19X9, the board of directors declared a 10% stock dividend. At the time of the declaration there were 1,450,000, $10 par value common shares outstanding with a fair market value of $16 per share. Retained earnings was $8,250,000, and paid-in capital totaled $5,800,000.

2. Record the journal entry recognizing the distribution of the stock dividend.

3.   Assume the same facts except that the board declared a 2-1 stock split. Show the stockholders' equity section before and after the split.

4.   Assume the same facts again except in this case the board declared a 50% stock dividend. Show the stockholders' equity section before and after the stock dividend.

5.   For each of the following items, state whether its effect will be to increase, decrease, or have no change in total stockholders' equity.

		Effect
a.	Issue preferred stock at a price greater than par value.	_____
b.	Declare the current year preferred stock dividend.	_____
c.	Pay the declared dividend in b.	_____
d.	Not declaring any dividends on cumulative preferred stock, thus having dividends in arrears.	_____
e.	Having a company call all callable preferred stock.	_____
f.	Declaring and issuing a 50% stock dividend.	_____
g.	Purchasing treasury stock.	_____
h.	Selling treasury stock for more than the purchase price.	_____
I.	Converting preferred stock to common stock.	_____

Matching

MATCH EACH TERM WITH ITS DEFINITION BY WRITING THE APPROPRIATE LETTER IN THE SPACE PROVIDED.

Terms

_____ 1. Authorized shares

_____ 2. Book value per share of common

_____ 3. Callable

_____ 4. Convertible

_____ 5. Corporate proxy

_____ 6. Cumulative

_____ 7. Date of record

_____ 8. Declaration date

_____ 9. Dilution

_____ 10. Dividend arrearages

_____ 11. Issued shares

_____ 12. Liquidating value

_____ 13. Outstanding shares

_____ 14. Participating

_____ 15. Payment date

_____ 16. Preemptive rights

_____ 17. Preferred stock

_____ 18. Stock dividends

_____ 19. Stock option

_____ 20. Stock split

_____ 21. Treasury stock

Definitions

A. A measure of the preference to receive assets in the event of corporate liquidation.

B. A characteristic of bonds or preferred stock that gives the holder the right to exchange the security for common stock.

C. The rights to acquire a pro-rata amount of any new issues of capital stock.

D. Accumulated unpaid dividends on preferred stock.

E. Issuance of additional shares to existing stockholders for no payments by the stockholders, and par value is usually adjusted.

F. A characteristic of preferred stock that provides increasing dividends when common dividends increase.

G. Reduction in stockholders' equity per share or earnings per share that arises from some changes among shareholders' proportional interests.

H. The aggregate number of shares potentially in the hands of shareholders.

I. The date dividends are paid.

J. Stock that has some priority over other shares regarding dividends or the distribution of assets upon liquidation.

K. Special rights usually granted to executives to purchase a corporation's capital stock.

L.   Shares in the hands of shareholders.

M.   The date the board of directors declares a dividend.

N.   The total number of shares that may legally be issued under the articles of incorporation.

O.   Stockholders' equity attributable to common stock divided by the number of shares outstanding.

P.   A characteristic of bonds or preferred stock that gives the issuer the right to redeem the security at a fixed price.

Q.   A corporation's issued stock that has subsequently been repurchased by the company and not retired.

R.   A distribution to stockholders of additional shares of any class of the distributing company's stock, without any payment to the company by the stockholders, and the par value is typically retained.

S.   A written authority granted by individual shareholders to others to cast the shareholders' votes.

T.   The date when ownership is fixed for determining the right to receive a dividend.

U.   A characteristic of preferred stock that requires that undeclared dividends accumulate and be paid in the future before common dividends.

Multiple Choice

SELECT THE BEST ANSWER AND ENTER THE IDENTIFYING LETTER IN THE SPACE PROVIDED.

_____ 1.　The ultimate power to manage a corporation almost always resides with the:

　　a.　Board of directors.
　　b.　Management.
　　c.　Common shareholders.
　　d.　Preferred and common shareholders.

_____ 2.　Outstanding shares may be defined as equal to:

　　a.　Authorized shares - treasury shares.
　　b.　Issued shares - treasury shares.
　　c.　Treasury shares + issued shares.
　　d.　Treasury shares + authorized shares.

_____ 3.　Upon liquidation of assets, which of the following is correct as to priority of claims?

　　a.　Liabilities, common shareholders, preferred shareholders.
　　b.　Preferred shareholders, common shareholders, liabilities.
　　c.　Common shareholders, preferred shareholders, liabilities.
　　d.　Liabilities, preferred shareholders, common shareholders.

_____ 4.　A call feature on a preferred stock:

　　a.　Gives the issuing company the right to purchase the stock back from the owner upon payment of the call price.
　　b.　Gives the owner the right to sell the stock back to the issuing company at the call price.
　　c.　Typically sets the redemption price 5% to 10% below the issuance price of the stock.
　　d.　None of the above are correct.

_____ 5.　Electronics, Inc.'s board of directors declared a dividend on October 1, 19X9, of $4.30 per share to stockholders of record December 31, 19X9. The dividend would be paid on January 15, 20X0. Electronics' year ends November 30. The corporation will record a liability on:

　　a.　January 15.
　　b.　December 31.
　　c.　November 30.
　　d.　October 1.

_____ 6.　When a small-percentage stock dividend occurs:

　　a.　Common stock is debited.
　　b.　Retained earnings is reduced by the par value of the common stock issued.
　　c.　Retained earnings is increased by the market value of the stock issued.
　　d.　Retained earnings is reduced by the market value of the stock issued.

_____ 7. When a large-percentage stock dividend occurs:

    a. Common stock is debited.
    b. Retained earnings is reduced by the par value of the common stock issued.
    c. Retained earnings is increased by the market value of the stock issued.
    d. Retained earnings is reduced by the market value of the stock issued.

_____ 8. When a board of directors decides to retire shares of stock:

    a. The journal entry reverses the original average paid-in capital per share and charges the additional amount to retained income.
    b. The journal entry reduces paid-in capital for the amount the corporation paid to repurchase the stock that was in excess of the par value.
    c. No journal entry is required when retiring stock.
    d. None of the above are correct.

_____ 9. When treasury shares are resold:

    a. The cost of the treasury stock is removed from the books.
    b. Additional paid-in capital may be debited or credited depending on the price received for the treasury stock.
    c. Gains or losses are not recorded in treasury stock transactions.
    d. All of the above are correct.

_____ 10. Conversion of preferred stock to common stock:

    a. May trigger a gain or loss.
    b. Is at the option of the issuing company.
    c. Rearranges the issuing corporation's owners' equity.
    d. None of the above are correct.

VI. Solutions Test Yourself

Questions

1. Stockholders are entitled to: vote, share in corporate profits, share residually in corporate assets upon liquidation, and acquire more shares of subsequent issues of stock to maintain their percentage of ownership.

   Perhaps the most important right of common shareholders is *limited liability*, which means that creditors of the corporation have claims only on the assets owned by the corporation, not on the assets of the owners of the corporation. (L. O. 1)

2. A state approves the articles of incorporation, which includes authorization of the number and types of capital stock that can be issued. The total number of shares that may be issued is known as *authorized* shares. When the company receives cash in exchange for stock certificates, the shares become *issued* shares. Shares that are issued and held by the stockholders are called *outstanding* shares. Shares that are issued but no longer outstanding because the company reacquired the shares by purchasing them from its own shareholders are called *treasury stock*. (L. O. 2)

3. Preferred stock is stock that has some priority over other shares regarding dividends or the distribution of assets upon liquidation. It generally has a specified dividend rate, which does not change over time and usually appears in the top part of the stockholders' equity section of the balance sheet

   The cumulative characteristic of preferred stock requires that undeclared dividends accumulate and be paid in the future before common dividends. The amount of dividends in arrears (dividend arrearages) is *not* a liability, because no dividends are owed until declared. However, dividends in arrears must be disclosed in a footnote to the balance sheet.

   In addition to the cumulative dividend feature, preferred stock usually has a liquidating value, which is the preference to receive assets in the event of corporate liquidation. The exact liquidating value is stated on the stock certificate, and is often the same as par value. In a liquidation when cash available exceeds the claims of creditors and preferred shareholders, the excess goes to the common shareholders as residual claim holders. When cash is insufficient to pay other claims, the common shareholders receive nothing.

   Each of the following characteristics affects the attractiveness of the security to potential investors. The issuing company chooses the mix of features that best meets its needs given the market conditions at the time the preferred stock is being offered.

   1. A participating preferred ordinarily receives a minimum dividend but also receives higher dividends when the company has a very good year and pays substantial dividends on common shares. This might be an attractive feature that a company with strong growth opportunities might use to make its preferred stock more attractive and, thereby, increase its price.

   2. A callable preferred gives the issuing company the right to purchase the stock back from the owner upon payment of the call price, or redemption price.

   3. A convertible preferred gives the owner the option to exchange the preferred for common. Convertible securities typically carry a lower dividend rate because the investor can convert when it benefits him or her to do so. (L. O. 3)

4. Treasury stock is a decrease in stockholders' equity; it is *not* an asset. The treasury stock account is a contra account to stockholders' equity. A separate treasury stock account is a deduction from total stockholders' equity on the balance sheet. Common stock at par value, additional paid-in capital, and retained income accounts remain untouched by treasury stock purchases.

    If treasury shares are resold below their cost, accountants tend to debit (decrease) additional paid-in capital for the difference.

    Although the specific accounting for transactions in a company's own stock may vary from company to company, one rule is constant: any differences between the acquisition costs and the resale proceeds of treasury stock must never be reported as losses, expenses, revenues, or gains in the income statement. Changes in a corporation's capitalization should produce no gain or loss but should merely require direct adjustments to the owners' equity. (L. O. 6)

5. To protect creditors, dividend-declaring power is restricted by either state laws or contractual obligations or both. Boards of directors can also voluntarily restrict their declarations of dividends.

    States typically do not permit dividends if stockholders' equity is less than total paid-in capital. Therefore, retained income must exceed the cost of treasury stock. If there is no treasury stock, retained income must be positive.

    Most of the time, restrictions of retained income are disclosed by footnotes. (L. O.7)

Exercises and Problems

1.

Preferred Dividends

Year	Net income	Declared	In arrears	Common Dividend	End. Balance Retained Earnings
					$200,000
19X9	$(100,000)	—	$ 40,000	—	100,000
20X0	(50,000)	—	80,000	—	50,000
20X1	-0-	—	120,000	—	50,000
20X2	200,000	$100,000	60,000	—	150,000
20X3	300,000	100,000	—	$ 80,000	270,000
20X4	450,000	40,000	—	230,000	450,000
				$310,000	

A. In 20X1 the total amount the company was in arrears was $120,000

B. The total amount of common stock dividends paid through 20X4 was $310,000

C. The balance in retained earnings at the end of year 20X4 was $450,000

2.

Retained earnings (1,450,000 X .10 X $16)	2,320,000	
Common stock (145,000 X $10)		1,450,000
Paid-in capital		870,000

3.

	Before	After
Common stock	$14,500,000	$ 14,500,000
Paid-in capital	5,800,000	5,800,000
Retained earnings	8,250,000	8,250,000
Total Stockholders' equity	$28,550,000	$28,550,000

The only change occurs to par value and the number of shares outstanding.

4.

	Before	After
Common stock	$14,500,000	$21,750,000
Paid-in capital	5,800,000	5,800,000
Retained earnings	8,250,000	1,000,000
Total Stockholders' equity	$28,550,000	$28,550,000

The difference in this situation is the transfer of par value of $7,250,000 from retained earnings to common stock for the shares distributed.
    (1,450,000 shares X .50 X $10 par = $7,250,000)

5.

a.	Increase		f.	No change
b.	Decrease		g.	Decrease
c.	No change		h.	Increase
d.	No change		I.	No change
e.	Decrease			

Matching

1.	N	L. O. 2	8.	M	L. O. 3	15.	I	L. O. 3
2.	O	L. O. 8	9.	G	L. O. 6	16.	C	L. O. 1
3.	P	L. O. 3	10.	D	L. O. 3	17.	J	L. O. 3
4.	B	L. O. 3	11.	H	L. O. 2	18.	R	L. O. 4
5.	S	L. O. 1	12.	A	L. O. 3	19.	K	L. O. 4
6.	U	L. O. 3	13.	L	L. O. 2	20.	E	L. O. 4
7.	T	L. O. 3	14.	F	L. O. 1	21.	Q	L. O. 2

Multiple Choice

1. c   Common shareholders hold the ultimate power to manage a corporation but in publicly held corporations, usually delegate that power to a board of directors and top management. (L. O. 1)

2. b   (L. O. 2)

3. d   (L. O. 3)

4. a   A call feature gives the *issuing* company the right to purchase the stock, at its option, back from the owner upon payment of the call price. Because of this, the redemption price is typically set 5% to 10% *above* the issuance price of the stock. (L. O. 3)

5. d   A liability is recorded on the declaration date, October 1. (L. O. 3)

6. d   Small-percentage stock dividends are accounted for at *market* value. (L. O. 5)

7. b   Large-percentage stock dividends are accounted for at *par* value. (L. O. 5)

8. a   (L. O. 6)

9. d   (L. O. 7)

10. c   (L. O. 7)

Chapter 12

INTERCORPORATE INVESTMENTS AND CONSOLIDATIONS

I. Learning Objectives

Proper management of resources may include holding investments in another company's securities. These investments may take the form of short-term investments of idle cash, or may be a substantial enough long-term investment to warrant compilation of consolidated statements. Whatever the case, it is necessary for a manager to be familiar with the proper accounting practices and procedures associated with short- and long-term investments. Use the following objectives as focal points to support your understanding of this chapter.

1. Account for short-term investments in debt securities and equity securities.

2. Report long-term investments in bonds.

3. Contrast the equity and market methods of accounting for investments.

4. Prepare consolidated financial statements.

5. Incorporate minority interests into consolidated financial statements.

6. Explain the economic and reporting role of goodwill.

7. Contrast the purchase method and the pooling-of-interests method of accounting for business combinations. (Appendix 12)

II.   Pretest

SELECT THE BEST ANSWER AND ENTER THE IDENTIFYING LETTER IN THE SPACE PROVIDED.

_____ 1.   The key point in deciding if an investment is to be classified as short-term or long-term is:

   a.   The investment can be converted to cash even if management intends to hold the investment for years.
   b.   Conversion to cash is immediately available when needed at the option of management.
   c.   The investment must be a cash equivalent.
   d.   None of the above is correct.

_____ 2.   Trading securities:

   a.   Are current investments that the company acquires with a short-term profit motive.
   b.   Are accounted for at market value.
   c.   Have related gains and losses recorded and recognized in the income statement as their value changes over time.
   d.   All of the above are correct.

_____ 3.   When a long-term investment in bonds is purchased at a discount, the amortization of the discount:

   a.   Increases the interest revenue of the investors.
   b.   Decreases the interest revenue of the investors.
   c.   Has no impact on the interest revenue of the investors.
   d.   None of the above are correct.

_____ 4.   If a long-term investment in bonds is sold on the open market prior to the maturity date:

   a.   Only gains may be recognized at the date of sale.
   b.   FASB #115 does not permit the sale of long-term investments prior to maturity date.
   c.   A gain or loss may be recognized depending on the book value and selling price of the bonds.
   d.   None of the above are correct.

_____ 5.   The equity method of accounting for an investment in equity securities of another company is required when the investor:

   a.   Owns few shares of stock and is a passive investor.
   b.   Has significant influence over the affiliated company.
   c.   Controls more than 50% of the other companies outstanding stock.
   d.   None of the above are correct.

_____ 6. Which of the following is *not* part of the definition of the equity method?   The equity method accounts for the investment:

    a.   At acquisition cost.
    b.   Adjusted for the investor's share of dividends.
    c.   Adjusted for the investor's share of earnings and losses of the investee subsequent to the date of investment.
    d.   All of the above are part of the definition of the equity method.

_____ 7. Which of the following is *not* a reason for having a subsidiary instead of a single legal entity?

    a.   Limiting the liabilities in a risky venture.
    b.   Saving income taxes.
    c.   Doing business in a foreign country.
    d.   All of the above are reasons for having a subsidiary instead of a single legal entity.

_____ 8. Which of the following statements is *true* of the concept of consolidated financial statements?

    a.   The subsidiary is entirely unaffected from an accounting standpoint by the parent's investment and subsequent accounting.
    b.   The consolidated entity keeps a separate set of books.
    c.   The subsidiary is dissolved as a separate legal concept.
    d.   None of the above are true.

_____ 9. Minority interests are:

    a.   The outside shareholders' interests in a parent corporation.
    b.   The interests of management in a subsidiary corporation.
    c.   The nonmajority shareholders' interest in a subsidiary corporation.
    d.   The nonmajority shareholders' interest in a parent corporation.

_____ 10. In consolidated financial statements, minority interests are:

    a.   Reported on the balance sheet as a liability.
    b.   Shown as a reduction to net income on the income statement.
    c.   Reported as a net reduction of the investment in the subsidiary on the balance sheet.
    d.   None of the above are correct.

_____ 11. An investing company is willing to pay more for a going concern than pay less for the individual assets that could produce the same products because:

    a.   Customers pay more for a known brand product.
    b.   Known brands are given more prominent display space.
    c.   Customers believe that known brands offer reliable quality.
    d.   All of the above are correct.

_____ 12. Which of the following is *not* true of goodwill amortization?

    a.   Current GAAP allows for the amortization of goodwill to be up to 40 years.
    b.   Current GAAP does not allow an immediate write-off of goodwill.
    c.   The periods over which goodwill can be amortized vary from country to country.
    d.   All of the above are true of goodwill.

_____ 13.   Which of the following is *not* part of the definition of pooling-of-interests? A pooling-of-interests:

    a.   Is a way to account for the combination of two corporations.
    b.   Is based on the market values of the acquired company's net assets.
    c.   Must occur in a single transaction.
    d.   All of the above are true of a pooling-of-interests.

_____ 14.   The purchase method:

    a.   Accounts for a business combination on the basis of the market prices actually paid.
    b.   Is a purchase of one company by another company.
    c.   Pays stockholders of the acquired company for their stock and they are no longer stockholders or owners.
    d.   All of the above are correct.

III. Answers to Pretest

1. b The decision as to whether an investment is short- or long-term must include the intention of management, and that the investment can be converted to cash immediately when needed. (L. O. 1)

2. d (L. O. 1)

3. a Amortization of bond discounts for an *investor increases* interest *revenue*. Amortization of a bond discount for the *issuer* of a bond *increases* interest *expense*. (L. O. 2)

4. c Whenever an asset is sold, a gain or loss may be recognized depending on the book value and selling price of the asset. This would, therefore, also be true for long-term investments. (L. O. 2)

5. b An affiliated company is a company that has 20% to 50% of its voting stock owned by another company. This presumes the investor has the ability to exert significant influence over the affiliated company. (L. O. 3)

6. d (L. O. 3)

7. d (L. O. 4)

8. a The consolidated entity does *not* keep a separate set of books. Both the subsidiary and parent are separate legal entities with separate accounting systems. (L. O.4)

9. c (L. O. 5)

10. b The minority interests' share of the subsidiarys' net income is deducted from the consolidated net income on the income statement. On the balance sheet the minority interest is usually shown as a separate item just above stockholders' equity. (L. O. 5)

11. d (L. O. 6)

12. d (L. O. 6)

13. b A pooling-of-interests is based on the *book* values of the acquired company's net assets (L. O. 7)

14. d (L. O. 7)

EVALUATION

The pretest contained two questions for each learning objective. If you did not answer both questions correctly for each learning objective, you should review the appropriate section of the textbook and study guide before you attempt the material after Part IV.

IV. Key Concept Review by Learning Objectives

L. O. 1: Account for Short-Term Investments in Debt Securities and Equity Securities

A. An Overview of Corporate Investments

    1.   When a firm has an excess of cash, sound management dictates that the cash be invested rather than remain idle.

    2.   Corporations frequently make both short- and long-term investments in debt securities issued by governments, banks, and other corporations.

    3.   Companies also invest in other corporations' equity securities. These investments are typically long-term, and when they are large enough, they allow the investing company varying degrees of control over the company issuing the securities.

    4.   After companies create intercorporate linkages, the accountant must develop ways to report on the financial results of these complicated entities.

    5.   All investments made by companies are classified on a balance sheet according to purpose, or intention.

        a.   An investment should be carried as a current asset if it is a short-term investment.

        b.   Other investments are classified as noncurrent assets and usually appear as either a separate investments category between current assets and property, plant, and equipment, or a part of other assets below the plant assets category.

B. Short-Term Investments

    1.   A **short-term investment** is a temporary investment of otherwise idle cash in **marketable securities**. Marketable securities are notes, bonds, or stocks that can be easily sold.

    2.   Short-term investments are *expected* to be completely converted into cash within a year after the balance sheet date on which they appear.

        a.   However, investments held beyond one year are still classified as current assets if management intends to convert them into cash *when needed*.

        b.   The key point is that conversion to cash is immediately available at the option of management.

    3.   **Short-term debt securities** consist largely of notes and bonds with maturities of one year or less. They represent interest-bearing debt of businesses and governments and may be held until maturity or may be resold in securities markets.

        a.   Debt security investments include short-term obligations of banks, called **certificates of deposit**, and **commercial paper**, which consists of short-term notes payable issued by large corporations with top credit ratings. They also include **U.S. Treasury obligations**, which refer to interest bearing notes, bonds, and bills issued by the federal government.

b.   Investors purchase debt securities to gain the interest income, which is recognized as it accrues.

4.   **Short-term equity securities** consist of capital stock in other corporations that are regularly traded on the New York and other stock exchanges. If the investing firm intends to sell the equity securities it holds within one year or within its normal operating cycle, then the securities are considered a short-term investment.

5.   Although these securities are initially recorded at cost, how they are reported after acquisition depends on whether they are classified as trading securities, available-for-sale securities, or held-to-maturity securities.

   a.   **Trading securities** are short-term investments of both debt and equity securities that the company acquires only with the intent to resell them shortly. These securities are accounted for at market value, and market valuation is the basis for valuation on the balance sheet.

   b.   **Held-to-maturity securities** are debt securities that the company purchases with the intent to hold them until they mature, and are classified according to the time remaining until they mature and are repaid. They are accounted for at amortized cost, not market value.

   c.   **Available-for-sale securities** include all debt and equity securities that fall between trading and held-to-maturity in terms of intent. The accounting is based on market values, which are reported on the balance sheet.

C.   Changes in Market Prices of Securities

1.   Changes in market value are ignored for held-to-maturity investments. Interest revenue appears directly on the income statement, increasing income and, therefore, increasing stockholders' equity.

2.   When marketable securities are held in a trading category or as available-for-sale they are carried in the financial statements using the **market method** where the reported asset values in the balance sheet are the market values of the publicly traded securities.

3.   For trading securities the changes in value appear as unrecognized gains or losses in the income statement.

4.   For available-for-sale securities the changes in value do not affect the income statement; rather the difference between historical cost and current market value are reported as valuation allowances in the owners' equity section of the balance sheet.

STOP & REVIEW:

Before continuing, carefully review **Exhibits 12-1 and 12-2**, and **journal entries** in the textbook.

L. O. 2: Report Long-Term Investments in Bonds

A. Bonds-Held-to-Maturity

1. Investors analyze bonds held-to-maturity in a parallel fashion to the issuer of bonds except that the investor typically does not keep a separate account for unamortized discounts and premiums.

2. For an investor, amortization of a discount *increases* the interest revenue of investors, and amortization of a premium *decreases* the interest revenue.

 **& REVIEW:**

Before continuing, carefully review **Exhibits 12-3** and **12-4** in the textbook.

C. Early Extinguishment of Investment

Gains or losses are recognized after all interest payments and amortization are recorded.

 **& REVIEW:**

Review **Exhibit 12-5** in the textbook before continuing.

> **STUDY TIP:**
> Remember that for the issuer to extinguish the bonds early, the bond must either grant the issuer the right to repay the debt early or the investor must chose to sell the bonds back to the issuer.

L. O. 3: Contrast the Equity and Market Methods of Accounting for Investments

The Market and Equity Methods for Intercorporate Investments

1. Long-term investments in the equity securities of one company are frequently made by another company. The investor's accounting depends on the relationship between the "investor" and the "investee" (or **affiliated company**).

2. The holder of a small number of shares in a company's stock is a passive investor and follows the market method, whereby the investment is carried at market and dividends are recorded as income when received. This type of investor cannot affect how the company invests its money, conducts its business, or declares and pays its dividends.

3. Once the investor has "significant influence" (about 20 - 25% ownership), the investor must use the **equity method**, which records the investment at acquisition cost and makes adjustments for the investors' share of dividends and earnings or losses of the investee after the date of investment. The carrying amount of the investment:

   a. Is increased by the investor's share of the investee's earnings.

   b. Is reduced by dividends received from the investee and by the investor's share of the investee's losses.

4. The market method is generally used to account for interests of less than 20% in an investee company. The equity method is generally used to account for a 20% to 50% interest in an investee company, and a more than 50% interest is accounted for through consolidation, which is based on the belief that the investor has control.

 **& REVIEW:**

Before continuing, carefully review **Exhibit 12-6** in the textbook.

L. O. 4: Prepare Consolidated Financial Statements

A. Consolidated Financial Statements

1. United States companies with substantial ownership of other companies constitute a single overall economic unit that is composed of two or more separate legal entities that almost always have a parent-subsidiary relationship. The **parent company** is the owner. The **subsidiary** is the "owned" company that is fully controlled by the parent.

2. The reasons to have subsidiaries as opposed to a single legal entity include: limiting the liabilities in a risky venture, saving income taxes, conforming with government regulations with respect to a part of the business, doing business in a foreign country, and expanding in an orderly way.

3. **Consolidated statements** combine the financial positions and earnings reports of the parent company with those of various subsidiaries into an overall report *as if* they were a single entity. The aim is to give the readers of the financial statements a better perspective than the readers could obtain by examining separate reports of individual companies.

B. The Acquisition

1. The purchase transaction when the parent company buys more than 50% of the outstanding voting shares of the subsidiary company is a simple exchange of one asset for another from the parent's perspective. The subsidiary is entirely unaffected from an accounting standpoint although it now has one majority owner with unquestionable control over all economic decisions the subsidiary may make in the future.

2. Each legal entity keeps its own set of books; the consolidated entity does not keep a separate set of books. Instead, working papers are used to prepare the consolidated statements.

3. The consolidated statements cannot show both the evidence of interest *plus* the detailed underlying assets and liabilities. This is avoided by eliminating entries on the consolidated worksheet, not on the books of the parent or subsidiary.

 **& REVIEW:**

Before continuing, carefully review **Exhibits 12-7** and **12-8,** and **the journal entries** in the textbook.

C.   After Acquisition

1.   After initial acquisition, the parent accounts for its long-term investment in the subsidiary by the same equity method used to account for an unconsolidated ownership interest of 20% through 50%.

2.   The only difference on the income statement is that under an unconsolidated ownership interest the parent's income statement shows its share of the investee company's net income or loss as a single item, whereas the consolidated income statement combines the detailed revenue and expense items for the parent and subsidiary.

STOP & REVIEW:

Carefully review **Exhibit 12-9** in the textbook.

D.   Intercompany Eliminations

When two or more companies are consolidated, double-counting needs to be avoided. The accountant needs to eliminate the intercompany receivables and payables, costs and revenues, and be sure the inventory is carried at its cost to the consolidated company.

STOP & REVIEW:

Carefully review the **continuing example** and **journal entries** in the textbook.

L. O. 5:   Incorporate Minority Interests into Consolidated Financial Statements

A.   Minority Interests

1.   **Minority interests** represent the rights of nonmajority shareholders in the assets and earnings of a company that is consolidated into the accounts of its major shareholder.

2.   The same basic procedures are followed regardless of whether the subsidiary is owned 100% or if there is a minority interest. However, the presence of a minority interest slightly changes the consolidated financial statements.

STOP & REVIEW:

Carefully review **Exhibits 12-10** and **12-11**, and **journal entries** in the textbook.

B.   Defining Control

Intercorporate investments occur worldwide, and different countries have made different choices about how to define control and about when to consolidate the financial results of two related companies.

L. O. 6:   Explain the Economic and Reporting Role of Goodwill

A.   Purchased Goodwill

   1.   When a parent company's total purchase price exceeds the sum of the fair market values of the identifiable individual assets less the liabilities of the subsidiary company such excess is called **goodwill**.

   2.   A parent would pay more for a subsidiary as a going concern rather than pay less for the same assets that would produce the same products because:

      a.   When customers consider a purchase, they know a known brand's quality and will pay more.

      b.   Known brands are given more prominent display space than unknown brands.

B.   Accounting for Goodwill

   The goodwill would appear in the consolidated balance sheet as a separate intangible asset account. It is usually amortized in a straight-line manner as an expense in the consolidated income statement over a period of not more than forty years.

STOP & REVIEW:

   Carefully review **Exhibit 12-12**, and **journal entries** in the textbook.

C.   Goodwill and Abnormal Earnings

   1.   A purchaser may be willing to pay more than the current values of the individual assets received because the acquired company is able to generate abnormally high earnings for a variety of reasons.

   2.   The final price paid by the purchaser of an ongoing business is the culmination of a bargaining process. There are steps for determining the maximum price.

STOP & REVIEW:

   Carefully review **Exhibit 12-13** in the textbook.

D.   Amortization of Goodwill

   1.   Current generally accepted accounting principles (GAAP) require that goodwill purchased after 1970 be amortized as an expense against net income over the period benefited, not to exceed forty years.

   2.   GAAP does not permit the lump-sum write-off of goodwill upon acquisition.

Perspective on Consolidated Statements

STOP & REVIEW:

   Before continuing, carefully review **Exhibit 12-14** and **related text** in the textbook.

The FASB requires that all subsidiaries be consolidated. One exception to that general rule is that a subsidiary shall not be consolidated if control is likely to be temporary or if that control does not rest with the majority owner.

Equity Affiliates and the Statement of Cash Flows

A company with equity affiliates may use the direct method or the indirect method to prepare its cash flow statement.

1. If the direct method is used, no special problem arises because only the cash received from the affiliate as a dividend appears.

2. If the indirect method is used, an adjustment to reported net income must be made for the investor's share of the investee's net earnings or losses that was included in the investor's net income.

 **& REVIEW:**

Review the **example** in the textbook.

Summary of Accounting for Equity Securities

 **& REVIEW:**

Carefully review **Exhibit 12-15** in the textbook before continuing.

> **STUDY TIP:**
> Study the "Summary Problems for Your Review" and solutions in the text before going on.

 **& REVIEW:**

Before continuing, review the objectives for this chapter and make sure you have a good understanding of each one.

Appendix 12: Pooling of Interest

L. O. 7: Contrast the Purchase Method and the Pooling-of-Interests Method of Accounting for Business Combinations

A. Nature of Pooling

1. The business combinations described thus far in this chapter were accounted for by using the **purchase method,** which is based on the *market prices* actually paid for the acquired company's assets.

    a. One company is obviously acquiring another and typically paying cash to do so.

b. The majority of shareholders of the acquired company sell their stock and go away; the owners of the purchaser now own a different, bigger company.

2. The **pooling-of-interests method** is a combination of two corporations based on the *book values* of the acquired company's net assets.

   a. Pooling is a uniting of ownership interests of two or more companies by the exchange of common stock. The recorded assets and liabilities of the fused companies are carried forward at their book values by the combined corporation.

   b. The combined corporation must completely adhere to a long list of restrictive conditions, including most importantly:

      1. The acquirer must issue voting common shares in exchange for substantially all (at least 90%) of the voting common shares of the acquired company.

      2. The acquisition must occur as a single transaction.

3. A detailed approach to the consolidation process for pooling is:

   a. Sum the individual assets and liabilities of both companies line by line.

   b. Sum the individual retained incomes.

   c. Adjust common stock at par and additional paid-in capital accounts.

 **& REVIEW:**

Before continuing, carefully review **Exhibits 12-16** and **12-17** in the textbook.

V. Test Yourself

Questions

1. Discuss the accounting for short-term debt and equity securities.

2. Explain the accounting for long-term bonds.

3. Discuss the equity method of accounting for investments.

4. Explain the preparation of consolidated financial statements.

5. Discuss the use of minority interests in consolidated financial statements.

Exercises and Problems

Data for use with #1 and #2

State Manufacturing acquired a 32% interest in Village Appliances for $705,000. During the following year Village Appliances had net income of $250,000 and distributed cash dividends of $75,000.

1. A. Compute the book value of State Manufacturing's investment in Village Appliances at the end of the period using the cost method.

   B. Compute the increase in State Manufacturing's stockholders' equity account by the cost method as a result of Village Appliances' operations during the period.

2. A. Compute the book value of State Manufacturing's investment in Village Appliances at the end of the period using the equity method.

   B. Compute the gross increase in State Manufacturing's stockholders' equity account by the equity method as a result of Village Appliances' operations during the period.

3. Snappy Dairy Products recently acquired an 80% voting interest in Jen and Barry's Ice Cream for the amount shown in the investment account.

Description	Snappy	J & B
Cash and other assets	$250,000	$225,000
Investment in J & B	180,000	—
Accounts payable, etc.	100,000	50,000
Stockholders' equity	400,000	225,000

   A. Compute the minority interests.

   B. Compute consolidated stockholders' equity.

   C. Compute consolidated cash and other assets.

   D. Compute consolidated net income for the first year after acquisition if Snappy earned $40,000, and J & B earned $27,000.

261

4. In 19X9 Island Computers purchased the assets of City Software for $1,250,000. The following data was available concerning City Software at the time of acquisition.

	Book Value	Fair Market Value
Cash	$ 50,000	$ 50,000
Accounts receivable	200,000	200,000
Inventory	300,000	400,000
Net fixed assets	500,000	450,000
Total	$1,050,000	$1,100,000

Compute the amount of goodwill that would be included in the consolidated statements upon completion of the acquisition.

5. On December 31, 19X9, General, Inc., repurchased on the open market all of its outstanding bonds. The bonds had a face value of $10,000 each, a 12% coupon rate, and 10 years left to maturity. General paid $10,500 for each of the outstanding bonds. At the time of the repurchase Motors, Inc., held 100 of the bonds which had a book value of $1,022,000. Compute the amount of the gain or loss that Motors would recognize on the early extinguishment of the bonds.

Matching

Terms

_____ 1. Affiliated companies

_____ 2. Available-for-sale securities

_____ 3. Consolidated statements

_____ 4. Equity method

_____ 5. Held-to-maturity securities

_____ 6. Market method

_____ 7. Minority interests

_____ 8. Parent company

_____ 9. Pooling-of-interests method

_____ 10. Purchase method

_____ 11. Short-term debt securities

_____ 12. Short-term equity securities

_____ 13. Short-term investments

_____ 14. Subsidiary

_____ 15. Trading securities

Definitions

A.   Debt securities that the investor expects to hold until maturity.

B.   A company owning more than 50% of the voting shares of another company.

C.   A temporary investment of otherwise idle cash in marketable securities.

D.   The method whereby the investment is carried at market and dividends received are recorded as revenues.

E.   A way of accounting for the acquisition of one company by another, based on the market prices paid for the acquired company's assets.

F.   A company that has 20% to 50% of its voting shares owned by another company.

G.   A corporation owned or controlled by another company through the ownership of more than 50% of the voting stock.

H.   Capital stock in other corporations held with the intention to liquidate within one year as needed.

I.   Combinations of the financial positions and earnings reports of the parent company with those of various subsidiaries into an overall report as a single entity.

J.   Current investments in equity or debt securities held for short-term profit.

K.   The outside shareholders' interests in a subsidiary corporation.

L.   Largely notes and bonds with maturities of one year or less.

M.   A way of accounting for the combination of two corporations based on the book values of the acquired company's net assets.

N.   Accounting for an investment at acquisition cost adjusted for the investor's share of dividends and earnings or losses of the investee subsequent to the date of investment.

O.   Investments in equity or debt securities that are not held for active trading but may be sold before maturity.

Multiple Choice

SELECT THE BEST ANSWER AND ENTER THE IDENTIFYING LETTER IN THE SPACE PROVIDED.

_____ 1.   Investments can be reported on the balance sheet as:

    a.   Current assets.
    b.   Noncurrent assets in a separate investment category.
    c.   Other assets.
    d.   All of the above are correct.

_____ 2.   Available-for-sale securities:

    a.   May include securities not held for active trading and securities that may be sold before maturity.
    b.   Are reported on the balance sheet at market value.
    c.   Unrealized gains and losses are carried in the stockholders' equity account.
    d.   All of the above are correct.

_____ 3.   The major justification for using the equity method instead of the market method is that:

    a.   It more appropriately recognizes increases and decreases in the economic resources that the investor can influence.
    b.   The reported net income of an equity investee is affected by its share of net income or net loss recognized by the investee.
    c.   The reported net income of the equity investor is affected by the dividend policies of the investee.
    d.   None of the above.

_____ 4.   A company accounts for its investment in another company's stock using the cost method. During 19X9 it received $5,000 in dividends as a result of this investment. The journal entry to record the receipt of these dividends would include:

    a.   A credit to long-term investments.
    b.   A debit to dividend revenue.
    c.   A credit to dividend revenue.
    d.   A credit to cash.

_____ 5.   A consolidated income statement:

    a.   Shows separately the revenues and expenses for both the parent and the subsidiary.
    b.   Combines the detailed revenue and expense items for the parent and the subsidiary.
    c.   Reports the subsidiary's net income as a single item.
    d.   None of the above are correct.

_____ 6. Which of the following is *not* considered when eliminating intercompany transactions?

    a. Receivables.
    b. Payables.
    c. Cost of goods available for sale.
    d. Merchandise inventory.

_____ 7. Minority interests:

    a. Do not permit consolidated statements.
    b. Are listed on the balance sheet as a separate item between liabilities and stockholders' equity.
    c. Are ignored unless they are 5% or more of the voting stock of the subsidiary.
    d. None of the above are correct.

_____ 8. A company paid $1,750,000 for a company that had a net book value of $1,250,000. The difference is referred to as:

    a. A long-term investment.
    b. Goodwill.
    c. Excess over book valuation.
    d. Investment coverage.

_____ 9. When two or more companies exchange voting stock in a single transaction sufficient enough to qualify for pooling-of-interests, at what value will the assets be recorded on the consolidated balance sheet?

    a. Fair market value at the date of the pooling.
    b. Book value prior to the pooling.
    c. Lower-of-cost-or-market at balance sheet date.
    d. Historical cost at the date of pooling.

_____ 10. When comparing purchase and pooling methods of accounting, which of the following is true?

    a. Asset values will be higher under pooling because of revaluation to generally higher fair market value.
    b. Retained earnings on the consolidated statements will be lower because the purchase method does not include retained earnings of the subsidiary.
    c. Both purchase and pooling methods include earnings from the beginning of the period in the consolidated statements.
    d. Under the pooling method, depreciation expense is based upon fair market values at the date of acquisition.

VI. Solutions to Test Yourself

Questions

1. Short-term debt securities consist largely of notes and bonds with maturities of one year or less. They represent interest-bearing debt of businesses and governments and may be held until maturity or may be resold in securities markets. Investors purchase debt securities to gain the interest income, which is recognized as it accrues.

    The investor's balance sheet shows short-term investments immediately after cash. Although these securities are initially recorded at cost, when their market values differ from cost there is a requirement to write them either up or down to their market value.

    Short-term equity securities consist of capital stock in other corporations that are regularly traded on the New York and other stock exchanges. If the investing firm intends to sell the equity securities it holds within one year or within its normal operating cycle, then the securities are considered a short-term investment.

    Current generally accepted accounting principles (GAAP) requires investments be classified in one of three categories: trading securities, available-for-sale securities, and securities-held-to-maturity. Trading securities are the current investments of both debt and equity securities that the company acquires with a short-term profit motive. These securities are accounted for at market value, and as the market value changes over time, gains and losses are recorded and recognized in the income statement. Market valuation is the basis for valuation on the balance sheet.

    Held-to-maturity securities are debt securities that the company purchases with the intent to hold them until they mature, and are classified according to the time remaining until they mature and are repaid. They are accounted for at amortized cost, not market value. Changes in market value are ignored for held-to-maturity investments. Interest revenue appears directly on the income statement, increasing income and, therefore, increasing stockholders' equity.

    Available-for-sale securities include all debt and equity securities that fall between trading and held-to-maturity in terms of intent. The accounting is based on market values, which are reported on the balance sheet. For available-for-sale securities the changes in value do not affect the income statement; rather the difference between historical cost and current market value are reported as valuation allowances in the owners' equity section of the balance sheet. (L. O. 1)

2. Investors analyze bonds held-to-maturity in a parallel fashion to the issuer of bonds except that the investor typically does not keep a separate account for unamortized discounts and premiums.

    For an investor, amortization of a discount *increases* the interest revenue, and amortization of a premium *decreases* the interest revenue. (L. O. 2)

3. Once the investor has "significant influence" (about 20 - 25% ownership), the investor must use the equity method, which accounts for the investment at acquisition cost adjusted for the investor's share of dividends and earnings or losses of the investee subsequent to the date of investment. The carrying amount of the investment:

    a. Is increased by the investor's share of the investee's earnings.
    b. Is reduced by dividends received from the investee and by the investor's share of the investee's losses.

266

The market method is generally used to account for interests of less than 20% in an investee company, the equity method to account for a 20% to 50% interest, and an interest of more than 50% is accounted for through consolidation which is based on the belief that the investor has control. (L. O. 3)

4. Consolidated statements combine the financial positions and earnings reports of the parent company with those of various subsidiaries into an overall report as if they were a single entity. The aim is to give the readers of the financial statements a better perspective than the readers could obtain by examining separate reports of individual companies.

    The purchase transaction when one company (the parent company) buys more than 50% of the outstanding voting shares of another company (the subsidiary company) is a simple exchange of one asset for another from the parent's perspective. The subsidiary is entirely unaffected from an accounting standpoint although it now has one majority owner with unquestionable control over all economic decisions the subsidiary may make in the future.

    Each legal entity has its individual set of books; the consolidated entity does not keep a separate set of books. Instead, working papers are used to prepare the consolidated statements. The consolidated statements cannot show both the evidence of interest *plus* the detailed underlying assets and liabilities. This is avoided by eliminating entries on the consolidated worksheet, not on the books of the parent or subsidiary.

    After initial acquisition, the parent accounts for its long-term investment in the subsidiary by the same equity method used to account for an unconsolidated ownership interest of 20% through 50%.

    The only difference on the income statement is that under an unconsolidated ownership interest the parent's income statement shows its share of the investee company's net income or loss as a single item, whereas the consolidated income statement combines the detailed revenue and expense items for the parent and subsidiary. (L. O. 4)

5. Minority interests represent the rights of nonmajority shareholders in the assets and earnings of a company that is consolidated into the accounts of its major shareholder.

    The same basic procedures are followed regardless of whether the subsidiary is owned 100% or if there is a minority interest. However, the presence of a minority interest slightly changes the consolidated financial statements. In consolidated income statements, minority interests' share of net subsidiary income is subtracted from net income to arrive at net income to consolidated entity. In consolidated balance sheets, the minority interest is usually shown as a separate item above stockholders' equity. (L. O.5)

Exercises and Problems

1.   A.   <u>$705,000</u>

         B. $75,000 X .32 = <u>$24,000</u>

2.   A.

Proportionate share of earnings:	($250,000 X .32)	$ 80,000
Proportionate share of dividends:	($75,000 X .32)	(24,000)
Net addition to investment account		$ 56,000
Plus: beginning balance investment account		705,000
Ending balance in the investment account		$ 761,000

         B. $250,000 X .32 = <u>$80,000</u>

3.   A.   Minority interest: $225,000 X .20 = <u>$45,000</u>

         B.   Only the stockholders' equity of the parent is included in the consolidated statements. The parent's investment account and the subsidiary's stockholders' equity accounts are eliminated on the consolidation worksheet. The minority interests would be shown separately on the balance sheet above stockholders' equity. The balance in the consolidated stockholders' equity account would be <u>$400,000</u>.

         C. $250,000 + $225,000 = <u>$475,000</u>

         D.

Parent's earnings	+	Subsidiary's earnings	-	Minority interest in earnings	=	Consolidated Net Income
$40,000	+	$27,000	-	.20($27,000)	=	<u>$61,600</u>

4.

Total purchase price	$1,250,000
Total fair market value	1,100,000
Goodwill	$ 150,000

5.

Book value	$1,022,000
Sales price (100 X $10,500)	1,050,000
Gain on early extinguishment	$ 28,000

Matching

1.	F	L. O. 3	6.	D	L. O. 3	11.	L	L. O. 1
2.	O	L. O. 1	7.	K	L. O. 5	12.	H	L. O. 1
3.	I	L. O. 4	8.	B	L. O. 4	13.	C	L. O. 1
4.	N	L. O. 3	9.	M	L. O. 7	14.	G	L. O. 4
5.	A	L. O. 1	10.	E	L. O. 7	15.	J	L. O. 1

Multiple Choice

1.   d   (L. O. 1)

2.   d   (L. O. 1)

3.   a   The reported net income of the *investor*, not investee, is affected by its share of the *investee's* net income or loss. Also, the net income of the investor is *not* affected by the receipt of dividends from the investee.   (L. O. 3)

4.   c   Using the cost method any dividends received would be recorded as dividend revenue. The investment account would be unaffected. (L. O. 3)

5.   b   A consolidated income statement is the summation of the individual revenue and expense accounts of two or more separate legal entities.   (L. O. 4)

6.   c   Cost of goods *sold*, not cost of goods *available for sale*, is an item that is considered in intercompany eliminations. (L. O. 4)

7.   b   (L. O. 5)

8.   b   From the textbook, "Such excess of purchase price over fair market value is called goodwill or purchased goodwill." (L. O. 6)

9.   b   Using the pooling-of-interest method assets are carried at book value prior to the combination. (L. O. 7)

10.   b   (L. O. 7)

Chapter 13

FINANCIAL STATEMENT ANALYSIS

I. Learning Objectives

Much of this text focuses on the theories and practices associated with construction of financial statements. The majority of this chapter deals with ratios and how to understand the financial statements as prepared under GAAP. To aid the reader in the decision-making process, attention is also given to understanding when special disclosure of nonrecurring items is necessary. Use the following learning objectives to guide your study of this important and interesting chapter.

1. Locate and use the many sources of information about company performance.

2. Analyze the components of a company using trend analysis and other techniques.

3. Use the basic financial ratios to guide your thinking.

4. Evaluate corporate performance using ROA and ROE.

5. Calculate EPS under complex circumstances.

6. Adjust for nonrecurring items.

7. Explain some effects on financial statements from translating foreign currencies.

II. Pretest

_____1.   Creditors are *least* concerned with:

      a.   Future security prices.
      b.   Profitability.
      c.   Short-term liquidity.
      d.   Creditors are concerned about all of the above.

_____ 2.   Investors are *least* concerned with:

      a.   Future security prices.
      b.   Profitability.
      c.   Short-term liquidity.
      d.   Investors are concerned about all of the above.

_____ 3.   Which of the following is *not* true of trend analysis? Trend analysis:

      a.   Examines changes over time.
      b.   Examines the relationships of percentage changes to each other.
      c.   Uses changes in dollar amount and percentage terms to identify patterns.
      d.   All of the above are true.

_____ 4.   Component analysis may concentrate on:

      a.   The relative size of current assets.
      b.   The gross margin percentage.
      c.   Different geographic areas of production.
      d.   All of the above.

_____ 5.   Which of the following is *not* a type of comparison for financial ratios?

      a.   Horizontal.
      b.   Time-series.
      c.   Bench mark.
      d.   Cross-sectional.

_____ 6.   Which of the following is a short-term liquidity ratio?

      a.   Quick ratio.
      b.   Current ratio.
      c.   Inventory turnover.
      d.   All of the above are short-term liquidity ratios.

_____ 7.   Operating performance is best measured by:

   a.   Return on equity ratio.
   b.   Price/earnings ratio.
   c.   Pretax operating rate of return on total assets.
   d.   None of the above.

_____ 8.   Which of the following statements is true?

   a.   When a company has a ROE greater than its interest rate, ROA exceeds ROE.
   b.   An unleveraged company has ROE higher than ROA.
   c.   The more stable the income, the less dangerous it is to trade on the equity.
   d.   All of the above are true.

_____ 9.   Which of the following is *not* an issue that complicates reporting and computation of earnings per share?

   a.   Preferred stock.
   b.   Common stock.
   c.   Stock issues and redemptions.
   d.   Possibility of exercise of options or various convertible securities.

_____ 10.   Which of the following statements is *not* true of diluted EPS?

   a.   It must always be presented on the income statement.
   b.   It assumes conversion of all potentially dilutive securities.
   c.   It is an expansion of the computation for EPS.
   d.   All of the above are true.

_____ 11.   Which of the following does *not* have to be shown on the income statement of the period in which it was recognized?

   a.   Special items.
   b.   Extraordinary items.
   c.   Accounting changes.
   d.   All of the above have to be shown on the income statement.

_____ 12.   Discontinued operations:

   a.   Involve the termination of a single plant or location.
   b.   Are reported separately, net of tax, in the income statement.
   c.   Related gains or losses should be reported as extraordinary items.
   d.   All of the above are true.

_____ 13.   When conducting business in various countries and doing business in various currencies, companies may have problems with differences in:

   a.   Accounting methods used.
   b.   Language of reporting.
   c.   Currency of measurement.
   d.   All of the above.

_____ 14.   Internationally, when analyzing financial statements which of the following does *not* affect the relative value of financial assets?

    a.   Security markets.
    b.   Tax laws.
    c.   Preferences among cultures.
    d.   All of the above affect the relative value of financial assets.

III. Answers to Pretest

1. a   Creditors are least concerned with future security prices. They are concerned with profitability and short-term liquidity. (L. O. 1)

2. c   Investors are least concerned with short-term liquidity. They are concerned with profitability and future security prices. (L. O. 1)

3. b   Each percentage change in trend analysis is independent of the other percentage changes, so this statement is incorrect. (L. O. 2)

4. d   (L. O. 2)

5. a   Horizontal comparisons for financial ratios do not exist. The other three choices are types of comparisons for financial ratios. (L. O. 3)

6. d   (L. O. 3)

7. c   (L. O. 4)

8. c   An unleveraged company has identical ROA and ROE. Also, when a company has an ROA greater than its interest rate, ROE exceeds ROA. (L. O. 4)

9. b   All the choices listed except for common stock are issues that might complicate the reporting and computation of earnings per share. Common stock is the basis for any owners' equity structure. (L. O. 5)

10. a   Fully diluted EPS is only presented on the income statement if the company has potentially dilutive securities. (L. O. 5)

11. d   (L. O. 6)

12. b   Discontinued operations involve the termination of a segment of the business, and not just a single plant or location. Gains or losses related to discontinued operations should be reported in conjunction with discontinued operations, and not as extraordinary items. (L. O. 6)

13. d   (L. O. 7)

14. d   (L. O. 7)

EVALUATION

The pretest contained two questions for each learning objective. If you did not answer both questions correctly for each learning objective, you should review the appropriate section of the textbook and study guide before you attempt the material after Part IV.

IV. Key Concept Review by Learning Objectives

L. O. 1: Locate and Use the Many Sources of Information about Company Performance

A.   Sources of Information About Companies

    1.   **Financial statement analysis** focuses on techniques used by analysts external to the organization being analyzed, although internal managers use many of the same methods. These analysts rely on publicly available information.

    2.   Publicly available information refers primarily to published information and analysis that are broadly available to analysts and investors.

    3.   A major source of information about an individual firm is the company's annual report. In addition to the financial statements, annual reports usually contain:

        a.   Footnotes to the financial statements.

        b.   A summary of the accounting principles used.

        c.   Management's discussion and analysis of the financial results.

        d.   The auditor's report.

        e.   Comparative financial data for a series of years.

        f.   Narrative information about the company.

    4.   To be useful, the financial statements and their accompanying footnotes and other disclosures must provide all significant or *material* information.

    5.   Companies also prepare reports for the Securities and Exchange Commission (SEC).

        a.   Form 10K — This form presents financial statement data in a standard format and is generally more comprehensive than the financial statements published in annual reports.

        b.   Form 10Q — This form includes quarterly financial statements, so it provides more timely information than the annual report, although the reports are less complete.

        c.   Other SEC reports are required for certain specified events and for issuance of common shares or debt.

    6.   Information that is more timely than annual reports and SEC reports is available from:

        a.   Company press releases and articles in the business press, such as the *Wall Street Journal, Business Week, Forbes, Fortune,* and *Barron's.* Companies provide the financial community with news about company developments. Members of the financial press decide which information in press releases will be interesting and important to their readers.

         b.   Services such as Value Line, Moody's Investors Services, and Standard and Poor's Industrial Surveys. Internet competitors are providing competing services electronically.

         c.   Stockbrokers, and private investment services and newsletters.

         d.   Credit agencies such as Dun & Bradstreet.

    7.   Heavy financial commitments are preceded by thorough investigations, including requests for **pro forma statements**, which are projected financial statements or other estimates of predicted results.

B.   Objectives of Financial Statement Analysis

    1.   Investors purchase capital stock expecting to receive dividends and an increase in the value of the stock. They are concerned with profitability, dividends, and future security prices.

    2.   Creditors make loans with the expectation of receiving interest and eventual repayment. Because creditors generally have specific fixed amounts to be received and have the first claim on assets, they are most concerned with assessing **short-term liquidity** and **long-term solvency**. They also assess profitability because profitable operations are the prime source of cash to repay loans.

         a.   Short-term liquidity refers to how much cash a company has on hand to meet current payments, such as interest, wages, taxes, etc.

         b.   Long-term solvency refers to a company's ability to generate cash to repay the principals on long-term debts to creditors as they mature.

    3.   Both investors and creditors bear the risk that they will not receive their expected return. They use financial statement analysis to:

         a.   Predict the amount of expected returns.

         b.   Assess the risks associated with those returns.

    4.   Financial statement analysis is useful to creditors and investors because past performance is often a good indicator of future performance, and current position is the base on which future performance must be built.

L. O. 2: Analyze the Components of a Company Using Trend Analysis and Other Techniques

A.   Evaluating Trends and Components of the Business

    1.   The methods used to analyze financial statement data focus on trend analysis and assessing the components of the business.

    2.   Trend analysis examines changes over time.

    3.   Component analysis can mean concentrating on the components of the financial statements themselves, or sorting out parts of the company's business.

B.   Trend Analysis

1.   Using the comparative data found in the financial statements and the annual report, financial analysts can examine in detail the changes in the past year and can examine longer-term trends in several important items.

STOP & REVIEW:

Before continuing, carefully review the **Oxley Company example** and **Exhibits 13-1, 13-2, and 13-3** in the textbook.

2.   Changes for each item must be interpreted carefully. Both the amount and the percentage changes should be examined.

3.   Changes in dollar amount and percentage terms are used to identify patterns. This procedure focuses the analysts' attention and encourages questions that probe for underlying causes.

C.   Common-Size Statements

1.   To aid comparisons with a company's prior years or comparisons of companies that differ in size, income statements and balance sheets are often analyzed using **common-size statements** in which the components are assigned a relative percentage, which are known as **component percentages.**

2.   The income statement percentages are usually based on sales = 100%. The behavior of each expense in relation to changes in total revenue is often revealing.

3.   The balance sheet percentages are usually based on total assets = 100%.

STOP & REVIEW:

Carefully review the continuing **Oxley Company example and Exhibit 13-4** in the textbook.

D.   Management's Discussion and Analysis

1.   Both trends and component percentages are generally discussed in a required section of annual reports called **management's discussion and analysis** (often called **MD&A**). This section explains the major changes in the income statement, liquidity, and capital resources.

2.   The space most companies devote to this section in annual reports has increased dramatically in recent years.

STOP & REVIEW:

Review **Exhibit 13-5** in the textbook.

E.   Segment Reporting

1.   Since the issuance by the FASB in 1976 of *Statement No. 14*, "Financial Reporting for Segments of a Business Enterprise," corporations must now disclose data about their operations in different industries and foreign countries, their export sales, and their major customers. The FASB is currently reconsidering how its segment rules will be written.

2.   The purpose of segment disclosures is to facilitate predicting of profitability, risk, and growth, which is sometimes difficult to evaluate from consolidated data.

 **& REVIEW:**

Review **types of disclosures required in Exhibit 13-6** in the textbook.

L. O. 3:   Use the Basic Financial Ratios to Guide Your Thinking

A.   Financial Ratios

The cornerstone of financial statement analysis is the use of ratios.

 **& REVIEW:**

Before continuing, carefully review **Exhibit 13-8: Some Typical Financial Ratios** in the textbook.

B.   Evaluating Financial Ratios

Evaluation of a financial ratio requires a comparison. There are three main types of comparisons:

      a.   With a company's own historical ratios, called **time-series comparisons**.

      b.   With general *rules of thumb* or **bench marks**.

      c.   With ratios of other companies or with industry averages, called **cross-sectional comparisons**.

C.   Ratios

      1.   Ratios are useful for financial analysis by investors because ratios capture critical dimensions of the economic performance of the entity.

      2.   Increasingly ratios are a tool that managers use to guide, measure, and reward workers.

      3.   The most commonly used liquidity ratio is the current ratio. The higher the current ratio, the more assurance the short-term creditor usually has about being paid in full and on time.

      4.   The quick ratio measures shorter-term liquidity. The numerator includes only those current assets that can quickly be turned into cash: cash, marketable securities, and accounts receivable. From management's perspective, a very high current ratio may be bad because the company may be maintaining higher levels of inventory and receivables than they should.

      5.   The average collection period and inventory turnover are ratios that are also closely watched, as liquidity is affected by how soon accounts receivable will be collected and how soon inventory will be sold.

      6.   Many analysts use sales *on account* in the denominator of the average collection period, as this focuses attention on how long it takes to collect credit accounts, in contrast to how long it takes to receive payment on sales in general.

7. Ratios of debt to assets and debt to equity are used for solvency evaluation. Both creditors and shareholders watch these ratios to judge the degree of risk of insolvency and the stability of profits.

8. Another solvency measure is the interest coverage ratio, which shows how much danger there is that operations will not generate operating income (before interest expense) at least as large as the company's interest expense.

9. The primary profitability measure is return on stockholders' equity (ROE). This ratio relates an accounting measure of income to the level of ownership capital used to generate the income.

L. O. 4:   Evaluate Corporate Performance Using ROA and ROE

A. Operating Performance and Financial Performance

1. *Financial management* is concerned with where the company gets cash and how it uses that cash to its benefit.   Borrowed funds create interest costs and affect net income, the numerator of the ROE ratio.

2. *Operating management* is concerned with the day-to-day activities that generate revenues and expenses. Ratios to assess operating efficiency should not be affected by financial considerations.

B. Operating Performance

1. In general, we evaluate the overall success of an investment by comparing what the investment returns to us with the investment we initially made.

2. In various settings it is useful to define income differently, sometimes as net earnings and sometimes as either pretax income from operations or earnings before interest and taxes (**EBIT**).

3. Because the measurement of *operating* performance should not be influenced by how assets are financed, it is best measured by **pretax operating rate of return on total assets** (also referred to as **return on total assets** or **ROA**).

$$\frac{\textit{Pretax operating rate}}{\textit{of return on total assets}} = \frac{\textit{Operating income}}{\textit{Average total assets available}}$$

4. The right side of the above equation consists of two important ratios:

a. **Operating income percentage on sales:**

$$\frac{\textit{Operating income}}{\textit{Sales}}$$

b. **Total asset turnover (asset turnover):**

$$\frac{\textit{Sales}}{\textit{Average total assets available}}$$

 **& REVIEW:**

Review **Exhibit 13-9** in the textbook.

C.   Financial Performance

    1.   Good financial performance requires an appropriate balance of debt and equity financing.

    2.   In addition to a decision about how much debt is appropriate, a firm must choose how much to borrow short term and how much to borrow by issuing bonds or other long-term debt.

D.   Trading on the Equity

    1.   Most companies have two basic types of long-term financing: long-term debt and stockholders' equity. The total of long-term financing is often called the **capitalization**, or simply **capital structure** of a corporation.

    2.   **Trading on the equity** (also referred to as using **financial leverage**, or in the U.K., **gearing**) means using borrowed money at fixed interest rates with the objective of enhancing the rate of return on common shareholders' equity.

    3.   When a company is unable to earn at least the interest rate on the money borrowed, the return on equity will be lower than for a debt-free company.

    4.   The more stable the income, the less dangerous it is to trade on the equity. The prudent use of debt is part of intelligent financial management.

STUDY TIP:
A debt-free, or unlevered, company has identical ROA and ROE.

STOP & REVIEW:

    Review **Exhibit 13-10** in the textbook before continuing.

E.   Income Tax Effects

    1.   Because interest payments are deductible as an expense for income tax purposes but dividends are not, if all other things are equal, the use of debt is less costly to the corporation than equity.

    2.   Failure to pay interest is an act of bankruptcy, which gives creditors rights to control or liquidate the company. Failure to pay dividends has less severe consequences.

STOP & REVIEW:

    Review the **example** in this section of the textbook.

F.   Measuring Safety

    1.   Investors in debt securities want assurance that future operations will easily provide enough cash to make the scheduled payments of interest and principal.

    2.   A ratio that focuses on interest-paying ability is **interest coverage** (sometimes called **times interest earned**).

$$Interest\ coverage = \frac{Income\ before\ interest\ expense\ and\ income\ taxes}{Interest\ expense}$$

3.   A rule of thumb or bench mark for debt investors is that the interest coverage should be at least five times even in the poorest year in a span of seven to ten years.

L. O. 5:   Calculate EPS Under Complex Circumstances

A.   Prominence of Earnings Per Share

Three issues that might complicate the reporting and computation of earnings per share (EPS) are:

1.   If preferred stock exists, the priority claims of those shareholders must be considered.

2.   If common stock is issued or redeemed during the year, the weighted-average number of shares must be calculated.

3.   If there are exchange privileges outstanding, such as stock options or convertible securities, their potential effect must be considered.

B.   Weighted-Average Shares and Preferred Stock

1.   Simple earnings per share is computed:

$$EPS\ of\ common\ stock = \frac{Net\ income}{Weighted\text{-}average\ number\ of\ shares\ outstanding}$$

2.   If the capital structure includes preferred stock that is nonconvertible, the dividends on preferred stock applicable to the current period, whether or not paid, should be deducted in calculating earnings applicable to common stock, as follows:

$$EPS\ of\ common\ stock = \frac{Net\ income - preferred\ dividends}{Weighted\text{-}average\ number\ of\ shares\ outstanding}$$

3.   Historical summaries of EPS must be made comparable by adjusting for changes in capitalization structure (i.e., stock splits and stock dividends).

STOP & REVIEW:

Review the **example** in this section of the textbook.

C.   Diluted EPS

1.   EPS calculations become a bit more complex when companies have convertible securities, stock options, or other financial instruments that can be exchanged for or converted to common shares.

2.   Diluted EPS assumes the conversion of all potentially dilutive securities.

STOP & REVIEW:

Review the **example** in this section of the textbook.

L. O. 6: Adjust for Nonrecurring Items

A.   Disclosure of Nonrecurring Items

   1.   When estimating the future, it is very important to distinguish the elements of the current financial statements that reflect recurring aspects of the firm from those that represent one-time events or items that will not continue.

   2.   There are four categories of these items: special items, extraordinary items, discontinued operations, and accounting changes.

B.   Special Items

   1.   **Special items** are expenses that are large enough and unusual enough to appear as a separately identified amount, reported on the income statement before tax.

   2.   The most common special item has been restructuring charges, which occur when a firm decides to substantially change the size or scope or location of a part of the business.

      a.   GAAP requires that the total costs be estimated and recorded when the plan is made, even if the costs will be incurred over an extended period of time.

      b.   The FASB and the SEC acted in 1994 to assure that restructuring changes did not include costs that will benefit future periods. Specifically, they cannot include relocation and training costs for people who will continue to work for the firm. These costs must still be properly matched to future revenues.

C.   Extraordinary Items

   Extraordinary items are items that are both *unusual in nature* and *infrequent in occurrence*, and are shown separately, net of tax, in the income statement. Casualties such as an earthquake, or government expropriation or prohibition, or early extinguishment of debt are examples of extraordinary items.

🛑 **STOP & REVIEW:**

   Review the appropriate section of **Exhibit 13-11** in the textbook.

D.   Discontinued Operations

   Discontinued operations involve the termination (closing or sale) of a business segment, not just of a single plant or location.   Discontinued operations are reported separately from the results of continuing operations, net of tax, in the income statement.

      a.   Any gain or loss from the disposal of a segment of a business should be reported in conjunction with the related results of discontinued operations and not as an extraordinary item.

b.   Amounts of applicable income taxes should be disclosed on the face of the income statement or in related notes. Revenues applicable to the discontinued operations should be disclosed separately in the related notes.

STOP & REVIEW:

Review the appropriate section of **Exhibit 13-11** in the textbook.

E.   Accounting Changes

    1.   The presentation of the effects of an accounting change is net of tax, and is separated from ongoing operations in the same section of the income statement that contains discontinued operations.

    2.   Changes of accounting method that are treated this way arise from FASB requirements. When the FASB changes its rules it often requires a major one-time recognition.

L. O.7: Explain Some Effects on Financial Statements From Translating Foreign Currencies

A.   Internationally, financial statement analysis is significantly complicated by a variety of factors, including differences in accounting methods, the language of reporting, and the currency of measurement.

B.   Different structures for security markets, different tax laws, and different preferences among citizens of different countries also all affect the relative value of financial assets.

STUDY TIP:
Study the "Summary Problem for Your Review" and solution
in the text before going on.

STOP & REVIEW:

Before continuing, review the objectives for this chapter and make sure you have a good understanding of each one.

V. Test Yourself

Questions

1. Discuss the many sources of information about company performance.

2. Explain the different objectives of financial statement analysis.

3. Describe trend analysis and other techniques used to analyze the components of a company.

4. Contrast operating performance and financial performance.

5. Briefly explain the four major categories of nonrecurring items.

Exercises and Problems

Data for use with #1 - #3

Learning Technologies, Inc.
Income Statement
For the year ended December 31, 19X9

Sales		$5,250,000
Cost of goods sold		1,837,500
Gross margin		$3,412,500
Operating expenses:		
Payroll expense	$1,000,000	
Rent expense	400,000	
Depreciation expense	105,000	
Miscellaneous expense	999,167	2,504,167
Operating income		$ 908,333
Deduct: Interest expense		75,000
Income before taxes		$ 833,333
Income taxes (40%)		333,333
Net income		$ 500,000

Learning Technologies, Inc.
Balance Sheet
December 31, 19X9

Assets

Current assets:

Cash		$ 65,000
Marketable securities		100,000
Accounts receivable		105,000
Inventory		320,000
Prepaid rent		40,000
Prepaid insurance		20,000
Total current assets		$ 650,000

Noncurrent assets:

Long-term investments		$385,000	
Land		310,000	
Equipment	$ 350,000		
Accumulated depreciation-equipment	(125,000)	225,000	
Plant	$1,050,000		
Accumulated depreciation-plant	370,000	680,000	
Total noncurrent assets			1,600,000
Total assets			$2,250,000

Liabilities and Stockholders' Equity

Current liabilities:

Accounts payable		$ 70,000
Notes payable		45,000
Accrued taxes		105,000
Total current liabilities		$ 220,000

Long-term liabilities:

Long-term mortgage		655,000
Total liabilities		$ 875,000

Stockholders' equity:

Common stock, $10 par, 100,000 shares authorized, 10,000 shares issued and outstanding	$100,000	
Paid-in capital in excess of par	410,000	
Retained earnings	865,000	1,375,000
Total liabilities and Stockholders' equity		$2,250,000

1. Based on the income statement and balance sheet for Learning Technologies, Inc., compute the component percentages for:

    a. Cash
    b. Cost of goods sold
    c. Rent expense
    d. Land
    e. Stockholders' equity

2. Based on the income statement and balance sheet for Learning Technologies, Inc., compute:

    a. Working capital
    b. Inventory turnover
    c. Total asset turnover
    d. Profit margin on sales
    e. Debt-to-equity ratio
    f. Return on assets
    g. Return on equity

3.   In 20X0, Price Corporation had sales of $2,400,000; cost of goods sold of $1,560,000; and operating expenses of $720,000. Common shares outstanding for the whole period were 60,000. The firm had 900 convertible bonds outstanding with a conversion ratio of 10 shares of common stock for each bond received. If the bonds were converted $10,000 in interest would be saved. What is EPS and diluted EPS?

4.   Montauk Co. had credit sales of $3,220,000 in 19X9. The average number of days it took Montauk to collect its receivables in 19X9 was 32 days. What is the average balance in accounts receivable? (Use a 360-day year.)

5.   Based on the following ratios, fill in the blank spaces on the accompanying balance sheet and partial income statement.

Balance sheet:

Cash	_____		Accounts payable	$ 75,000
Accounts receivable	_____		Long-term debt	_____
Inventory	_____		Common stock	$200,000
Total current assets	_____		Retained earnings	_____
Fixed assets	_____		Total liabilities and	_____
Total assets	_____		Stockholders' equity	$600,000

Income statement:

| Sales | _____ | | Cost of goods sold | _____ |

Debt ratio	50%
Quick ratio	.90
Total asset turnover	4x
Average collection period	9 days
Gross profit margin	40%
Current ratio	2.5

Matching

MATCH EACH TERM WITH ITS DEFINITION BY WRITING THE APPROPRIATE LETTER IN THE SPACE PROVIDED.

Terms

_____ 1. Asset turnover

_____ 2. Bench mark

_____ 3. Capitalization

_____ 4. Common-size statements

_____ 5. Component percentages

_____ 6. Discontinued operations

_____ 7. EBIT

_____ 8. Extraordinary items

_____ 9. Financial statement analysis

_____ 10. Interest coverage

_____ 11. Long-term solvency

_____ 12. Operating income percentage on sales

_____ 13. Pretax operating rate of return on total assets

_____ 14. Pro forma statement

_____ 15. Return on total assets

_____ 16. Short-term liquidity

_____ 17. Special items

_____ 18. Trading on the equity

Definitions

A. Analysis and presentation of financial statements in percentage form to aid comparability.

B. An organization's ability to generate enough cash to repay long-term debts as they mature.

C. A carefully formulated expression of predicted results.

D. Items that are unusual in nature and infrequent in occurrence, which are shown separately, net of tax, in the income statement.

E. Expenses that are large enough and unusual enough to warrant separate disclosure.

F. General rules of thumb specifying appropriate levels for financial ratios.

G. The termination of a business segment reported separately, net of tax, in the income statement.

H. An organization's ability to meet current payments as they become due.

I. Income before interest expense and income taxes divided by interest expense.

J. Earnings before interest and taxes.

K. Operating income divided by average total assets available.

L. Owners' equity plus long-term debt.

M. Using financial statements to assess a company's performance.

N.   Using borrowed money at fixed interest rates with the objective of enhancing the rate of return on common equity.

O.   Sales divided by average total assets available.

P.   Operating income divided by sales.

Q.   Income before interest expense divided by average total assets.

R.   Financial statements expressed in component percentages.

Multiple Choice

SELECT THE BEST ANSWER AND ENTER THE IDENTIFYING LETTER IN THE SPACE PROVIDED.

_____ 1.   In addition to the financial statements, annual reports usually contain:

      a.   Footnotes to the financial statements and the auditor's report.
      b.   Management's discussion and analysis of the financial results.
      c.   Narrative information about the company.
      d.   All of the above are included in an annual report.

_____ 2.   The report for the SEC that includes quarterly financial statements is:

      a.   Form 10F.
      b.   Form 10K.
      c.   Form 10Q.
      d.   Form 10W.

_____ 3.   Which of the following is the least timely source of business information?

      a.   Annual report.
      b.   _Business Week._
      c.   Value Line.
      d.   Moody's Investors Services.

_____ 4.   Which of the following is _not_ a reason financial statement analysis is useful to creditors and investors?

      a.   Past performance is often a good indicator of future performance.
      b.   Current position is the base on which future performance must be built.
      c.   Future trends can always be accurately predicted.
      d.   All of the above are reasons financial statement analysis is useful.

_____ 5.   Both trends and component percentages are discussed in what required section of an annual report?

      a.   Footnotes.
      b.   Management's discussion and analysis.
      c.   Summary of financial policies.
      d.   Auditor's report.

_____ 6.   The ratio that measures earnings available to the holder of a share of common stock is:

      a.   Earnings per share.
      b.   Return on stockholders' equity.
      c.   Price-Earnings.
      d.   None of the above.

_____ 7. Which of the following is *not* a long-term solvency ratio?

    a.   Debt to equity.
    b.   Debt to assets.
    c.   Return on equity.
    d.   Interest coverage.

_____ 8. Which of the following statements is true?

    a.   Net income attributable to common shareholders can be substantially higher if debt is used.
    b.   Net income is higher if preferred shares are used, as opposed to bonds.
    c.   Failure to pay interest is an act of bankruptcy, which gives creditors rights to control or liquidate the company.
    d.   All of the above are true.

_____ 9. Which of the following is *not* true of EPS?

    a.   It must always be presented on the income statement.
    b.   It is calculated as if common stock equivalents that dilute EPS were converted.
    c.   Its computation may include other potentially dilutive securities.
    d.   All of the above are true.

_____ 10. An example of an extraordinary item is:

    a.   An earthquake.
    b.   Retirement of debt due in the current year.
    c.   The effects of a strike.
    d.   All of the above are examples of extraordinary items.

VI. Solutions to Test Yourself

Questions

1. Financial statement analysis focuses on techniques used by analysts external to the organization being analyzed, although internal managers use many of the same methods. These analysts rely on publicly available information, which refers primarily to published information and analysis that are broadly available to analysts and investors.

    A major source of information about an individual firm is the company's annual report. In addition to the financial statements, annual reports usually contain:

    a. Footnotes to the financial statements.
    b. A summary of the accounting principles used.
    c. Management's discussion and analysis of the financial results.
    d. Comparative financial data for a series of years.
    e. Narrative information about the company.
    f. The auditor's report.

    To be useful, the financial statements and their accompanying footnotes and other disclosures must provide all significant or *material* information.

    Companies also prepare reports for the Securities and Exchange Commission SEC).

    a. Form 10K - This form presents financial statement data in a standard format and is generally more comprehensive than the financial statements published in annual reports.
    b. Form 10Q - This form includes quarterly financial statements, so it provides more timely information than the annual report, although the reports are less complete
    c. Other SEC reports are required for certain specified events and for issuance of common shares or debt.

    Information that is more timely than annual reports and SEC reports is available from:

    a. Company press releases and articles in the business press, such as the *Wall Street Journal, Business Week, Forbes, Fortune,* and *Barron's.*
    b. Services such as Value Line, Moody's Investors Services, and Standard and Poor's Industrial Surveys.
    c. Stockbrokers, and private investment services and newsletters.
    d. Credit agencies such as Dun & Bradstreet. (L. 0. 1)

2. Investors purchase capital stock expecting to receive dividends and an increase in the value of the stock. They are concerned with profitability, dividends, and future security prices.

    Creditors make loans with the expectation of receiving interest and eventual repayment. Because creditors generally have specific fixed amounts to be received and have the first claim on assets, they are most concerned with assessing short-term liquidity and long-term solvency. They also assess profitability because profitable operations are the prime source of cash to repay loans.

    Both investors and creditors bear the risk that they will not receive their expected return. They use financial statement analysis to predict the amount of expected returns, and assess the risks associated with those returns.

Financial statement analysis is useful to creditors and investors because past performance is often a good indicator of future performance, and current position is the base on which future performance must be built. (L. 0. 1)

3 .   The methods used to analyze financial statement data focus on trend analysis and assessing the components of the business. Trend analysis examines changes over time. Component analysis can mean concentrating on the components of the financial statements themselves, or sorting out parts of the company's business.

Using the comparative data found in the financial statements and the annual report, financial analysts can examine in detail the changes in the past year and can examine longer-term trends in several important items. Changes for each item must be interpreted carefully. Both the amount and the percentage changes should be examined.

Changes in dollar amount and percentage terms are used to identify patterns. This procedure focuses the analysts' attention and encourages questions that probe for underlying causes.

To aid comparisons with a company's previous years and especially to aid the comparison of several companies that differ in size, income statements and balance sheets are often analyzed using component percentages, which result in commonsize statements.

The income statement percentages are usually based on sales = 100%. The behavior of each expense in relation to changes in total revenue is often revealing.

The balance sheet percentages are usually based on total assets = 100%.

Both trends and component percentages are generally discussed in a required section of annual reports called management's discussion and analysis (often called MD&A). This section explains the major changes in the income statement and the major changes in liquidity and capital resources. The space most companies devote to the section in annual reports has increased dramatically in recent years.

Since the issuance by the FASB in 1976 of *Statement No. 14*, "Financial Reporting for Segments of a Business Enterprise," corporations must now disclose data about their operations in different industries and foreign countries, their export sales, and their major customers.

The purpose of segment disclosures is to facilitate predicting of profitability, risk, and growth, which is sometimes difficult to evaluate from consolidated data. (L. 0. 2)

4.   *Financial management* is concerned with where the company gets cash and how it uses that cash to its benefit. Borrowed funds create interest costs and affect net income, the numerator of the ROE ratio.

Operating management is concerned with the day-to-day activities that generate revenues and expenses. Ratios to assess operating efficiency should not be affected by financial considerations. (L. 0. 4)

5.   As security analysts evaluate the prospects of the firm relative to the future, it is very important to distinguish the elements of the current financial statements that reflect recurring aspects of the firm from those that represent one-time events or items that will not continue. There are four categories of these items: special items, extraordinary items, discontinued operations, and accounting changes.

Special items are expenses that are large enough and unusual enough to warrant separate disclosure, and are reported on the income statement before tax. The most common special item has been restructuring charges, which occur when a firm decides to substantially change the size or scope or location of a part of the business. GAAP requires that the total costs be estimated and recorded when the plan is made, even if the costs will be incurred over an extended period of time. The FASB and the SEC acted in 1994 to assure that restructuring changes did not include costs that will benefit future periods. Specifically, they cannot include relocation and training costs for people who will continue to work for the firm.

Extraordinary items are items that are both unusual in nature and infrequent in occurrence, which are shown separately, net of tax, in the income statement. Casualties such as an earthquake, or government expropriation or prohibition, or early extinguishment of debt are examples of extraordinary items.

Discontinued operations involve the termination of a business segment, and are reported separately, net of tax, in the income statement. Any gain or loss from the disposal of a segment of a business should be reported in conjunction with the related results of discontinued operations and not as an extraordinary item. Amounts of applicable income taxes should be disclosed on the face of the income statement or in related notes. Revenues applicable to the discontinued operations should be disclosed separately in the related notes.

Accounting changes are changes of accounting methods that arise from FASB requirements. When the FASB changes its rules it often requires a major one-time recognition.

The presentation of the effects of an accounting change is net of tax, and is separated from ongoing operations in the same section of the income statement that contains discontinued operations. (L. 0. 6)

Exercises and Problems

1. Component percentages:

   a. Cash = $65,000 / $2,250,000 = 2.88%

   b. Cost of goods sold = $1,837,500 / $5,250,000 = 35%

   c. Rent expense = $400,000 / $5,250,000 = 7.62%

   d. Land = $310,000 / $2,250,000 = 13.78%

   e. Stockholders' equity = $1,375,000 / $2,250,000 = 61.1%

2.
   a. Working capital = Current assets — current liabilities
      $430.000   = $650,000   — $220,000

   b. Inventory turnover = Cost of goods sold / Average inventory
      5.74   = $1,837,500   / $320,000

   c. Total asset turnover =   Sales   / Total assets
      2.33   = $5,250,000   / $2,250,000

   d. Profit margin on sales = Net income /   Sales
      9.52%   = $500,000 / $5,250,000

   e. Debt-to-equity = Total liabilities /   Stockholders' equity
      63.64%   = $875,000   / $1,375,000

f.   Return on assets = Operating income before taxes / Total assets

$$\underline{40.37\%} \quad = \qquad \$908{,}333 \qquad\qquad / \qquad \$2{,}250{,}000$$

g.   Return on equity = Net income / Total stockholders' equity

$$\underline{36.36\%} \quad = \quad \$500{,}000 \quad / \quad \$1{,}375{,}000$$

3.

Sales	$2,400,000
Cost of goods sold	(1,560,000)
Operating expenses	(720,000)
Net income	$ 120,000

EPS:

$120,000 / 60,000 shares = $2 per share

Diluted EPS:

$120,000 + $10,000 / 60,000 shares + (10 shares X 900 bonds)

$130,000   /   34,500 share = $1.88 per share

4.   Average collection period = Average receivables / Average daily sales

     32   = Average receivables / $3,220,000 / 360 days

     32   = Average receivables / $8,944 (rounded)

     32 X $8,944   = $286,208 average receivables

5.   Balance sheet:

Cash	$ 7,500 (10)	Accounts payable	$ 75,000
Accounts receivable	60,000 (9)	Long-term debt	225,000 (3)
Inventory	120,000 (6)	Common stock	200,000
Total current assets	187,500 (2)	Retained earnings	100,000 (4)
Fixed assets	412,500 (5)	Total liabilities and	
Total assets	$600,000 (1)	Stockholders' equity	$600,000

Income statement:

Sales	$2,400,000 (7)	Cost of goods sold	$1,440,000 (8)

(1)   Total assets = Total liabilities + Stockholders' equity (given)

          Total assets = $600,000

(2)   Total current assets / Total current liabilities = 2.5 Current ratio

          Total current assets / $75,000   = 2.5

          Total current assets = 2.5 X $75,000

          Total current assets = $187,500

(3)   Total liabilities / Total assets = .50 Debt ratio

          Total liabilities / $600,000   = .50

          Total liabilities = .5 X $600,000

          Total liabilities = $300,000

          Total liabilities — Current liabilities = Long-term debt

          $300,000   — $75,000 (given) = $225,000

(4)   Total liabilities &
Stockholders' equity — Total liabilities — Common stock = Retained earnings
$$\$600{,}000 \quad - \quad \$300{,}000 \quad - \quad \$200{,}000 \quad = \quad \underline{\$100{,}000}$$

(5)   Total assets — Total current assets = Fixed assets
$$\$600{,}000 \quad - \quad \$187{,}500 \quad = \quad \underline{\$412{,}500}$$

(6)   Current assets — Inventory / Current liabilities = .9 Quick ratio
$$\$187{,}500 - \text{Inventory} / \$75{,}000 = .9$$
$$\$187{,}500 - \text{Inventory} = \$75{,}000 \text{ X } .9$$
$$\$187{,}500 - \text{Inventory} = \$67{,}500$$
$$\$187{,}500 - \$67{,}500 = \text{Inventory}$$
$$\underline{\$120{,}000} = \text{Inventory}$$

(7)   Sales / Total assets = 4 times Total asset turnover
Sales / $600,000 = 4 times
Sales = 4 X $600,000
Sales = $\underline{\$2{,}400{,}000}$

(8)   Sales   X (1 — gross margin %) = Cost of goods sold
$$\$2{,}400{,}000 \text{ X } .60 = \text{Cost of goods sold}$$
$$\underline{\$1{,}440{,}000} = \text{Cost of goods sold}$$

(9)   Average accounts receivable / Average days sales   = 9 days Average collection period
Average accounts receivable / $2,400,000/360 days = 9 days
Average accounts receivable / $6,666.66   = 9 days
Average accounts receivable = 9 X $6,666.66
Average accounts receivable = $\underline{\$60{,}000}$

(10)   Cash = Total current assets — Inventory — Accounts receivable
Cash = $187,500   — $120,000 — $60,000
Cash = $\underline{\$7{,}500}$

Matching

1.	O	L. O. 4	7.	J	L. O. 4	13.	K	L. O. 4
2.	F	L. O. 3	8.	D	L. O. 6	14.	C	L. O. 1
3.	L	L. O. 4	9.	M	L. O. 1	15.	Q	L. O. 4
4.	R	L. O. 2	10.	I	L. O. 4	16.	H	L. O. 1
5.	A	L. O. 2	11	B	L. O. 1	17.	E	L. O. 6
6.	G	L. O. 6	12.	P	L. O. 4	18.	N	L. O. 4

Multiple Choice

1.   d   (L. O. 1)

2.   c   Form 10Q includes quarterly financial statements, which provide more timely information than annual reports or Form 10K. (L. O. 1)

3.   a   The annual report is the least timely source of business of those listed. This is because annual reports are issued well after the events being reported have occurred. (L. 0. 1)

4.   c   Future trends cannot always be *accurately* predicted, no matter how good the input. (L. 0. 1)

5.   b   (L. 0. 2)

6.   a   Earnings per share measure earnings available to the holder of a share of common stock. (L. 0. 3)

7.   c   Return on equity is a profitability ratio, not a long-term solvency ratio. (L. 0. 3)

8.   d   (L. 0. 4)

9.   c   EPS includes only common stock equivalents that dilute EPS. Other potentially dilutive securities are included in diluted EPS. (L. 0. 5)

10.   a   An earthquake is the only item listed that qualifies as an extraordinary item. (L. 0. 6)

Chapter 14

CONCEPTUAL FRAMEWORK AND MEASUREMENT TECHNIQUES

I. Learning Objectives

The purpose of accounting is to bring together financial data in a cost-effective manner that is understandable to the reader, and is useable for effective decision making. This chapter gathers some of the concepts introduced in earlier chapters, and adds others to provide a more complete picture of the concepts that underlie accounting. It also provides a synopsis and integration of the international diversity that characterizes accounting practice, as well as variations of methods of measuring income with GAAP. Use the following learning objectives as a guide in studying this chapter.

1. Describe the FASB's conceptual framework.

2. Identify the qualities that make information valuable.

3. Explain how accounting differences could produce differing income for similar companies.

4. Differentiate between financial capital and physical capital.

5. Incorporate changing prices into income measurement using four different methods.

6. Compare U.S. GAAP with other countries' standards.

II. Pretest

_____ 1.　The FASB's conceptual framework:

    a.　Provides solutions to all the reporting issues faced by the FASB.
    b.　Aids the exercise of judgment.
    c.　Provides objective criteria for financial reporting issues.
    d.　None of the above is correct.

_____ 2.　The process of setting accounting standards includes:

    a.　The development of a conceptual framework.
    b.　The gaining of general acceptance and support.
    c.　The application of a conceptual framework to specific issues using logic and fact gathering.
    d.　All of the above are included in the process of setting accounting standards.

_____ 3.　The overriding criterion for choosing reporting alternatives is:

    a.　Cost/benefit.
    b.　Logic.
    c.　Accuracy.
    d.　Reasonableness.

_____ 4.　When the inclusion or correct presentation of information would probably change the judgment of a reasonable person the information is:

    a.　Reliable.
    b.　Relevant.
    c.　Material.
    d.　Neutral.

_____ 5.　The timing of income is influenced most by the:

    a.　Accrual accounting basis.
    b.　Recognition principle.
    c.　Cost recovery principle.
    d.　All of the above.

_____ 6.　Which of the following is _not_ an exception to the idea that delivery triggers the recording of revenue?

    a.　Percentage-of-completion method.
    b.　Installment sales.
    c.　Completed contract method.
    d.　All of the above are exceptions.

_____ 7.   The historical-cost basis for measuring income:

a.   Produces misleading results during a time of rising prices.
b.   Is always accurate and reasonable.
c.   Has never been a concern that the FASB has addressed.
d.   None of the above are correct.

_____ 8.   A concept of income measurement whereby income emerges only after recovering an amount that allows physical operating capability to be maintained is:

a.   Financial capital maintenance.
b.   Physical capital maintenance.
c.   Invested capital maintenance.
d.   None of the above are correct.

_____ 9.   Dollar measurements that are restated in terms of current purchasing power are:

a.   Nominal dollars.
b.   Current dollars.
c.   Constant dollars.
d.   None of the above.

_____ 10.   Holding gains or losses are increases (or decreases):

a.   In the replacement costs of the assets held during the current period.
b.   In the current costs of the assets held during the past few years.
c.   In the historical costs of the assets held during the current period.
d.   None of the above are correct.

_____ 11.   Which of the following basic aspects of accounting are consistent throughout the world?

a.   Double-entry systems.
b.   Accrual accounting.
c.   The income statement and balance sheet as required financial statements.
d.   All of the above.

_____ 12.   Which of the following accounting areas is different throughout the world?

a.   Financial reporting of income taxes.
b.   Financial statement accounting for inflation.
c.   Influence of tax law on financial reporting.
d.   All of the above.

III. Answers to Pretest

1. b   The conceptual framework does *not* provide solutions to all reporting issues faced by the FASB, and there are no objective criteria for the FASB to use in making decisions for financial reporting. The framework does, however, aid the exercise of judgment. (L. O. 1)

2. d   (L. O. 1)

3. a   Cost/benefit is the overriding factor for choosing reporting alternatives. The perceived benefits of an accounting method must exceed their perceived costs for society as a whole. (L. O. 2)

4. c   Deciding if information is *material* is resolved by professional judgment on a case-by-case basis. (L. O. 2)

5. b   Revenue recognition, which is a major feature of accrual accounting, as it determines when income will be reported. (L. O. 3)

6. c   Completed contract method *does* require revenue to be recorded on delivery so it is not an exception. (L. O. 3)

7. a   As the historical-cost basis for measuring income ignores inflation, it can produce misleading results during a time of rising prices. (L. O. 4)

8. b   (L. O. 4)

9. c   (L. O. 5)

10. a   (L. O. 5)

11. d   (L. O. 6)

12. d   (L. O. 6)

EVALUATION

The pretest contained two questions for each learning objective. If you did not answer both questions correctly for each learning objective, you should review the appropriate section of the textbook and study guide before you attempt the material after Part IV.

IV. Key Concept Review by Learning Objectives

L. O. 1:   Describe the FASB's Conceptual Framework

A.   FASB's Conceptual Framework

1.   Between 1978 and 1984, the Financial Accounting Standards Board (FASB) issued four statements of *Financial Accounting Concepts* relating to business enterprises. These statements provide the conceptual framework used by the FASB.

2.   The principal task of the FASB is accounting policy making, which is choosing the accounting measurement and disclosure methods required for financial reporting.

3.   The conceptual framework aids the exercise of judgment; it does not provide solutions to all the reporting issues faced by the FASB.

4.   The process of setting accounting standards includes the development of a conceptual framework, its application to specific issues via exercises in logic and fact gathering, and the gaining of general acceptance and support.

STOP & REVIEW:

Carefully review **Exhibit 14-1** before continuing.

B.   Lessons From History

1.   Until the late 1930's, when Congress created the SEC, accounting practices in the United States evolved in accordance with the best professional judgment of CPAs and managers. Today, the SEC is legally charged with setting accounting standards but has delegated that responsibility to the FASB.

2.   The FASB's task is not only technical but also political or educational. It must tackle the task of obtaining general acceptance, particularly by the SEC and Congress.

3.   In many countries accounting standards are set by a government agency. In the U.S., most accounting reporting requirements are determined by the FASB, with the backing of the SEC. If Congress, which maintains oversight of the SEC, becomes unhappy with progress in the setting of financial accounting standards, it could specifically change the role of the FASB.

4.   Although there will probably be more government exercise of authority through the SEC in the future, it remains likely that during the next ten years the FASB will continue to be the major single influence on changes in financial accounting standards.

L. O. 2:   Identify the Qualities That Make Information Valuable

A.   Choosing Among Reporting Alternatives

1.   The overriding criterion for choosing reporting alternatives is *cost/benefit*. A policy-making body such as the FASB must do its best to issue pronouncements whose perceived benefits exceed their perceived costs for the whole of society.

2.   The costs of providing information include costs to both providers and users. The benefits of accounting information exist, but they are harder to pinpoint than the costs.

3.   An important concept in judging benefits of accounting information is *decision usefulness*. If accounting information is not useful in making decisions, it provides no benefit.

 **& REVIEW:**

Review **Exhibit 14-2** in the textbook.

B.   Aspects of Decision Usefulness

1.   *Relevance* and *reliability* are qualities that make accounting useful for decision making.

   a.   **Relevance** refers to whether or not the information will make a difference to the decision maker.

   b.   **Reliability** means that the information can be counted on to represent faithfully the condition of the company given the rules in use.

2.   For information to be relevant, it must help decision makers by having either *predictive value* (predict the outcomes of future events) or *feedback value* (confirm or update past predictions), and must be available on a timely basis.

3.   *Verifiability, neutrality*, and *validity* enhance reliability.

   a.   **Verifiability** means that information can be checked to make sure it is correct, and that the measured amounts will have the same value each time the measurement is made.

   b.   **Validity** (also called **representational faithfulness**) means the information provided represents the events or objects it is supposed to represent.

   c.   **Neutrality**, or freedom from bias, means that information is objective and is not weighted unfairly.

4.   *Comparability* and *consistency* are the final items affecting usefulness. Information is more useful if it can be compared with similar information about other companies or with similar information for other reporting periods.

C.   Overview of Key Concepts

 **& REVIEW:**

Before continuing, carefully study **Exhibit 14-3.**

STUDY TIP:
Exhibit 14-3 is a handy guide for recalling and comparing major ingredients of accounting's conceptual framework.

L. O. 3: Explain How Accounting Differences Could Produce Differing Income For Similar Companies

A. Measuring Income

    The primary method underlying U.S. GAAP is the historical-cost method. Disputes often occur in applying this method. Most of these disputes center on timing.

B. Revenue Recognition

    1. The timing of income is influenced most by the *recognition* principle, which is a major feature of accrual accounting because it determines when revenues and the associated costs will be recorded.

    2. Generally, revenue is recorded when goods or services are *delivered* to customers. There are some exceptions to this:

        a. Long-term construction projects are often accounted for using the *percentage-of-completion method*, which recognizes revenues, related costs, and resulting net income over the life of the contract in proportion to the work accomplished.

        b. In rare cases, revenue is recorded in proportion to cash collections under long-run installment contracts.

C. Expense Recognition

    1. GAAP allows accountants to choose when to recognize certain expenses. Comparing two companies can be difficult if each chooses a different method for recognizing major expenses.

    2. For stockholder reporting purposes, the choice of accounting policies can have a dramatic effect on operating income before taxes. Some companies choose the accounting policies that maximize operating income while other companies choose more conservative policies.

    3. Until accounting measurements become better standardized, accountants and corporate executives should view increased disclosure and amplified description as the most pressing requirements in financial reporting.

STOP **& REVIEW:**

    Review **Exhibit 14-4 and 14-5** in the textbook.

D. Statement of Accounting Policies

    1. Information about the accounting principles, practices, procedures, or policies is essential for the intelligent analysis of financial statements.

    2. Companies must include a description of all significant accounting policies as an integral part of the financial report. The disclosure usually appears as a separate Summary of Significant Accounting Policies preceding the footnotes of financial statements.

Review **Exhibit 14-6** in the textbook.

L. O. 4: Differentiate Between Financial Capital and Physical Capital

A.   Income Measurements When Prices Change

Accountants tend to agree that sometimes historical costs do not measure income properly, and that income is best described as the return on capital invested by shareholders. By examining the relationship of income to capital in greater detail circumstances can be discovered where historical cost leads to incorrect and misleading measures of income.

B.   Income or Capital

1.   Income is an entity's increase in wealth during a period; that is, the amount that could be paid out to shareholders at the end of the period and still leave the entity as *well off* as it was at the beginning of the period.

2.   Shareholders invest capital and expect a return *on* the capital and an eventual return *of* the capital.

   a.   To measure the shareholders' *return on capital*, the company must first measure the resources required to maintain invested capital at its original level.

   b.   Any profit above and beyond this level of maintained capital is income.

3.   **Financial capital maintenance** is a concept of income measurement whereby income emerges only after financial resources are recovered.

4.   **Physical capital maintenance** is a concept of income measurement whereby income emerges only after recovering an amount that allows physical operating capability to be maintained.

C.   Complaints About Historical Cost

1.   Many business executives insist that our traditional historical-cost basis for measuring income produces misleading results during a time of rising prices.   These overstated profits also cause their companies to pay more income taxes than they should.

2.   In response to these concerns on the usefulness of traditional historical-cost financial statements, the FASB issued *Statement No. 33*, "Financial Reporting and Changing Prices."

   a.   The statement required no changes in the primary financial statements but did require large companies to include supplementary inflation-adjusted schedules in their annual reports.

   b.   By 1987 inflation had subsided and the FASB decided that inflation-adjusted disclosures would no longer be required.

3.   However, a basic knowledge about reporting the effects of changing prices is useful for the following reasons:

a. High inflation is still present in many countries, and most accounting reports in those countries report the effects of inflation.

b. Higher inflation rates will return to the U.S. sooner or later, and readers of financial statements will again become concerned with inflation-adjusted statements.

c. The cumulative effect of even a 2% or 3% inflation rate is substantial.

d. Understanding the limitations of traditional financial statements is enhanced by knowing how inflation affects (or does not affect) such financial statements.

L. O. 5: Incorporate Changing Prices into Income Measurement Using Four Different Methods

A. Alternatives to Historical-Cost Measurement

1. When prices of resources do not change, financial and physical capital maintenance give identical measures of income. Some price changes are a result of **inflation**, a general decline in the purchasing power of the dollar or a general increase in the average cost of goods and services.

2. Changing prices, and particularly inflation, have caused accountants to consider two types of changes in financial reporting:

   a. Switch from measuring transactions in **nominal dollars**, which are dollar measurements that are not restated for fluctuation in the general purchasing power of the monetary unit, to **constant dollars**, which are dollar values restated in terms of current purchasing power.

   b. Instead of reporting the **historical cost** of an asset use the **current cost**. Historical cost is the amount originally paid to acquire an asset while current cost is generally the cost to replace it.

3. Using historical costs implies maintenance of financial capital, current costs imply *physical* capital maintenance.

4. The two approaches, which can be applied separately or in combination, address separate but related problems caused by changing prices:

   a. Constant-dollar disclosures account for *general* changes in the purchasing power of the dollar.

   b. Current-cost disclosures account for changes in *specific* prices.

5. The two approaches create four alternatives for measuring income:

   a. Historical cost/nominal dollars

   b. Current cost/nominal dollars.

   c. Historical cost/constant dollars.

   d. Current cost/constant dollars.

305

B.   Historical Cost/Nominal Dollars

   1.   This method measures invested capital in nominal dollars. It is the most popular approach to income measurement and is the primary method in U.S. GAAP. It is commonly called the historical-cost method.

   2.   Income is not recognized until an asset is sold; intervening price fluctuations are ignored.

STOP & REVIEW:

   Review the appropriate columns of **Exhibit 14-7** in the textbook.

C.   Current Cost/Nominal Dollars

   1.   The focus of this method is on income from continuing operations, and emphasizes that operating income should be income that is "distributable" to shareholders while maintaining physical capital.

   2.   This method has especially strong advocates in the United Kingdom and Australia.

   3.   Critics of traditional accounting claim that the historical-measure of income from continuing operations is misleading because it overstates the net amount of distributable assets.

STOP & REVIEW:

   Review the appropriate columns of **Exhibit 14-7** in the textbook

D.   Holding Gains and Physical Capital

   1.   The current-cost method stresses a separation between *income from continuing operations* and *holding gains* (or *losses*), that are increases (or decreases) in the replacement costs of the assets held during the current period.

   2.   The current-cost method recognizes the impact of intervening price fluctuations on a company when the values of its assets change.

   3.   Accountants differ sharply on how to account for holding gains. The advocates of a physical concept of capital maintenance claim that *all* holding gains (both those gains related to the units sold and the gains related to the units unsold) should be excluded from income and become a part of stockholders' equity called **revaluation equity**.

STOP & REVIEW:

   Review **Exhibit 14-8** and the appropriate columns of **Exhibit 14-7** in the textbook.

E.   Historical Cost/Constant Dollars

   1.   Essentially, the income measurements in each year are restated in terms of *constant dollars* (which possess the same general purchasing power of the current year) instead of the *nominal dollars* (which possess different general purchasing powers of various years.

2. General indexes may be used to restate the amounts of the historical-cost/nominal dollar method. A **general price index** compares the average price of a group of goods and services at one date with the average price of a similar group at another date.

3. **Specific price indexes** are used as a means of approximating the current costs of particular assets or types of assets.

STOP & REVIEW:

Review the appropriate columns of **Exhibit 14-7** in the textbook.

F. Maintaining Invested Capital

1. The historical-cost/constant dollar approach is *not* a fundamental departure from historical costs. Instead it maintains that all historical costs to be matched against revenue should be restated on some constant-dollar basis so that all revenues and all expenses are expressed in dollars of the same (usually current) purchasing power.

2. The restated historical-cost approach harmonizes with the concept of *maintaining the general purchasing power* of the invested capital in total, rather than maintaining "specific invested capital," item by item.

STOP & REVIEW:

Review the **example** in the textbook.

G. Current Cost/Constant Dollars

1. In this method the nominal gains reported under the current cost/nominal dollar method are adjusted so that only gains in constant dollars are reported.

2. There is general agreement among the theorists that using constant dollars would be an improvement if for no other reason than improved comparability.

STOP & REVIEW:

Review the appropriate columns of **Exhibit 14-7** in the textbook.

. O. 6: Compare U.S. GAAP With Other Countries' Standards

A. Accounting Standards Throughout the World

Although differences exist among countries, the most basic aspects of accounting are consistent throughout the world: double-entry systems, accrual accounting, and the income statement and balance sheet are used worldwide. Therefore, similarities in financial reporting exceed the differences.

B. Differences in Tax and Inflation Accounting

1. One major area of difference in financial reporting is the influence of the income tax law on reporting to shareholders.

a. In the U.S. the methods used for reporting to tax authorities differ from those used for reporting to shareholders.

b. Tax reporting and shareholder reporting are identical, or tax law has a major influence on financial reporting in many countries, such as France, Germany, Japan, and Argentina.

2. Another significant difference among countries is the extent to which financial statements account for inflation.

   a. In the U.S., there is no longer required supplementary disclosure of inflation-adjusted numbers because the FASB concluded that the costs exceeded the benefits.

   b. Many countries such as Brazil require full or partial adjustments for inflation for reporting to both shareholders and tax authorities.

   c. The countries that have experienced the lowest inflation rates have been the slowest to recognize inflation in their accounting statements. Japan has no recognition of inflation, and Germany has recommended supplementary disclosures, but few companies have responded.

C. Accounting Principles in Selected Countries

1. Accounting practices differ among countries for a variety of reasons, among them differences in government, economic systems, culture, and traditions.

2. The Companies' Laws in the United Kingdom provide general guidance for accounting standards, and the Accounting Standards Board, a private-sector body sponsored by the accountancy profession, specifies details. U.K. companies can use either historical-cost or current-cost accounting, or a mixture of the two.

3. France leads the way in standardized accounting. Companies must use a National Uniform Chart of Accounts, and financial reporting requirements are extensive.

4. Tax law dominates financial reporting in Germany; whatever is reported to shareholders must also be reported to tax authorities. Therefore, accounting standards are based on statutes and court decisions, and they are not necessarily directed at producing statements useful for decision making.

5. Accounting and finance play a smaller role in Japanese companies and in the Japanese economy than in other industrialized countries. Accounting is dominated by the central government, especially the Ministry of Finance.

6. The growing globalization of business enterprises and capital markets is creating much current interest in common, worldwide standards. The International Federation of Accountants (IFAC) is leading the way toward more standardization of accounting measurement and reporting practices throughout the world, although there are too many cultural, social, and political differences among countries to expect complete worldwide standardization of financial reporting in the near future.

STUDY TIP:
Study the "Summary Problems for Your Review" and solutions in the textbook.

STOP & REVIEW:

Before continuing, review the objectives for this chapter and make sure you have a good understanding of each one.

V. Test Yourself

Questions

1. Describe the FASB's conceptual framework.

2. Identify the qualities that make information valuable.

3. Explain how identical companies can report different net incomes because of their choice of accounting methods.

4. Describe the major differences between financial capital and physical capital.

5. Discuss examples of accounting standards in other countries that differ from those in the United States.

Exercises and Problems

1. The Source purchased 400 chairs for inventory at $30 each. One year later 125 were sold for $60 each. Replacement cost at the time was $34 each. The general-price-level-index had increased 10%. Calculate the amount of income from continuing operations using the current cost/constant dollar method.

2. Murphy Interiors purchased 500 flats of tile for inventory at a cost of $200 each. One year later, Murphy sold 100 of the flats for $280 each. Current replacement costs were $265 each. The general-price-level-index had increased 10% during this period. Using the historical cost/constant dollar approach, calculate the amount of income from continuing operations.

3. Golden Oak purchased 100 doorstops at a cost of $30 each. One year later Golden Oak was able to sell 75 of the doorstops for $80 each to tourists. Current replacement cost was $40 each. The general-price-level-index had risen 5% during the period. Calculate the amount of income from continuing operations using the historical cost/nominal dollar method.

Data for use with #4 and #5

Halesite Motors, Inc., was incorporated with $3,300,000 of capital in the form of cash. The entire amount was used to purchase inventory shortly after incorporation. The company had a very good year and sold all of the inventory for $8,000,000 one year later. Current cost of the inventory was $3,300,000 at the time of sale.

4. Under financial capital maintenance, calculate income.

5. Calculate income using the physical capital approach.

Matching

MATCH EACH TERM WITH ITS DEFINITION BY WRITING THE APPROPRIATE LETTER IN THE SPACE PROVIDED.

Terms

_____ 1. Constant dollars

_____ 2. Current cost

_____ 3. Financial capital maintenance

_____ 4. General price index

_____ 5. Historical cost

_____ 6. Inflation

_____ 7. Neutrality

_____ 8. Nominal dollars

_____ 9. Physical capital maintenance

_____ 10. Relevance

_____ 11. Reliability

_____ 12. Revaluation equity

_____ 13. Specific price index

_____ 14. Validity

_____ 15. Verifiability

Definitions

A.   A concept of income measurement whereby income emerges only after recovering an amount that allows physical operating capability to be maintained.

B.   A quality of information such that there would be a high extent of consensus among independent measures of an item.

C.   A part of stockholders' equity that includes all holding gains that are excluded from income.

D.   An index used to approximate the current costs of particular assets, or types of assets.

E.   Those dollars that are not restated for fluctuations in the general purchasing power of the monetary unit.

M. Dollar measurements that are restated in terms of current purchasing power.

N. Choosing accounting policies without attempting to achieve purposes other than measuring economic impact: freedom from bias.

O. An index that compares the average price of a group of goods and services at one date, with the average price of a similar group at another date.

Multiple Choice

SELECT THE BEST ANSWER AND ENTER THE IDENTIFYING LETTER IN THE SPACE PROVIDED.

_____ 1. The principal task of the FASB is:

    a. To be a conduit between the business community and the Securities and Exchange Commission (SEC).
    b. To review financial statements to insure adherence to GAAP.
    c. To discuss and recommend changes in GAAP to the SEC, which will make the final decision on a particular issue's acceptance and implementation.
    d. Accounting policy making.

_____ 2. A major role of the conceptual framework is to:

    a. Provide the answers to questions and issues that come before the FASB.
    b. Clearly define the role and function of the FASB.
    c. Enhance the likelihood that proposed statements will be generally accepted.
    d. Classify all prior and future pronouncements within well defined areas of accounting.

_____ 3. The capability of information to make a difference to the decision maker means the information is:

    a. Reliable.
    b. Relevant.
    c. Material.
    d. Neutral.

_____ 4. For information to be relevant it must:

    a. Have predictive value.
    b. Be timely.
    c. Have feedback value.
    d. All of the above.

_____ 5. Which one of the following does _not_ enhance reliability?

    a. Materiality.
    b. Verifiability.
    c. Neutrality.
    d. Validity.

_____ 6. Recording financial effects in the periods affected regardless of when cash is received or paid is known as:

    a. Continuity.
    b. Recognition.
    c. Accrual accounting.
    d. Matching.

_____ 7. Information is material when it affects:

    a. A company's inventory.
    b. A company's tangible assets.
    c. A company's income statement and balance sheet.
    d. The judgment of a reasonable person.

_____ 8. The method that applies a general price index number to historical costs is the:

    a. Historical cost/nominal dollar method.
    b. Historical cost/constant dollar method.
    c. Current cost/nominal dollar method.
    d. Current cost/constant dollar method.

_____ 9. The most popular approach to income measurement is commonly called the:

    a. Historical-cost method.
    b. Constant dollar method.
    c. Replacement cost method.
    d. Cost indexing method.

_____ 10. Which of the following is _not_ a reason accounting practices differ among countries?

    a. Government.
    b. Religion.
    c. Economic systems.
    d. All of the above are reasons for differing accounting practices.

VI. Test Yourself

Questions

1. Between 1978 and 1984, the Financial Accounting Standards Board (FASB) issued four statements of *Financial Accounting Concepts* relating to business enterprises. These statements provide the conceptual framework used by the FASB. The conceptual framework aids the exercise of judgment; it does not provide solutions to all the reporting issues faced by the FASB.

   The process of setting accounting standards includes the development of a conceptual framework, its application to specific issues via exercises in logic and fact gathering, and the gaining of general acceptance and support. (L. O. 1)

2. The overriding criterion for choosing reporting alternatives is *cost/benefit*. A policy-making body such as the FASB must do its best to issue pronouncements whose perceived benefits exceed their perceived costs for the whole of society.

   The costs of providing information include costs to both providers and users. The benefits of accounting information exist, but they are harder to pinpoint than the costs. An important concept in judging costs and benefits is *materiality*, which is a problem that is usually resolved by professional judgment on a case-by-case basis.

   Relevance and *reliability* are qualities that make accounting useful for decision making. For information to be relevant, it must help decision makers by having either *predictive value* or *feedback value*, and must be available on a timely basis.

   Verifiability, neutrality, and *validity* enhance reliability.

   Comparability and *consistency* are the final items affecting usefulness. (L. O. 2)

3. GAAP allows accountants to choose when to recognize certain expenses. Comparing two companies can be difficult if each chooses a different method for recognizing major expenses.

   For stockholder reporting purposes, the choice of accounting policies can have a dramatic effect on operating income before taxes. Some companies choose the accounting policies that maximize operating income while other companies choose more conservative policies.

   Until accounting measurements become better standardized, accountants and corporate executives should view increased disclosure and amplified description as the most pressing requirements in financial reporting. (L. O. 3)

4. Income is an entity's increase in wealth during a period; that is, the amount that could be paid out to shareholders at the end of the period and still leave the entity as well off as it was at the beginning of the period.

   Shareholders invest capital and expect a return on the capital and an eventual return of the capital. To measure the shareholders' *return on capital*, the entity must measure the resources required to maintain invested capital at its original level. Excess resources resulting from the period's operations are income.

   Financial capital maintenance is a concept of income measurement whereby income emerges only after financial resources are recovered.

Physical capital maintenance is a concept of income measurement whereby income emerges only after recovering an amount that allows physical operating capability to be maintained. (L. O. 4)

5. Accounting practices differ among countries for a variety of reasons, among them differences in government, economic systems, culture, and traditions.

The Companies' Laws in the United Kingdom provide general guidance for accounting standards, and the Accounting Standards Board, a private-sector body sponsored by the accountancy profession, specifies details. U.K. companies can use either historical-cost or current-cost accounting, or a mixture of the two.

France leads the way in standardized accounting. Companies must use a National Uniform Chart of Accounts, and financial reporting requirements are extensive.

Tax law dominates financial reporting in Germany; whatever is reported to shareholders must also be reported to tax authorities. Therefore, accounting standards are based on statutes and court decisions, and they are not necessarily directed at producing statements useful for decision making.

Accounting and finance play a smaller role in Japanese companies and in the Japanese economy than in other industrialized countries. Accounting is dominated by the central government, especially the Ministry of Finance.

The growing globalization of business enterprises and capital markets is creating much current interest in common, worldwide standards. The International Federation of Accountants (IFAC) is leading the way toward more standardization of accounting measurement and reporting practices throughout the world, although there are too many cultural, social, and political differences among countries to expect complete worldwide standardization of financial reporting in the near future. (L. O. 6)

Exercises and Problems

1.	Sales (125 X $60)		$7,500
	Cost of goods sold (125 X $34)		4,250
	Income from continuing operations		$3,250

2.	Sales (100 X $280)		$28,000
	Cost of goods sold (100 X $200 = $20,000 X 110/100)		22,000
	Income from continuing operations		$ 6,000

3.	Sales (75 X $80)	$6,000	
	Cost of goods sold (75 X $30)	2,250	
	Income from continuing operations	$3,750	

4. Income based upon the concept of financial capital maintenance is measured after financial resources, in nominal dollars, are recovered.

Sales	$8,000,000
Cost of goods sold	3,000,000
Operating income	$5,000,000

5. Physical capital maintenance relies on valuations based on replacement costs.

Sales	$8,000,000
Cost of goods sold	3,300,000
Operating income	$4,700,000

Matching

1.	M	L. O. 5	6.	G	L. O. 5	11.	J	L. O. 2
2.	L	L. O. 5	7.	N	L. O. 2	12.	C	L. O. 5
3.	F	L. O. 4	8.	E	L. O. 5	13.	D	L. O. 5
4.	O	L. O. 5	9.	A	L. O. 4	14.	H	L. O. 2
5.	I	L. O. 5	10.	K	L. O. 2	15.	B	L. O. 2

Multiple Choice

1. d (L. O. 1)

2. c (L. O. 1)

3. b (L. O. 2)

4. d (L. O. 2)

5. a Materiality does not enhance reliability, which is the quality of information that assures decision makers that the information captures the conditions or events it purports to represent. (L. O. 2)

6. c Accrual accounting records financial effects in the appropriate *periods*. Matching relates revenues and expenses to each other in a *particular* period. (L. O. 2)

7. d Although material information may specifically affect the items listed, in general, if an item is material it means it would effect the judgment of a reasonable person. (L. O. 2)

8. b The historical cost/constant dollar approach attempts to restate the original cost in terms of current purchasing power in order to arrive at an income measure that more closely reflects current dollar values. (L. O. 5)

9. a Historical cost/nominal dollar is the most popular approach in the United States, and is a generally accepted accounting principle. (L. O. 5)

10. b Religion is not a reason for differing accounting practices throughout the world, although culture and traditions are reasons for differing accounting practices. (L. O.6)